To Our Parents:
Margaret and Fred
Jack and Donna

Contents

Preface

Exchange rate issues have been a consistent focus of research at the Institute. John Williamson and I launched the target zone proposal in a co-authored chapter in *Trade Policy in the 1980s* (1983), and Williamson developed the concept further in both *The Exchange Rate System* (revised 1985) and *Targets and Indicators: A Blueprint for the International Coordination of Economic Policy* (1987, with Marcus H. Miller). Ronald McKinnon presented a complementary approach in *An International Standard for Monetary Stabilization* (1984).

The effectiveness of exchange rate changes in promoting trade adjustment has been assessed by William R. Cline in *United States External Adjustment and the World Economy* (1989) and by Paul Krugman in *Has the Adjustment Process Worked?* (1991). This relationship also played an important role in the analyses in *Deficits and the Dollar* by Stephen Marris (revised 1987) and in my *The United States–Japan Economic Problem* (revised 1987, with William R. Cline), *America in the World Economy* (1988), and *Reconcilable Differences? United States–Japan Economic Conflict* (1993, with Marcus Noland). Yoichi Funabashi described the currency policy deliberations of the major industrial countries in *Managing the Dollar: From the Plaza to the Louvre* (1988). I. M. Destler and C. Randall Henning analyzed the politics of the issue in *Dollar Politics: Exchange Rate Policymaking in the United States* (1989).

This new study by Kathryn M. Dominguez and Jeffrey A. Frankel is, however, our first effort to directly address the issue of intervention policy. It challenges the conventional wisdom that such policy is largely ineffective, as embodied officially in the Jurgensen Report to the Finance

Ministers of the Group of Five major industrial countries in 1983. It thus has significant implications for exchange-rate policies around the world and for potential reforms of the international monetary system. It is a particular pleasure for the Institute to have Dr. Frankel rejoin our list of authors; his *The Yen/Dollar Agreement: Liberalizing Japanese Capital Markets* (1984) remains the definitive study of that important episode of recent international monetary history.

The Institute for International Economics is a private nonprofit institution for the study and discussion of international economic policy. Its purpose is to analyze important issues in that area, and to develop and communicate practical new approaches for dealing with them. The Institute is completely nonpartisan.

The Institute is funded largely by philanthropic foundations. Major institutional grants are now being received from the German Marshall Fund of the United States, which created the Institute with a generous commitment of funds in 1981, and from the Ford Foundation, the William and Flora Hewlett Foundation, the William M. Keck, Jr. Foundation, the C. V. Starr Foundation, and the United States–Japan Foundation. A number of other foundations and private corporations also contribute to the highly diversified financial resources of the Institute. About 16 percent of the Institute's resources in our latest fiscal year were provided by contributors outside the United States, including about 7 percent from Japan.

The Board of Directors bears overall responsibility for the Institute and gives general guidance and approval to its research program, including identification of topics that are likely to become important to international economic policymakers over the medium run (generally, one to three years), and which thus should be addressed by the Institute. The Director, working closely with the staff and outside Advisory Committee, is responsible for the development of particular projects and makes the final decision to publish an individual study.

The Institute hopes that its studies and other activities will contribute to building a stronger foundation for international economic policy around the world. We invite readers of these publications to let us know how they think we can best accomplish this objective.

C. FRED BERGSTEN
Director
July 1993

Acknowledgments

This study grew out of joint work on the effects of intervention that we began in 1989, when Jeff was visiting the Kennedy School of Government. We are grateful to the Institute for International Economics and the National Bureau of Economic Research for providing meeting places over the subsequent years where we were able to continue our collaboration.

Over the course of our investigation of intervention policy, we have benefited from the support and comments of many scholars and policymakers. We are grateful to the officials at the US Treasury, Federal Reserve, Bundesbank, Swiss National Bank, and Banca d'Italia who worked on our behalf to provide us with daily data on intervention operations. We are especially grateful to Dr. Edwin Truman and Ralph Smith at the Federal Reserve Board, Margaret Green at the Federal Reserve Bank of New York, Jim Lister at the US Treasury, Dr. Franz Scholl at the Bundesbank, and Dr. Jean-Pierre Roth at the Swiss National Bank for their roles in granting us access to information about how intervention policy decisions are made and implemented in the United States, Germany, and Switzerland. Of course, the views expressed in this book should not be interpreted as reflecting those of any of these institutions or members of their staffs.

We wish to thank Stanley Black, Pietro Catte, Richard Cooper, Giampaolo Galli, Dale Henderson, Peter Kenen, Salvatore Rebecchini, and members of the October 1991 Institute Study Group for many helpful comments and suggestions on previous drafts of this study. We are especially grateful to Hali Edison and Maurice Obstfeld, who read the entire manuscript and offered extensive comments. We, however, remain responsible for any errors and omissions that remain in the book.

Numerous research assistants worked over the years to create the news variables documented in the appendix. We are thankful to Julia Lowell, Julia Marsh, Regina Ruepke, and Marjut Ruti for their painstaking work combing the financial press for reports of exchange rate policy.

We are also grateful to the publications staff at the Institute for their help in producing the book, to Valerie Norville for truly outstanding editing, and especially to C. Fred Bergsten for his support, extensive comments, and persistent prodding to bring this study to completion. Finally, we are grateful to James Hines and Jessica Stern for all their patience throughout this project.

Introduction: New Data to Reconsider an Old Question

The word "intervention," in the context of international politics, conjures up images of the government sending in the US Cavalry to impose order on a local situation perceived to have gotten out of hand. "Intervention" in the context of economics usually connotes action by the government to impose its will where the private market is perceived to be unable to function well on its own. Actions that some regard as requiring government intervention may, of course, be regarded by others as unwarranted interference.

Intervention in the foreign exchange market does not typically represent the same application of overwhelming force that the government has at its disposal for other political or economic problems. There was a time when the United States and other governments set the price of foreign exchange by fiat and were able to maintain their commitment to buy or sell however much foreign exchange was necessary to enforce that declared exchange rate. But that time, which began when the post-war world monetary system was established at Bretton Woods, New Hampshire, ended in 1971 when the exchange value of the dollar that had prevailed for 25 years was abandoned.

Today, the volume of activity in international financial markets is so great, and its power so strong, that governments cannot realistically hope to impose their wills on it. Central banks still intervene in the foreign exchange market, buying foreign currency in exchange for domestic currency to help keep the domestic currency from appreciating, or buying domestic currency to keep it from depreciating, as the case may be. But they cannot expect that their actions alone will determine the direction of the market. The most they can hope to accomplish is to nudge the market in the desired direction.

Another analogy from the American West may be more appropriate than the arrival of the Cavalry. The foreign exchange market is a herd of steers, and central banks are herd dogs. They bark and nip at the heels of the steers, with the aim of moving the herd in the desired direction.

Is such intervention effective? The conventional wisdom offers an unequivocal answer. Intervention in the foreign exchange market has little or no effect, except to the extent that it implies changes in countries' money supplies. In the latter case, intervention is just a particular variety of monetary policy. The conventional wisdom thus says that intervention does not offer the authorities an *independent* policy tool for influencing the foreign exchange market. To continue the cattle analogy, a herd dog is just one animal among hundreds and is not a large one at that. For all its noisy barking, according to the conventional wisdom, it has no substantial effect on the direction of the herd. There are also cowhands on horseback: they represent monetary policy. There is no question that they are powerful enough to direct the herd, and the dogs can often be interpreted as stand-ins for the cowhands. But the hypothesis says that the dogs have no power independent of that of the cowhands—that is, operations in the foreign exchange market have no power independent of monetary policy.

In the early 1980s, the belief that intervention was not an effective policy tool was widely shared among academic economists, central bankers, and market participants. In the first-term Reagan administration, the ineffectiveness of intervention was an article of faith, and the US government accordingly refrained from buying or selling foreign exchange (with some minor exceptions). In 1985, however, attitudes at the US Treasury shifted abruptly. US authorities began to intervene again in the markets in collaboration with other countries' central banks, most visibly as decided at the meeting of G-5 economic leaders at the Plaza Hotel in September. Since that time, intervention has taken place regularly. Foreign exchange traders have taken note of it. They are observed to react to reports of intervention, leaping for their computer terminals as vigorously as to any other sort of news. Most traders, and most involved central bankers, believe that this intervention has at times had important effects. The authors of this study believe that the time is right for a reconsideration of the conventional wisdom as to the ineffectiveness of foreign exchange intervention.

Our study uses a number of data sources that have not been used in mainstream economic analysis on this subject. One kind of data is so intrinsic to the subject of the study that it should be highlighted from the start. That is data on the daily intervention operations of three major central banks. Daily data are required if one hopes to illuminate the intricacies of the market; the usual monthly or quarterly statistics that central banks publish only allow the sort of tests that are far too coarse. Yet most major central banks have in the past declined to make available daily data on their intervention operations.

It is often possible to infer daily intervention from public sources by matching up contemporary wire service or newspaper reports with the official numbers released at the end of the quarter. But this technique is not 100 percent accurate. More importantly, one of our major goals in this study is to disentangle the effects of intervention that is "discreet"—that is, secret—from the effects of intervention that is publicly reported. For this, one needs the actual data.

We are thus pleased that officials in the German and US governments have agreed to depart from past practice and make the daily intervention data available. (The Swiss National Bank already had a policy of making all such information public.) The general temptation to "hoard" information is both widespread and understandable. We are thus especially grateful to the German and American officials involved for agreeing to release the intervention data and thereby allowing economists outside the central banks to study the issue more effectively. These officials had a sufficiently broad perspective to appreciate the potential benefits, in the form of increased understanding of the economic phenomena at work. We hope that our study is in some measure worthy of the confidence that they showed.

A Brief History of Intervention Since 1973

The Start of the Floating-Rate Era

There have been radical changes over the years in how foreign exchange intervention is viewed. It is not only the question of whether intervention is a powerful or useful policy tool that has changed; the perspective has also changed on whether it is a policy tool at all.

In the 1960s, when all major industrialized countries had currencies that were convertible into foreign currency at a fixed exchange rate, intervention was not viewed as a discretionary policy instrument available in governments' policy tool kits. Intervention, rather, was a passive act in which governments were thought to have no choice: if the net supply of foreign currency coming from the private sector fell short of the net demand at the particular exchange rate to which the country had committed itself, then the central bank necessarily had to make up the difference, supplying out of its reserves the foreign currency that the private sector wanted.

The Bretton Woods system of fixed exchange rates broke down when it became apparent that the quantity of international reserves in the vaults at Fort Knox—and, more importantly, in the Federal Reserve System—would not be sufficient to continue satisfying the excess demand that existed at the exchange value of the dollar that prevailed in 1971, or even in 1973. One view is that an eventual breakdown was the inevitable consequence of a fixed-rate system in which the currency of one country (the United States) served as the reserve currency for other countries. But the proximate cause of the breakdown was excessive

US macroeconomic expansion in the late 1960s and an unwillingness to accept the discipline of the resulting balance of payments deficits.

The floating-rate system that followed was not the pure float of economists' theories, in which central banks refrain from all operations in the foreign exchange market, but a "managed float" in which the authorities regularly intervened to try to influence the value of their currencies. In July 1973, central banks agreed at Basel to coordinate intervention. However, the Nixon administration allowed the dollar to reflect the reverberations of the subsequent 1973–74 oil shock. The floating-rate era's first major episode of intervention in the US foreign exchange market came in late 1974 and early 1975. US, German, and Swiss authorities bought dollars to moderate the currency's depreciation. This intervention episode was considered to have helped achieve the goal of stabilizing the dollar (Greene 1983a).

The Late 1970s: Talking Down, and then Rescuing, the Dollar

The substantial depreciation of 1977–78 began with a deliberate attempt by Treasury Secretary Michael Blumenthal and others in the Carter administration to "talk down" the dollar. In the absence of a willingness among trading partners to undertake macroeconomic expansion at as rapid a rate as was the United States, a depreciation of the dollar was at the time viewed as the natural way of staving off the then-record US trade deficits that were beginning to emerge. But the decline soon got out of control. The depreciation of the late 1970s is now usually thought of in the economic arena as a symptom of excessive US monetary expansion and in the political arena as one of many symbols of the "malaise" that is popularly associated with the Carter administration.

An anti-inflation program announced by President Carter on 24 October 1978 was received poorly by the financial markets, and the dollar slide accelerated. Finally, on 1 November a "dollar rescue package" was launched. Monetary policy was tightened. At the same time, the United States built up a $30 billion fund for intervention, partly by initiating swap arrangements with foreign central banks and partly by issuing "Carter bonds" in Germany and Switzerland. The New York trading desk bought over $600 million in intervention operations on 1 November. By the end of the day, the dollar had risen 10 percent against the mark. Japan, Germany, and Switzerland joined the United States in concerted intervention operations over the next few weeks. (Indeed, they had been buying dollars since late 1977.) By the end of the month, the operation appeared a complete success. But in December the dollar lost much of the ground it had gained, despite new intervention that was almost as large as November's.[1] The episode was interpreted as showing that intervention could have substantial effects but that these effects would be only temporary if they were not soon backed up with genuine policy changes (Greene 1983b, 40; Marston 1988, 101–03 and 105).

The yen began abruptly to depreciate against the dollar at the end of 1978, and the Japanese authorities responded with heavy sales of dollars throughout 1979 and early 1980 and with relaxation of existing controls against capital inflow.

The First Reagan Administration (1981–84)

The reversal of the down phase in the dollar began, not with the coming of Ronald Reagan, but with the earlier monetary tightening by Federal Reserve Chairman Paul Volcker. In October 1979 the Fed announced a change in its open market procedures that was designed to combat inflation and motivated partly by the need to restore the dollar to international respectability. For the subsequent several years, Volcker showed his determination to let interest rates rise however far they had to rise to defeat the inflation of the 1970s.

The dollar began its long appreciation in 1980. In the autumn, US authorities responded by buying foreign currencies. But the aim was to repay foreign-currency obligations that remained outstanding from the earlier operations rather than to prevent the appreciation (Greene 1983a).

First Phase of the Reagan Dollar Appreciation: 1981–82

During the 1981–82 period, the US long-term government bond rate averaged 13.3 percent, a two-point increase relative to 1980. US interest rates among a weighted average of trading partners' rates rose as well, but not by as much: the US differential averaged 1.9 percent over 1981–82 compared with 0.6 percent in 1979–80. The real (that is, inflation-adjusted) interest rate differential rose even more, by between 2 and 3 points, depending on the measure of expected inflation used (Frankel 1985). Between 1980 and 1982, the increase in the relative attractiveness of dollar assets in the eyes of global investors brought about an appreciation of the US dollar by 29 percent in nominal terms and 28 percent in real terms. Evidence of the textbook-perfect effects of the monetary contraction was seen not only in the rise of the dollar, but also more broadly in the recession of 1981–82. The traditional channel of monetary transmission to the real economy, the negative effect of an increase in interest rates on the construction industry and other interest rate–sensi-

---

1. This was the month when the second oil shock hit.

tive sectors, was subsequently joined by the modern channel of transmission: the negative effect of an increase in the value of the dollar on export industries and other exchange rate–sensitive sectors.

Second Phase of Dollar Appreciation: 1983–84

The trough of the recession came at the end of 1982; a recovery began in 1983 that was both vigorous and destined to be long-lived. The dollar continued on its previous upward path. Between 1982 and 1984 it appreciated another 17 percent in nominal terms and 14 percent in real terms. The textbooks had no trouble explaining why global investors continued to find dollar assets increasingly attractive: the US long-term real interest rate continued to rise until its peak in mid-1984. The differential vis-à-vis trading partners during 1983–84 averaged about 1 percentage point higher than in the previous two years. Nor did the textbooks have much trouble explaining the source of this increase in US real interest rates. As the Reagan administration cut income tax rates, indexed tax brackets for inflation, and began a massive buildup of military spending, the budget deficit rose from 2 percent of GNP in the 1970s to 5 percent of GNP in the mid-1980s. (The sharp increase in the budget deficit in 1982 could be largely blamed on the recession. But by 1985 the increase was mostly structural.) The increased demand for funds that these deficits represented readily explains the increase in US interest rates, the inflow of capital from abroad, and the associated appreciation of the dollar.

At the same time, the effects of the ever-loftier dollar began to be felt in earnest among those US industries that rely on exports for customers or that compete with imports. The affected sectors on the export side included particularly agriculture, capital goods, and aircraft and other transportation equipment; on the import side they included textiles, steel, motorcycles, and consumer electronics; and on both sides they included semiconductors and automobiles. Overall, the effects on exports and imports added up to a $67 billion trade deficit in 1983, double the record levels of 1977–78. This too was a prediction of the standard textbook model. The fiscal expansion was essentially "crowding out" private spending on American goods, not only in the interest rate–sensitive sectors through the traditional route, but also in the exchange rate–sensitive sectors through the modern route.

The Noninterventionist Policy of the First Reagan Administration

Throughout this period, 1981–84, the Reagan administration had an explicit policy of laissez faire (or benign neglect) toward the foreign exchange market. The policy was noninterventionist in the general sense that the movement of the dollar was not seen as requiring any sort of government response, or indeed to be a problem. The policy was also noninterventionist in the narrower sense that the authorities refrained from intervening in the foreign exchange market—that is, from the selling (or buying) of dollars in exchange for marks, yen, or other foreign currencies. Under Secretary for Monetary Affairs Beryl Sprinkel announced in the third month of the administration that the government intended not to undertake such intervention except in the case of "disorderly markets." Lest anyone think that the qualifying phrase was sufficiently elastic to include common fluctuations in the exchange rate, he explained that the sort of disorderly markets the administration had in mind was that resulting from the March 1981 shooting and wounding of the president (Destler and Henning 1989, 20). Newspapers occasionally carried reports of intervention—for example, in August 1983. The historical data in fact reveal a number of occasions between 1981 and 1984 when US authorities intervened in the market, but the interventions were small in magnitude.

For Sprinkel, a long-time member of the monetarist "Shadow Open Market Committee" and follower of Milton Friedman, the matter was a simple case of the virtues of the free market. Under floating exchange rates, the price of foreign currency is whatever it has to be to equilibrate the demand and supply of foreign currency in the market; it is, virtually by definition, the "correct price." Attempts by the monetary authorities to intervene in the foreign exchange market to keep the value of the currency artificially high or artificially low are unsound gambles with the taxpayers' money, as likely to be counterproductive as attempts by the Department of Agriculture to intervene in the market for grain to keep the price of grain artificially high or artificially low.[2]

Indeed, according to the monetarist model, intervention would not have any effect in the market to the extent that it was "sterilized," i.e., to the extent that it left money supplies unchanged. This is the position Sprinkel took when his French counterpart Michel Camdessus tried to argue the desirability of foreign exchange intervention in preparations for the 1982 Summit of the Group of Seven (G-7) heads of state at Versailles (Putnam and Bayne 1987, 133). The French argued that foreign exchange intervention did provide an independent and useful tool. The Americans agreed to form an intergovernmental working group to study the question (and to enact a process of "multilateral surveillance" by the Group of Five). The subsequent findings of the working group, the so-called Jurgensen Report, which is further discussed below, tended to support the Sprinkel position.

---

2. So convinced was Sprinkel of the evil of intervention, that, partly to save his successors from temptation, he gave away to the International Monetary Fund the deutsche mark and yen reserves that he had inherited from the Carter administration, instead of Special Drawing Rights (SDRs), as the US share of the 1984 increase in quota subscription.

But there were other free-market conservatives in the starting team at Treasury in the early 1980s, the supply-siders, who believed in the need to stabilize the exchange rate, just as firmly as the monetarists believed in the desirability of leaving it to be determined by the market. The issue was settled firmly on the side of nonintervention by Secretary of the Treasury Donald Regan. He had neither a monetarist nor a supply-sider philosophy. Rather, Regan saw the issue more in terms of politics and personalities. In the absence of any guidance from the White House, Regan saw his role as defending himself and the president from any suggestions that the status quo with respect to the dollar was a bad thing or that it required a response. He subscribed to the "safe haven" view that the pattern of capital inflow, dollar appreciation, and trade deficit was the result of the favorable investment climate created by the Reagan tax cuts and regulatory changes, in opposition to the textbook view that this pattern was the result of a fiscal expansion and an increase in real interest rates.

When the heads of state of the G-7 countries met again at Williamsburg, Virginia, 28–30 May 1983, the Europeans complained to Reagan about America's budget deficit and its effects, such as high interest rates. But Reagan and Regan responded that the strong dollar and US trade deficits were not problems and in any case were not due to high interest rates and fiscal expansion (Putnam and Bayne 1987, 179).

Within the first Reagan administration, the view that the strong dollar was the result of the differential in real interest rates was put forward early and often by Martin Feldstein, the chairman of the Council of Economic Advisers from 1982 to 1984. His view was that the source of the increase in real interest rates was the increase in the federal structural budget deficit and consequent shortfall of national saving. Federal Reserve Chairman Paul Volcker held a similar view.[3] This explanation for the appreciating dollar and widening trade deficit was increasingly accepted as the correct one by other members of the president's cabinet. Representatives of trading partners' governments also tended to share this view. But it was rejected by the Treasury and some White House aides, principally on the grounds that the emphasis on the "twin deficits" amounted to "selling short" America and the president's policies.

The "Bubble": June 1984–February 1985

From mid-1984 to February 1985, the dollar appreciated another 20 percent. This final phase of the currency's ascent differed from the earlier phases not only in that the appreciation was at an accelerated rate, but also in that it could not readily be explained on the basis of economic

---

3. As did C. Fred Bergsten (1984a) and a growing number of other observers.

fundamentals, whether by means of the textbook theories or otherwise. The interest rate differential peaked in June, and thereafter moved in the wrong direction to explain the remainder of the upswing in the dollar. Two influential studies (Krugman 1985; Marris 1985) claimed that the foreign exchange market had been carried away by an irrational "speculative bubble."[4] The trade deficit reached $112 billion in 1984 and continued to widen. Many who had hitherto supported freely floating exchange rates began to change their minds.

Managing the Dollar (1985–91)

The Plaza Sea-Change: 1985

The pivotal event in the making of exchange rate policy in the 1980s was the shift from a relatively doctrinaire laissez-faire policy during the first Reagan administration to a more flexible policy of activism during the second administration. By 1985, the dollar had soared to so high a level, and the US trade balance had plummeted to so low a level, that the political process demanded some sort of response. For many in Congress, the response demanded by the trade deficit was a more aggressive trade policy. For many others, the danger that Congress would enact damaging protectionist legislation, or that the Democrats would seize on the trade deficit as an effective campaign issue, became an argument for trying to do something about the dollar. At the same time, a new team of policymakers took the helm at the Treasury, and they were not restricted in the choice of strategies by either of the two constraints binding their predecessors: an economic ideology that forbade intervention in the foreign exchange market or a guiding principle that anyone who considered side effects of the existing macroeconomic policy mix such as the strong dollar to be a "problem" lacked the requisite loyalty to the president's program.

An obvious point from which to date the switch is 22 September 1985, when finance ministers and central bank governors from the G-5 countries met at the Plaza Hotel in New York and agreed to try to bring the dollar down.[5] The Plaza Agreement was certainly the embodiment of the new regime. But we would prefer to date the start of the new era

---

4. Contemporaneous statements by economists that the dollar was greatly overvalued included presentations by Krugman, Bergsten, and Richard Cooper to a prominent Federal Reserve System conference in Jackson Hole, Wyoming, just one month before the Plaza meeting. Another reference on "the dollar as an irrational speculative bubble" that dates from this year is Frankel and Froot (1987).

5. The story of the Plaza is described in detail in Funabashi (1988, 9–41).

from the beginning of that year. With the inauguration of the second Reagan administration, Donald Regan and Beryl Sprinkel left the Treasury (for the White House and Council of Economic Advisers, respectively). James Baker became secretary of the Treasury, and his aide Richard Darman became deputy secretary. Both men had already developed at the White House a reputation for greater pragmatism than other more ideological members of the administration. In January confirmation hearings, Baker explicitly showed signs of the departure with respect to exchange rate policy, stating at one point that the Treasury's previous stance against intervention was "obviously something that should be looked at . . ." (quoted in Destler and Henning 1989, 41–42)

Another reason to date the change from early in 1985 is that the dollar peaked in February and had already depreciated by 13 percent by the time of the Plaza meeting. Some, such as Feldstein (1986), would argue that the gap in timing shows that exchange rate "policy" in fact had little connection with the actual decline of the dollar, which was instead determined in the private marketplace regardless of what efforts governments made to influence it. But, notwithstanding that official policy did not change until September,[6] there are two respects in which the bursting of the bubble at the end of February may have been in part caused by policy change.

First, it was widely anticipated that Baker and Darman would probably be more receptive to the idea of trying to bring down the dollar than their predecessors had been. If market participants have reason to believe that policy changes to reduce the value of the dollar will be made in the future, they will move to sell dollars today in order to protect themselves against future losses, which will cause the dollar to depreciate immediately, in advance of actual policy changes.

Second, some intervention was agreed upon at a G-5 meeting in Washington, DC, attended by Baker and Darman on 17 January, and it did take place subsequently (Funabashi 1988, 10).[7] The US operations, though small in magnitude, were fully reported in the newspapers. The European central banks, particularly the Germans, intervened heavily to sell dollars in foreign exchange markets in February and March.[8] The

---

6. A June 1985 meeting of G-10 deputies in Tokyo, for example, concluded that there was no need for international monetary reform, and also endorsed the 1983 finding of the Jurgensen Report that intervention did not offer a very useful tool to affect exchange rates (Obstfeld 1990; Dobson 1991).

7. Surprisingly, the G-5 public announcement on 17 January used language that, on the surface at least, sounds more pro-interventionist than that used later in the Plaza announcement: the G-5 "in light of recent developments in foreign exchange markets, reaffirmed their commitment made at the Williamsburg Summit to undertake coordinated intervention in the markets as necessary."

8. Intervention was particularly strong on 27 February and appeared to have an impact on the market (Frankel 1985, 213). Our daily data, graphed in figure 5.6, show that the Bundesbank also intervened in January and, especially, in early March.

true daily data that are now available show that not all the German intervention that took place during this period was reported at the time. But the February intervention received particular attention and by virtue of timing appears a likely candidate for the instrument that pricked the bubble. It is in turn likely that the accession of Baker to the Treasury in January and the G-5 meeting were the developments that encouraged the Germans to renew their intervention efforts at that time.

It was not entirely clear at the time whether a major shift in policy regarding willingness to intervene had taken place. In June, a G-10 meeting of finance ministers and central bankers expressed confidence in freely floating exchange rates.

On 22 September the G-5 ministers, partly in response to an apparent incipient renewed rise in the dollar, met at the Plaza Hotel. They agreed upon an announcement that "some further orderly appreciation of the nondollar currencies is desirable" and that they "stand ready to cooperate more closely to encourage this when to do so would be helpful," language that by the standards of such communiqués is considered (at least in retrospect) to have constituted strong support for concerted intervention, even though the word "intervention" did not appear. A figure of 10 to 12 percent depreciation of the dollar over the near term had been specified as the aim in a never-released "nonpaper" drafted by Assistant Secretary David Mulford for a secret preparatory meeting of G-5 deputies in London on 15 September and (according to American government sources) was accepted as the aim by the G-5 ministers at the Plaza.[9] Substantial intervention took place over the subsequent two months. The dollar sales by the Federal Reserve and Bank of Japan were larger than they had been in February. The Bundesbank, feeling it had already done its share the preceding winter, did not sell as many dollars. In November, the Bundesbank was reported to be defending itself against charges that it was not intervening as much as the Germans had promised at the Plaza. Our data, however, show Bundesbank intervention to be as large as Fed intervention on most days that fall, particularly in the case of substantial dollar sales by both in mid-October (see chapter 5, figure 5.7).

Although the Plaza Agreement is widely perceived as having strikingly reversed the position of the G-7, particularly the United States, on the question of the effectiveness of intervention, there was in fact no discus-

---

9. The "nonpaper" also specified the total scale of intervention to be undertaken over the subsequent six weeks (up to $18 billion) and the allocation among the five countries (Funabashi 1988, 16–21). Intervention actually undertaken by the end of October turned out to be $3.2 billion on the part of the United States and $5 billion on the part of the other four countries, plus over $2 billion on the part of G-10 countries that were not represented at the Plaza, particularly Italy (*Federal Reserve Bank of New York Quarterly Review* 10, Winter 1985–86, 47).

sion in the deliberations or in the communiqué as to whether the intervention undertaken should be sterilized. Indeed, there was not much discussion at the major meetings as to what sort of monetary policies would be appropriate to support exchange rate objectives. The exception is that the Plaza Agreement called for Japanese monetary policy to "exercise flexible management with due attention to the yen exchange rate" (Funabashi 1988, 265; Dobson 1991, 82). When the Bank of Japan raised its discount rate soon after the Plaza, it claimed a reduction in the yen-dollar rate as its objective, although others were less sure that this was truly its motive.

On the Monday that the Plaza announcement was made public, the dollar fell a sudden 4 percent against a weighted average of other currencies (slightly more against the mark and the yen). Substantial intervention was reported in the newspapers the next day. Subsequently, the dollar resumed a gradual depreciation at a rate similar to that of the preceding seven months.[10] Interest rates continued to decline gradually, despite fears on the part of Volcker and many others that a depreciation might discourage international investors from holding dollars and thereby force interest rates up. Before long, the Plaza had widely become considered a great public success.

In 1986 the maneuvering that went on outside G-7 meetings was more substantive than the maneuvering that went on inside. Baker was repeatedly quoted in the press as "talking the dollar down," in large part as a weapon to induce the trading partners to cut interest rates. This was a tack very much reminiscent of an earlier Treasury secretary, Michael Blumenthal. The implicit pitch went something like: "We would prefer that you expand your economies and thereby import more from us so that reduction of the US deficit can be achieved in a way consistent with growth for all parties. But if you are not willing to go along, then I am afraid we are just going to have to let the dollar depreciate more, in which case your exports to us will fall."

In March and April, the Federal Reserve Board coordinated reductions in the discount rate with other major central banks; the aim was to stimulate the world economy without risking the sort of free-fall in the value of the dollar that Chairman Volcker was beginning to fear. The Tokyo Summit of G-7 leaders in May focused more on other macroeconomic indicators than on exchange rates per se.

The Germans and Japanese intervened in the foreign exchange market to try to support the dollar but complained that "these efforts were in vain, not least because statements by US officials repeatedly aroused the impression on the markets that the US authorities wanted the dollar to

---

10. Because the rate of depreciation in the six months after the Plaza was no greater than in the six months before the Plaza, Feldstein (1986) argued that the change in policy had no effect. This logic is far from conclusive, however.

depreciate further. Moreover, until the Louvre Accord in early February 1987 the Americans hardly participated in the operations to support their currency" (*Report of the Deutsche Bundesbank for the Year 1986*, 63, quoted in Obstfeld 1990). Indeed, the United States did not intervene at all in 1986. Meanwhile, Fed Chairman Volcker was also being quoted (periodically in 1986 and early 1987) as favoring the current level for the exchange rate, in apparent opposition to Baker. Volcker's fear was that an uncontrolled fall of the dollar would raise inflation and interest rates.

By September 1986 the yen-dollar rate had declined from its peak of about 260 to 154. Japanese exporters were feeling heavily squeezed. At an unannounced rendezvous in San Francisco, Japanese Finance Minister Kiichi Miyazawa met with Baker. They made a deal under which the exchange rate would be stabilized in its current range, and in return, the Japanese would undertake greater fiscal expansion. The agreement was not announced until 31 October. In the interim, the yen had depreciated back to about 162 yen to the dollar. The Americans suspected the Japanese of deliberate manipulation so as to lock in a more favorable rate and returned to talking down the dollar.

The Louvre Accord and the Return of Dollar Stability

Following a further decline of the dollar, the next meeting of G-7 finance ministers was held at the Louvre in Paris on 21–22 February 1987 (minus Italy, which declined to attend in protest against its exclusion from an informal G-5 meeting that had already worked out the agreement). The Baker-Miyazawa agreement now proved to be something of a dry run for the Louvre Accord. The ensuing communiqué showed that the United States had agreed that the dollar should be stabilized "around current levels." In return, Japan had agreed to expand domestic demand, a promise it was to fulfill in May, and Germany and some of the others had agreed more narrowly to cut taxes. One interpretation as to why Germany and the others were willing to participate at the Louvre when they had not been earlier is that the Baker-Miyazawa agreement demonstrated the readiness of the United States and Japan to proceed with a "G-2," and the Germans and others did not want to be left out.

The Bank of Japan intervened in support of the dollar in massive quantities, both before and after the Louvre meeting. In smaller quantities, the Bundesbank, the Fed, and the Swiss National Bank (SNB) bought dollars as well (figure 5.8). Monthly data also show heavy intervention by the United States and the other two major central banks in March and April (as is evident in figure 1.1, or Dobson 1991, 107). In the US case, with dollar purchases reported to begin 28 January, these were the first interventions since the heavy operations of 1985 on the opposite side of the market.

Figure 1.1 Intervention in the mark-dollar exchange rate and interventions by G3 central banks,[a] 1984–91

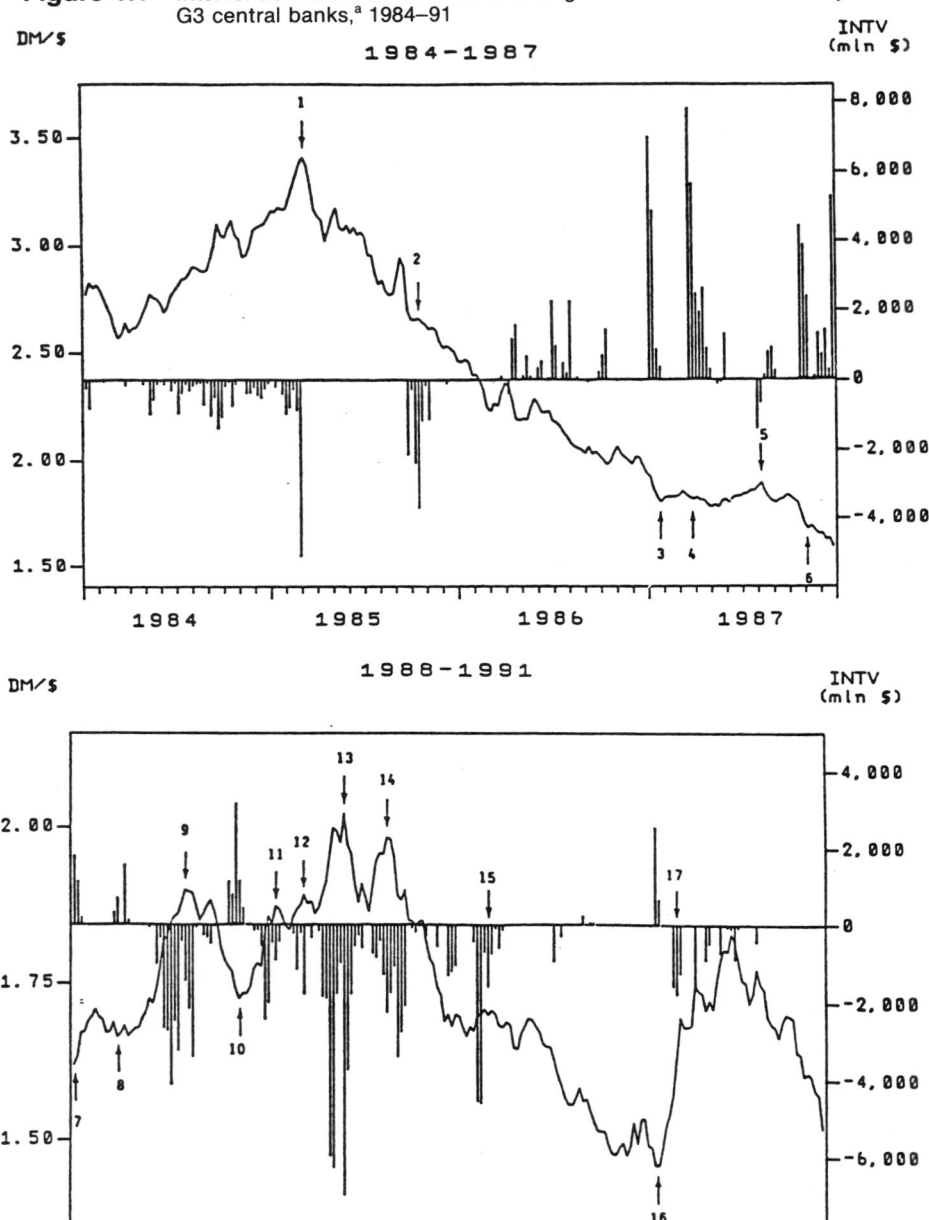

a. Weekly data. Intervention is defined as ($ purchases-DM purchases)/2.

Source: Catte, Galli, and Rebecchini (1992b).

16 DOES FOREIGN EXCHANGE INTERVENTION WORK?

A question of importance for evaluating the Louvre Accord concerns quantitative bands. The communiqué that was released after the meeting, as with all G-7 meetings, contained little hard information and conveyed the major policy change with a few understated words: "The Ministers and Governors agreed that the substantial exchange rate changes since the Plaza Agreement will increasingly contribute to reducing external imbalances and have now brought their currencies within ranges broadly consistent with underlying economic fundamentals. . . . Further substantial exchange rate shifts among their currencies could damage growth and adjustment prospects in their countries." As with the Plaza Agreement, participants denied to the press that any specific quantitative target range had been set (*Wall Street Journal*, 23 February 1987, 3). Subsequent newspaper reports spoke of the range or target zone that had been set at the Louvre and made guesses as to what it might be. Most knowledgeable observers surmised that probably no explicit quantitative range had in fact been agreed upon. This view was overturned, however, when Funabashi (1988, 183–87) reported that the Louvre participants had after all set a "reference range" of 5 percent around the current levels: 1.825 marks to the dollar and 153.5 yen to the dollar.[11]

The advantage of having kept the target range secret was borne out when the dollar broke out of the lower end of the range. By April 1987, the scheduled time of a G-7 meeting, the yen-dollar rate had fallen 7 percent from the Louvre baseline. Japanese Finance Minister Miyazawa was forced to accept Baker's proposal to "rebase" at the current level of 146 yen to the dollar, with the same width of the reference-range bands as before.

The US commitment at the Louvre to oppose further depreciation of the dollar might be supposed to show up in three ways, besides the announcement of the agreement itself: an absence of statements by the secretary of the Treasury "talking down the dollar," purchases of dollars in foreign exchange intervention operations, and a tighter monetary policy. From then on, Baker did indeed refrain from talking down the dollar, beginning with comments on 10 February. As mentioned, the United States also did indeed intervene substantially in the foreign exchange market in the aftermath of the Louvre, buying dollars to discourage further depreciation. Finally, US interest rates did indeed begin

---

11. More precisely, a narrower margin of plus or minus 2½ percent, after which point intervention would be called for on a voluntary basis, and a wider margin of plus or minus 5 percent, at which point a collaborative policy response would be obligatory. Such meetings are notorious for each country emerging with its own view as to what was agreed upon, and there is always the possibility that the 5 percent target range was a US proposal about which some countries, such as Germany, were unenthusiastic. No legal or quasi-legal documents are signed at such meetings.

a gradual rise in February (reversing a three-year downward trend), although the Federal Reserve was motivated more by a desire to choke off inflation, which was beginning to edge up slightly again, than by a commitment to support the dollar. Perhaps as a result of these three steps, the dollar appreciated, particularly against the mark, from the date of the Louvre until mid-March (at one point inducing a small amount of Fed intervention in March to dampen the appreciation).

Financial Markets Fear a Dollar Plunge: 1987

Many analysts had been warning for some time of the possibility of a "hard landing," which could be defined as a fall in the dollar that, because it is caused by a sudden portfolio shift out of dollar assets, is accompanied by a sharp increase in interest rates that have a contractionary effect on economic activity.[12] Two events shook financial markets in 1987; each of them began with the markings of such a portfolio shift. First, in the spring, there was a fall in demand for US bonds, perhaps led by nervous foreign investors. This shift in portfolio demand led to a depreciation of the dollar, despite April comments by Baker and concerted intervention in support of the dollar, and it also led to an abrupt decline in bond prices and an increase in interest rates.

Second, world stock markets crashed on 19 October 1987. One of the many hypotheses offered to explain the crash was that the markets feared that the Fed would deliberately raise interest rates to try to keep the dollar from falling through a floor set at the Louvre (Feldstein 1988; Obstfeld 1990).[13]

Many observers on 19 October at first feared that the hard landing was at hand. But in large part due to the rapid reaction of the Federal Reserve, interest rates fell rather than rose, and there was no subsequent slowdown in economic activity. The Fed was prepared to allow a sharp decline in the dollar if the alternative was insufficient liquidity to avert a financial crisis (though the dollar, surprisingly, did not depreciate on 19 October).

Consultations among the various governments began immediately, but in the absence of a clear idea as to what macroeconomic policy commitments could be made, and with respect to US fiscal policy in particular, no G-7 meeting was scheduled. Dollar depreciation was again a concern, with steady intervention in support of the dollar throughout fall 1987 having little apparent effect (figures 5.9 and 5.19).

---

12. For example, see Marris (1985). This was also a major concern of Paul Volcker's.

13. This explanation was partly inspired by Chairman Alan Greenspan's move to raise interest rates earlier in the year.

Two months after the stock market crash, G-7 representatives decided in a "Telephone Accord" to try to breathe new life into the Louvre Agreement. Paragraph 8 of their 22 December 1987 communiqué (which the G-7 was later to repeat word for word in an April 1988 meeting of ministers and in the communiqué of the Toronto Summit of leaders in June 1988) modified slightly earlier statements in favor of exchange rate stability. It included new wording: ". . . either excessive fluctuation of exchange rates, a further decline of the dollar, or a rise in the dollar to an extent that becomes destabilizing to the adjustment process could be counterproductive . . ." (Dobson 1991, table 4.8; *New York Times*, 8 January 1988, 26) The asymmetry of the language, describing the undesirability of a rise in a more qualified way than the undesirability of a fall, was a deliberate signal that the group wanted to put a floor under the dollar at its current level. The markets were initially unimpressed, but heavy around-the-clock intervention in support of the dollar in early January 1988, in an episode that has been called the G-7 "bear squeeze" or "bear trap" (Destler and Henning 1989, 66) was apparently quite effective at combating dollar weakness.[14]

Periodically in 1987 and 1988, Japan's Ministry of Finance used administrative guidance to encourage Japanese institutional investors to hold more US assets than they might choose on profit-maximizing grounds in order to keep the dollar from depreciating further than it already had by then. This happened, in particular, in response to the US bond-market decline in the spring of 1987.

Dollar Rallies: 1988 and 1989

The dollar began to appreciate after the intervention of late December 1987 and early January 1988. The early months of 1988 saw more statements from German, US, and Japanese policymakers opposing dollar depreciation.

In mid-June, the currency began to climb more determinedly. The long-awaited favorable effects of the 1985–86 depreciation were finally beginning to show up in the trade figures. The dollar's strength in mid-year, leading up to the November presidential election, led some observers to suggest that Japanese and other authorities were supporting the US currency in order to help candidate George Bush win the election and thus head off the danger of protectionist trade policies under the Democrats. But the data show that the Fed and Bundesbank were actually intervening moderately heavily to *reduce* the value of the dollar during

---

14. The intent of the intervention was to provide a "bridge" until substantial improvements in the US trade deficit materialized, at which time market sentiment in favor of the dollar could take over. This plan worked quite well (Dobson 1991).

the summer. It wasn't until the dollar began to depreciate in October, and particularly after the election in November, that the Fed began to buy dollars (figures 5.10 and 5.20).

When Baker left the Treasury to run the Bush presidential campaign and Nicholas Brady was appointed secretary, de facto management of exchange rate policy was passed to Mulford, the assistant secretary for international affairs (later promoted to a new position of under secretary for international affairs in the Bush administration). At the time, he reassured the G-7 that Baker's departure would not alter US exchange rate policy. Mulford (1991, 17) has more recently distinguished between the period from September 1985 to December 1987, a "formative" phase of G-7 coordination, and a second period from 1988 to 1991, "in which the process is firmly in place, and people have tried to make it work." The argument is made that the exchange rates prevailing at the time of the Louvre in February 1987 did not incorporate a sufficiently depreciated dollar to be sustainable for long, but that by the beginning of 1988 the exchange rate (the mark-dollar rate, at least) had fallen to a level that was sustainable. In retrospect, however, it is no easier to identify a target zone, even a relatively broad one, into which the dollar was confined during the period starting in 1988, than during the period starting a year earlier at the Louvre.

A new dollar rally began in May 1989. The data show that the Fed sold dollars in every month of that year; in May and June, the magnitudes were the largest of the 1980s (figure 1.2). For the first time since 1985–86, the official message switched from a desire for "exchange rate stability around recent levels" back to an implication that the current strength of the dollar was not justified (Dobson 1991). In May and June, Treasury Secretary Brady and President Bush expressed concern over the dollar's strength. But an observed dampening effect on the dollar over the summer proved to be only temporary.

Statements by other authorities led to a perception of conflicting goals and a breakdown in the coordination process.[15] A Washington ministerial meeting in September 1989 produced a communiqué stating that the G-7 ". . . considered the rise in recent months of the dollar inconsistent with longer run fundamentals," and the communiqué was followed by heavy dollar sales, which continued on into early 1990.[16] The Bank of Japan was especially active, as figure 1.3 shows.

It was around this time that the direction of the yen and the mark diverged. The yen weakened against the dollar at the end of the decade

---

15. For example, an 18 May *Wall Street Journal* story reported mixed signals from central banks on resolve to stem the dollar rally (see also Dobson 1991, 100–14).

16. The Federal Reserve, however, was not in favor at this time of acting to lower the value of the dollar (Dobson 1991, 115; *Financial Times*, 9 and 25 October 1989).

Figure 1.2 Daily intervention in 1989.

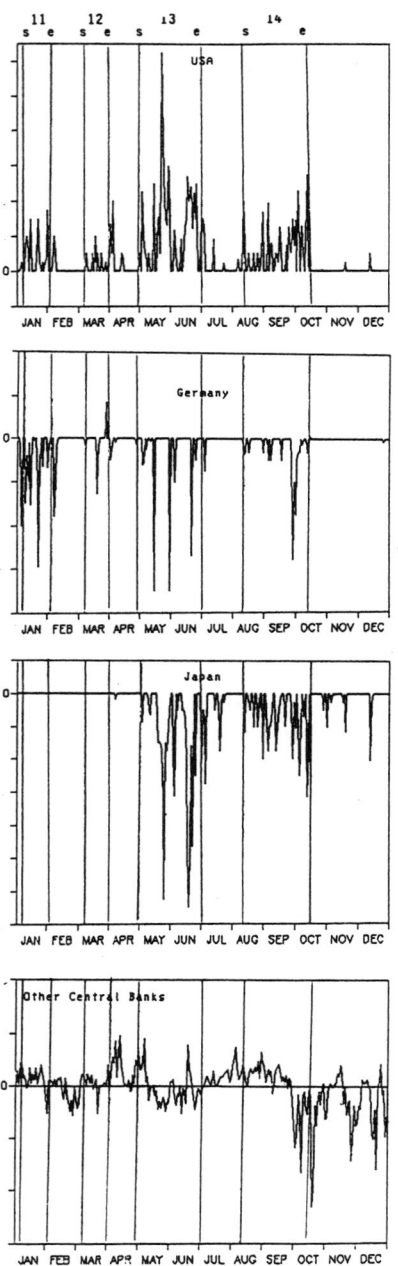

Figure 1.3 Daily intervention in 1990.

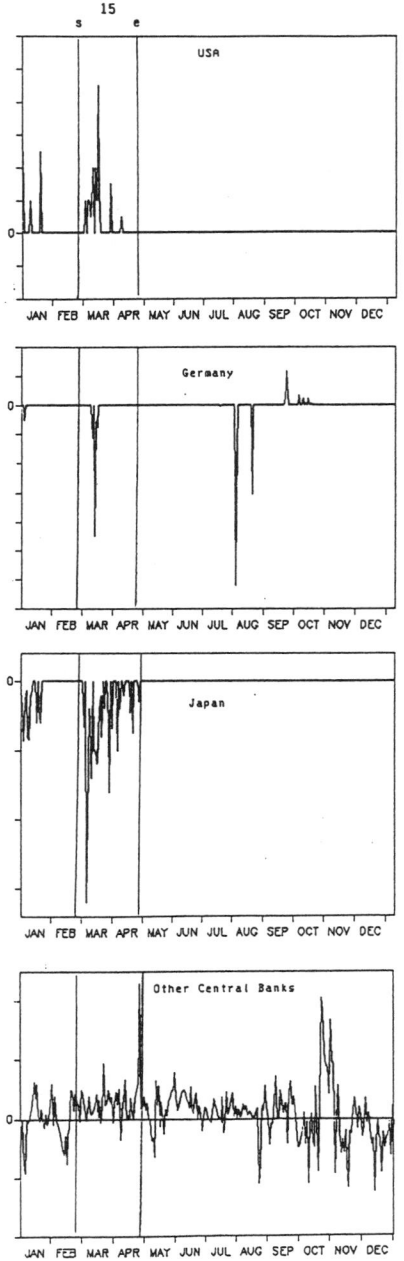

Source: Catte, Galli, and Rebecchini (1992a).

in association with political scandals in Japan in 1989 and an investor shift out of Japanese security markets in early 1990. Further difficulties for the yen arose when Bank of Japan and Ministry of Finance officials were reported as being at odds over monetary policy, favoring and opposing a tightening of monetary policy, respectively. Faced with a depreciating yen, the Japanese government was reported as believing that, having supported the US currency earlier, the Americans should now return the favor and support the yen. US authorities had bought yen and marks in 1988 and 1989 to dampen the appreciation of the dollar. But a Paris G-7 meeting in early April 1990 produced no support for Japan, beyond a statement that the ministers had "discussed . . . the decline of the yen against other currencies and its undesirable consequences for the global adjustment process" (Dobson 1991, table 4.8).

The mark, in contrast to the yen, began to strengthen when the Berlin Wall fell in November 1989 and German interest rates began to rise. The trend of mark appreciation—including against other European currencies—continued in 1990, even while the European countries sought to work out the details of a plan for European Monetary Union that would ban movements in exchange rates among the member currencies.

Combat Zone

The dollar depreciated in 1990, especially after the Iraqi invasion of Kuwait in August, reaching a trough on 13 February 1991, just before the launching of the ground war by the United States and its allies. On 4 February 1991, the authorities, convinced that the depreciation had gone too far, began to buy dollars in an operation that was apparently successful at putting the dollar back on an upswing. Intervention was coordinated between the Fed and Bundesbank, as can be seen in figure 1.4. If intervention was indeed a factor in bringing about this turnaround, then this brief episode is noteworthy in the respect that the amount of intervention involved was considerably smaller than the previous successful episodes such as the Plaza, the Louvre, the bear squeeze, and the other episodes of 1988 and 1989 (*Federal Reserve Bank of New York Quarterly Review* 1991, various issues).[17]

The subsequent dollar appreciation was particularly strong against the mark, as the German difficulties with absorption of the Eastern *länder*, which had been denied by officialdom, began to become more apparent to all. By this time, the yen's difficulties of 1989 and 1990 had subsided.

Just before a mid-July G-7 economic summit in London, the authorities (including many European central banks) once again intervened to sell

---

17. It is, of course, possible that the turnaround would have occurred even without the intervention.

Figure 1.4 Daily intervention in 1991.

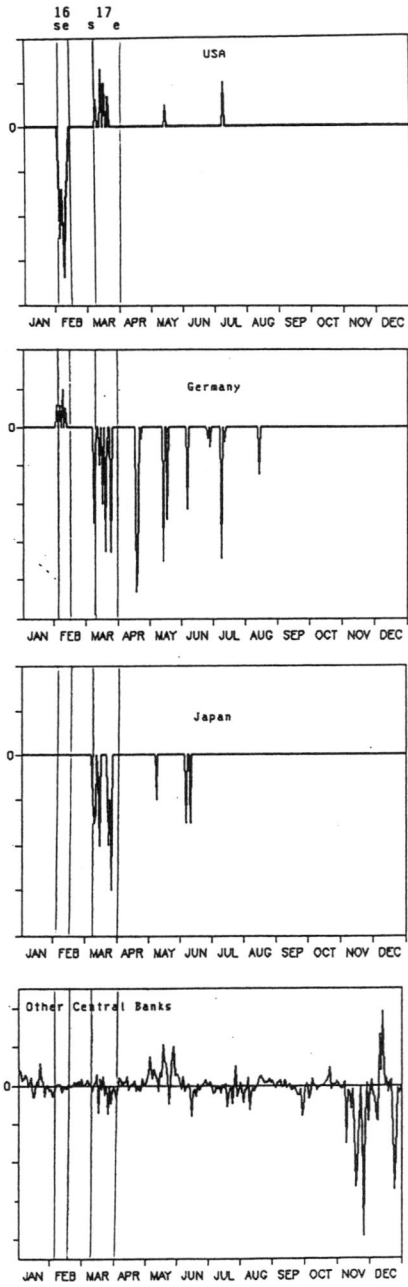

Source: Catte, Galli, and Rebecchini (1992a).

dollars, convinced that the upswing had now gone too far. This intervention, which *The New York Times* called an ambush, again met with apparent success. It was unusual in that administration officials confirmed to the press that the intervention had taken place.

The apparent successful placing of a floor under the dollar in February 1991 and a ceiling over it in July renewed talk that a possible (broad) target zone or "reference range" might be in effect for the dollar. Williamson (1985) had proposed earlier that the major currencies adopt a target zone with a ± 10 percent width. Bergsten (1991) suggested that the dollar–deutsche mark rate had acted over 1990–91 as if a ± 12 percent zone (centered on 1.65) were in effect. In any case, one can agree that the swings of recent years look small when compared with the big cycle of 1981–86 (figures 5.14 and 5.15).

Talk of a dollar target zone, viewed very skeptically by most at the time of the Louvre and earlier, had become somewhat more plausible by the start of the 1990s, in part due to the apparent success of the target zone of the European Monetary System. The EMS had gone into effect in March 1979, replacing its failed predecessor target zone, the "Snake." The apparent success of the EMS at accomplishing a degree of stabilization of European currencies in the first half of the 1980s—and, more importantly, the continued success at avoiding realignments in the second half of the 1980s, even after France, Italy, and some of the smaller countries phased out their capital controls—convinced some that intervention could help stabilize exchange rates. By December 1991, the European leaders felt confident enough of their success to agree at Maastricht on the terms for European Monetary Union (EMU).

High German Interest Rates Win Out: 1992

In the fall of 1992, however, the European exchange markets were rocked by a crisis that called into question the confident success surrounding the EMS, let alone the more ambitious plan for EMU. It chastened many of those who believed in the ability of central banks to impose their wills on the market.

Doubts about EMU had arisen when the Danish population voted against the Maastricht treaty in June, and they began to build as the date for a French referendum (21 September) approached. These doubts were manifested as mounting speculation in favor of the mark and against the weaker currencies. The speculation forced a devaluation of the lira on 14 September and then forced both the lira and pound to drop out of the EMS altogether, and Spain to devalue, on 17 September.

The importance of the crisis had mainly to do with the Europeans themselves. Repercussions for the dollar were of second-order importance. Nevertheless, there were several implications and lessons for the dollar. There may have been a direct implication, in that upward pressure on the mark against weaker European currencies was associated with upward pressure on the mark against the dollar. It is an old "rule of thumb" that a dollar depreciation is correlated with this sort of pressure on the European cross-rates, presumably because speculators treat the dollar and mark as substitute international currencies. But however the short-term patterns of speculation are interpreted,[18] the lesson for the longer term is that the macroeconomic fundamentals ultimately determine events. This is true both for European currencies and for the dollar.

German interest rates had continued to rise in 1992. (They had been rising steadily since 1988.) No concession was made to the European partners, despite Maastricht. The British and others would have preferred easier money in order to respond to a deepening recession but were obliged to raise their interest rates whenever the Bundesbank raised theirs. The unhappy public in the United Kingdom and other countries was ultimately not willing to sustain a deep recession just to keep up with the Germans. At least, speculators strongly suspected that the public was ultimately not willing to make this sacrifice, and they had no incentive to wait patiently until the drama played itself out. Hence the September crisis.

If other Europeans raised interest rates to match the Germans only with reluctance, the United States had no inclination to do so at all. US interest rates had been declining since 1988—steeply since late 1990— the same period over which German interest rates had been rising. The two crossed in 1990. The gap in short-term rates then steadily widened, with the Fed easing monetary policy in a year of recession and election, until it exceeded 6 points in July 1992. It might be a tribute to the effectiveness of the intervention of February 1991 that the dollar was still firm as late as January-February 1992, when the Fed and the Bank of Japan thought it necessary to sell dollars for yen.

Eventually, the large interest differential vis-à-vis Germany constituted too strong a lure for investors to resist. The dollar began to depreciate against the mark again in April, producing some concerted dollar purchases on 24 April and continued as the Bundesbank again raised interest rates and the United States again lowered them. The differential climbed above 6 points in July. The Fed, together with at least 12 other central banks, intervened 20 July to slow the dollar's slide (with some success, in part because it caught many speculators by surprise). Both the market's flirtation with an all-time low for the deutsche mark–dollar rate and concerted intervention to prevent this continued in August. The low was punctured, and the rate hit 1.40 on 24 August, despite repeated

---

18. Somewhat surprisingly, the dollar on the peak crisis day actually appreciated. The explanation financial analysts gave was that turbulence in the European markets was sending investors to the dollar as a safe haven.

intervention which, though not especially large, was coordinated. The dollar did not begin to revive until October. By that time, interest rates were being nudged upward by expectations of a Bill Clinton victory in the United States and were easing in Europe, where Italy and the United Kingdom had been freed of the need to tighten, and the Bundesbank, their point having been made, could afford to lighten up as well.

In other words, high German interest rates ultimately won out both against the other European currencies and against the dollar. A willingness in Europe to sacrifice some degree of monetary independence allowed Italy, the United Kingdom, and Spain to keep their currencies in line with Germany's from 1990[19] until September 1992. But the willingness to sacrifice independence was not complete, and without it, intervention could not save the system. In the United States, a relaxed but steady pattern of intervention apparently succeeded during the same two-year period in keeping the dollar inside a band that, on the one hand, was much wider than the Europeans' but on the other hand required little or no sacrifice of monetary policy. When widening monetary fundamentals caught up with the markets, however, neither the relaxed American readiness to intervene nor the European half-willingness to supplement intervention with monetary policy was sufficient to stem the tide.

---

19. German Monetary Union occurred in July 1990, and the United Kingdom joined the EMS in October.

Does a Free-Floating System Work Well?

Arguments over Free-Floating Exchange Rates

Many of the arguments regarding the desirability of using intervention policy to stabilize the exchange rate harken to the classic debate over the relative merits of two polar cases: a system in which exchange rates are determined by government authorities versus one in which they are determined freely by the private market. As summarized in the previous chapter, each administration since the end of the Bretton Woods fixed-rate system has wrestled with the issue of exchange rate volatility. Before turning to a discussion in succeeding chapters of whether intervention policy is an effective tool, it is necessary to consider whether such a tool is really needed.

Pro-Stability Arguments

The classic arguments in favor of exchange rate stability generally fall into two categories. The more traditional argument is that freely floating exchange rates tend to be volatile. The risk created by exchange rate uncertainty discourages imports, exports, borrowing, and lending. Thus, if exchange rates could be stabilized, it would help promote these international economic activities.

The other argument, which has received more emphasis since the high-inflation experience of the 1970s, is that fixing the exchange rate is an effective way of providing a nominal anchor to monetary policy. A credible commitment by the monetary authorities to pegging the exchange rate will convince people that inflation is unlikely; lower expectations of inflation will then feed through the system (via, for example, moderated wage demands) to yield a lower actual inflation rate for any given level of output. The foundation of the European Monetary System and further proposed steps toward European Monetary Union have been motivated in large part by the desire of Italy, France, and other inflation-prone countries to attain the benefits of a nominal anchor.

Of these arguments, the cost of exchange rate uncertainty is the more relevant for the question of whether the United States should seek to stabilize the dollar. Going all the way to a fixed exchange rate, or at least to a narrow band, which is probably necessary to obtain the benefits of a nominal anchor, is not currently a very practical option for the United States.[1]

Arguments for Market Float

There are also a number of distinct arguments in favor of purely floating exchange rates. A simple laissez-faire view is that exchange rates should be determined in private markets, without government interference, for the same reason that the price of wheat should be determined in private markets without government interference. Changes in the market price are the result of changes in demand or supply. If the government attempts to suppress them by stabilizing the price, it is merely "papering over" the disturbance. Where the change in demand or supply is permanent, such intervention merely postpones the day of adjustment. Where it is temporary, such intervention merely transfers the burden of uncertainty to somewhere else in the economy.

A parallel view, which recognizes market imperfections such as sticky prices and wages, is that it is easier to adjust the exchange rate to respond to new developments in the economy than to adjust wages and prices. Imagine, for example, that a country suffers a loss in demand for its products. It is easier to restore competitiveness in world markets with one simple devaluation than by reducing all nominal wages and prices in the economy one by one, a process that may be slow, painful, and accompanied by unemployment and an excess supply of goods. According to a famous analogy, it is easier to change the exchange rate than to change thousands of individual wages and prices for the same reason that it is easier to switch to daylight savings time than it is to change

---

1. An argument that is related to the nominal anchor point is that a highly variable exchange rate is more inflationary than a moderately variable exchange rate, via a ratchet effect: prices are "sticky" in the downward direction, so that the upward movement in domestic prices caused by a depreciation is larger than the downward movement caused by an appreciation of equal magnitude. There is, however, little empirical evidence in favor of this hypothesis.

thousands of individual schedules for work, transportation, entertainment events, and so on.

A third view is that a country typically has more policy goals that it would like to pursue, such as full employment and low inflation, than it has independent policy instruments to use, such as fiscal and monetary policy. Some measure of the balance of payments is an important goal for most countries as well.

It used to be said that a floating exchange rate would automatically equilibrate the trade balance and thereby free up the other policy instruments to pursue important internal economic goals. Similarly, a floating exchange rate is said to free countries to pursue their goals independently of each other. The exchange rate adjusts automatically to insulate one country from disturbances in another.

These arguments are, in a sense, at least 20 years out of date: the existence of large capital flows between countries means that floating exchange rates imply neither trade balance equilibrium nor insulation from foreign disturbances. It is true that floating exchange rates have eliminated as a goal the need to obtain equilibrium in the overall balance of payments (the balance of trade in goods and services *plus* the balance in private capital flows and other financial transactions). But in the meantime, we have in a sense acquired a new goal: there is a perceived need to obtain equilibrium in the trade balance.

The argument for attempting to stabilize the dollar boils down to a claim that the variability of floating rates imposes a high cost on international transactions. The argument in favor of pure floating is based on the claim that any such uncertainty is intrinsic in the system—that any excessive instability in the exchange rate is merely a reflection of instability in macroeconomic policies—and that it cannot be simply suppressed without creating greater costs elsewhere. To evaluate the weight of the arguments in greater detail, we need to consider first whether exchange rate volatility imposes real costs and then whether the volatility experienced since 1973 has been greater than it need be.

Real Effects of Exchange Rate Volatility

It is easy enough to dispose of one simplistic argument that was often made 20 years ago when officials and analysts contemplated how the new floating-rate system would work: that movements in variable nominal exchange rates would neatly offset movements in countries' price levels and would thus not have real effects. To the contrary, a very small fraction of movements in nominal exchange rates have been offset by movements in prices. Movements in nominal exchange rates have, rather, translated almost fully and in almost all instances into movements in real exchange rates. These, in turn, have major effects on the profitability of exports, the attractiveness of overseas investment, etc.

Some argue that movements in real exchange rates are always the cause rather than the effect of movements in nominal exchange rates. But these arguments are implausible. Whenever an exchange rate is switched from a fixed-rate regime to a floating-rate regime, the variability of both the real and nominal rate is observed to increase. It is clear here that nominal movements are causing real movements rather than the other way around.

Hedging Foreign Exchange Risk on the Forward Market

Before the advent of floating rates, the dominant fear was that exchange rate uncertainty would impose heavy costs on international trade. Importers who contracted to buy from abroad at a price set in foreign currency would face the risk of an unexpected increase in the price of foreign exchange between the time the contract was signed and the time payment was due. Thus they would be uncertain how much they were going to have to pay in domestic currency. Similarly, exporters who contracted to sell abroad at prices set in foreign currency would face the risk of an unexpected decrease in the price of foreign currency. Thus they would be uncertain how much they were going to earn in terms of domestic currency. To the extent that importers and exporters are risk-averse, this uncertainty would impose a cost and discourage them from undertaking trade.

Governments often view currency integration as a way to encourage trade integration. In the case of the European Community, promoting intraregional trade has been a major motivation behind the drive to stabilize exchange rates.

After 20 years of experience with floating rates, most analysts discount the risk argument. It is not that floating rates have not created a great deal of uncertainty; they have. It is rather that this uncertainty is commonly thought to impose relatively small costs on firms. Firms can readily protect themselves against exchange risk by hedging, or "covering," on the forward exchange market. The markets in forward exchange—and other derivatives such as futures, options, and swaps—have developed in scope and grown in size with the need for them: more currencies are included, trading takes place in more locations, and transactions costs tend to be smaller than was the case 20 years ago.

The argument that any given firm can fully protect itself by hedging misses the point that someone must take the other side of the contract, and that this someone will charge a price for taking the risk off the firm's hands. The price in terms of the bid-ask spread or other direct transactions costs is very small, though even here it is not necessarily negligible from the viewpoint of a small importer or exporter. But the importer may have to pay an exchange risk premium, an excess of the forward price over the expected future spot price, for the privilege of unloading foreign currency exposure.

The same logic holds for investors who buy foreign securities or undertake direct investment abroad. They expose themselves to the risk that the value of these assets in terms of domestic currency will drop when the price of foreign exchange drops. They can protect themselves by hedging, selling the foreign currency forward. But they may have to pay an exchange risk premium to do so.

There is some reason to believe that such exchange risk premiums are relatively small. Much of exchange risk is "diversifiable": the domestic importer who wishes to buy foreign exchange forward will, through the intermediation of the market, find a natural partner in the foreign importer who wishes to buy domestic exchange (sell foreign exchange) forward. Similarly, the investor who wishes to sell foreign exchange forward will find a ready partner in the foreign investor who wishes to buy foreign exchange forward. The market-clearing equilibrium forward price at which all parties end up trading may not be far off from the expected future spot price that would prevail in the absence of uncertainty.[2]

Evidence on the Foreign Exchange Risk Premium

What do econometric estimates of the exchange risk premium reveal? They give very different answers for its magnitude, depending on the approach taken and the sample period used. The ambiguity comes in measuring investors' expectations of the future spot exchange rate. Under the "rational expectations methodology," investors' *ex ante* expectations are inferred from *ex post* changes in the exchange rate. These tests indicate that a large fraction (often equal to or greater than 100 percent) of movement in the forward discount constitutes movement in a risk premium. This would imply, for example, that the dollar had to pay a positive risk premium in the 1980s vis-à-vis the mark or yen. (This follows because the dollar sold at a forward discount against these foreign currencies.) It would also imply that the risk premium reversed sign in the 1990s.

---

2. If the exchange risk premium is positive from the viewpoint of domestic residents $[F - E(S_{t+1}) > 0]$, it is likely that it is negative from the viewpoint of foreign residents $[1/F - E(1/S_{t+1}) < 0]$. What determines which currency charges a positive risk premium? It is the one that is in excess supply, in the sense that the share of outstanding assets denominated in that currency, which must be held in the marketplace, exceeds a particular benchmark. If investors diversify optimally, the benchmark share is called the "minimum-variance portfolio" and is closely related to the importance of that country's goods in investors' consumption patterns.

But there is reason to be skeptical of this approach to measuring expectations over short periods. An alternative approach, measuring investors' expectations from survey data, tends to throw doubt on the usefulness of the rational expectations methodology. In the case of the five major currencies against the dollar, no fraction of variation in the forward discount represents variation in the risk premium. (Variation in the forward discount represents, rather, variation in the expectations that market traders hold of future changes in the exchange rate.) In one respect, the conclusion is the same as under the rational expectations methodology: there is evidence of a gap between the forward rate and the expected future spot rate. But the behavior of the risk premium is very different. The survey data approach suggests, for example, that US assets were viewed as less risky than German and Japanese assets in the 1980s rather than more (Dominguez 1986; Froot and Frankel 1989).

Even those approaches that make a guess at the magnitude of risk aversion and tend to produce a small estimate for the risk premium in terms of how many basis points one has to give up to eliminate exposure may carry the implication that this is enough to have a major effect on the behavior of risk-averse investors. A tax of 0.50 percentage points on gross sales abroad might be enough to have a perceptible effect on the incentive to export. Ultimately, whether exchange rate variability has an effect on trade is an empirical question that should be examined directly.

Effect of Exchange Rate Variability on Trade Flows

It is natural, after 20 years of experience with floating rates, to want to look directly for an effect on trade. Trade volumes have increased since 1973, despite the increase in exchange rate variability. But many other things have changed at the same time. A number of empirical studies have tried to sort out the effects (Hooper and Kohlhagen 1978; Kenen and Rodrik 1986; Akhtar and Hilton 1984; Caballero and Corbo 1989; the literature is surveyed in Edison and Melvin 1990). Some find modest negative effects on trade, but the results are mixed.

The majority of the studies use time series. Given that it probably takes many years before a pattern of variability is fully reflected in trade, it is perhaps not surprising that there is a limited amount that can be learned from a few decades of data. An alternative to the time-series approach is to study the role of bilateral exchange rate variability in a cross-section of bilateral trade flows. Frankel and Wei (1992) study 1,953 pairs of trading partners and find an effect (using ordinary least-squares estimation) that, though relatively small, is statistically significant in 1980: the estimated effect on the volume of trade of hypothetically eliminating all fluctuations in real exchange rates worldwide in 1980 was 2.7

percent. (This equals an average standard deviation of monthly exchange rate changes of .333 times an estimated coefficient of 8.04.[3])

The cross-section approach has a problem of its own, however: at least part of the observed correlation is probably attributable to reverse causality. An attempt to isolate the exogenous component of bilateral exchange rate variability (using as the instrument bilateral differences in money supply variability) reduces the estimated impact on trade considerably. Furthermore, by either estimation technique, the effect seems to have disappeared later in the 1980s. One possible explanation is the increased use of futures, options, and other instruments for hedging.

Misalignments

Recent detractors of free-floating rates have tended to be more concerned about large medium-term "misalignments" than about short-term volatility. The argument is that large swings such as the 1981–85 appreciation of the dollar have had serious consequences. The proximate effect, of course, is that American exporters and import-competing firms lose competitiveness on world markets and the US trade balance deteriorates sharply. It is too simplistic to count the number of jobs lost in exchange rate–sensitive sectors because there are jobs gained in other sectors. But reallocations in the labor market and other such adjustments may have long-term costs. When domestic firms in a given industry contract and their foreign competitors expand, effects may persist even beyond the subsequent reversal in the exchange rate. Once American firms lose market share, they may have trouble winning it back. These long-lasting effects, sometimes referred to as "hysteresis," occur via the industry's capital stock (how large and up-to-date it is), distribution networks, marketing channels, and consumer tastes. There is also the argument that import-sensitive sectors hurt by an overvalued dollar may be able to win protective barriers that impose a high cost on everyone else and that are not dismantled when the exchange rate returns to normal.

Have Exchange Rates Behaved as They Were Supposed To?

We have already noted that exchange rates have been highly volatile since 1973. It would be a mistake to conclude from this observation alone, however, that they have necessarily been more volatile than they should be. Since the exchange rate is the relative price of countries'

---

3. Other studies with a cross-section dimension are De Grauwe (1988), Abrams (1980), and Brada and Mendez (1988).

moneys, it is natural that it should be volatile in the same way as the prices of other assets, such as gold, stocks, and bonds. The price will change from moment to moment, every time there is a change in supply or demand.

Milton Friedman (1953) predicted that floating exchange rates would be stable if monetary policies were stable and would be variable if policies were variable. To discern whether exchange rates have been "excessively variable," it is not enough simply to compare the variability of the exchange rate with the variability of the money supply (or with the variability of likely macroeconomic determinants of money demand, such as output). There are several excellent theoretical reasons for believing that observed changes in the money supply of a given magnitude can be accompanied by observed changes in the exchange rate of a larger magnitude, even when the markets are operating well.

Magnification and Overshooting in Models of Exchange Rates

The simplest model of exchange rates, the monetarist model, ignores any international barriers, frictions, or imperfect substitutabilities that might segment domestic goods markets from foreign goods markets, or domestic assets from foreign assets. Even in such a perfect-markets model, the magnification effect can imply a large change in the exchange rate associated with a small change in the money supply. The magnification effect operates when money market developments cause investors to expect a substantial change in the future rate of money growth. Even if the current observed change in the money supply is small, an expectation of rapid money-supply growth will lead to expectations that the domestic currency will lose value. To protect themselves against expected capital losses, investors will register a lower demand for domestic assets and a higher demand for foreign assets. This will cause the domestic currency to depreciate immediately, even before the feared money growth has taken place.

A great limitation of the monetarist model is that it can only explain changes in the nominal exchange rate that are matched by changes in price levels. It cannot explain changes in the real exchange rate. Since most variation in the foreign exchange market is of the latter type, the appeal of the model is limited. The monetarist model is considered to be most applicable to hyperinflation. But the basic lesson of the magnification effect remains valid: large changes in the exchange rate can be observed even in the absence of large changes in the money supply when there are developments that change investors' expectations of future monetary conditions.

An even more important reason to expect high variability in the exchange rate is the overshooting effect. This effect arises in models where adjustment to equilibrium is not instantaneous. In the case of the renowned sticky-price monetary model of Dornbusch (1976), the prices of goods and services do not adjust instantaneously to an increase in demand that occurs when there is an increase in the money supply. This means that an increase in the nominal money supply in the short run translates into an equal increase in the real money supply, which works to lower real interest rates. The decline in interest rates, in comparison with expected rates of return abroad, discourages investors from holding domestic securities, which in turn causes a large depreciation of the currency. The currency generally depreciates to a level beyond its long-run equilibrium. This is the overshooting effect. The result is that the short-run change in the exchange rate is greater than the change in the money supply.

An additional source of overshooting can arise in the portfolio-balance model. Here the focus is on the fact that the country's net international investment position can only change gradually. (The year's change in the international investment position is the current account.) In other words, the country enters each period with given holdings of foreign assets, which it has accumulated in the past. Consider an increase in the US money supply. It changes the share of American investors' portfolios allocated to dollars versus foreign assets. The value of the currency falls in response to the increase in the supply of the currency. The change in the exchange rate will be greater in the short run, when the international investment position is predetermined, than in the long run, when it has had time to adjust. This is similar to the pattern in the sticky-price monetary model, only now the investment position adjusts gradually via the current account, whereas in the monetary model it is the price level that adjusts, via excess demand for goods.

The lesson for our purposes is the same in both the overshooting model and the portfolio-balance model: the theories imply that a permanent 1 percent increase in the money supply will change the exchange rate by more than 1 percent. Intuitively, if some variables in the system are not free to adjust in the short run (the price level or the stock of foreign assets), then the exchange rate, which is free, will adjust more than proportionately in order to compensate. But the theory does not tell us exactly how much more. For this reason, when we observe that the variance of changes in the exchange rate exceeds the variance of changes in the money supply, we have no way of concluding whether exchange rate volatility is "excessive," or whether this is simply the overshooting phenomenon at work.

To restate the point, any resemblance of the word "overshooting" to a value judgment on how well floating exchange rates function is purely coincidental. An analogy will illustrate how the phenomenon could be entirely consistent with efficient, well-functioning markets. Consider a shortage in the world orange juice market due, for example, to a loss of supply from Brazil. The price of orange juice rises more in the short run than in the long run. The reason is that the supply of oranges in California is relatively fixed in the short run. Over time, if the disturbance in the world market persists, more orange trees will be planted and harvested, and the gradual increase in supply will drive the price of oranges back down. One might say that the price of oranges initially "overshot" its new long-run equilibrium. Yet there is nothing inefficient about this. Oranges were genuinely scarce in the short run, and an efficient allocation of resources required the signals that were sent by the high price.

So it may be with the foreign exchange market. Or, it may not: in the case of macroeconomics, such market imperfections as the stickiness of wages and prices imply that there is no automatic presumption that laissez-faire is best. This is different from the case of oranges, where—in the absence of imperfections such as marketing boards—there is in fact a presumption that the price fluctuations are optimal and that the government should leave the market to function on its own.

Do Exchange Rates Operate as They "Should"? Econometric Tests

How then to tell whether fluctuations in the foreign exchange market are efficient? Some interesting questions concern how much flexibility in the exchange rate is desirable even under the assumption that the markets left to themselves operate as theory says they should. These are discussed in chapter 3. First, we consider briefly some efforts to tell whether the markets are operating as theory suggests. These econometric tests are of two kinds.

Many studies have tested whether the forward exchange rate is an unbiased predictor of the future spot exchange rate. These are usually called tests of "efficiency" in the foreign exchange market. They are in fact joint tests of three propositions simultaneously:

- investors' forecasts are optimal (this is the rational expectations hypothesis, which is a component of most standard models of exchange rate determination);

- speculators do not require compensation for risk when they buy a currency that they expect to be worth more than the forward rate (this is the no-risk-premium hypothesis mentioned above[4]);

---

4. The risk premium is also key to the question of whether sterilized foreign exchange intervention can have an effect on the market, as in the portfolio-balance model, or whether only money supply changes have an effect, as in the monetary models. The question of whether intervention is an effective tool to control the exchange rate, the central focus of this study, is addressed in chapters 6 and 7. Here we are only considering whether there is a need for such a tool.

- there are no substantial transactions costs or other barriers discouraging investors from buying the currency.

These three propositions together would imply that the forward rate is the optimal forecast of the future spot rate, fully reflecting available information.

Despite the label "efficiency," these tests are not much help in telling us whether the free-floating system maximizes the desirable allocation of resources. Even if one failed to find evidence of bias in the forward rate, the leap to drawing judgments about the efficient allocation of resources is a large one (e.g., Tobin 1978; Dornbusch 1982 and 1986). Imperfections in goods and labor markets, and a role for monetary policy, are facts of life. The "theory of the second best" says that when imperfections occur in some markets, intervention in others that lack relevance may be preferable to laissez-faire. In some contexts, this point has a decidedly academic flavor. But in the foreign exchange market, it has more relevance.

The usual finding, in any case, is that the forward rate is in fact a biased forecast of the future spot rate. This finding is clearly not due to failure of the transaction-costs proposition above: transactions costs are directly observable and are known to be small. Some believe the finding of bias is due to a failure of the rational expectations proposition, others to the existence of a risk premium. Either way, the conventional empirical model, whereby the exchange rate is determined solely by current monetary factors plus rational expectations of future monetary conditions, is called into question.

In addition to these "market efficiency" tests, a second body of empirical evidence consists of attempts to estimate complete equations of exchange rate determination. If exchange rate movements were indeed attributable to changes in macroeconomic conditions as in the models reviewed above, one should be able to verify this by complete econometric tests of the models. The monetary models, for example, say that one should be able to explain the exchange rate by means of such contemporaneous variables as money supplies, income levels, interest rates, and inflation rates. Many medium-term swings can be explained by these fundamentals. Figure 2.1, for example, illustrates that some major movements of the differential in real interest rates (of the United States minus a weighted average of major trading partners' interest rates) have been matched by corresponding major movements in the real value of the dollar, just as the overshooting model says: downward from 1976 to 1978, sharply upward from 1980 to 1984, sharply downward from 1985 to 1986, and again downward (more gently) from 1988 to 1991. The explanatory power of the econometric equations overall is quite unimpressive, however, especially in the short run. This finding tends to undermine the argument that exchange rates only vary to the extent

Figure 2.1 Exchange value of the dollar and interest rate differential, 1973–91

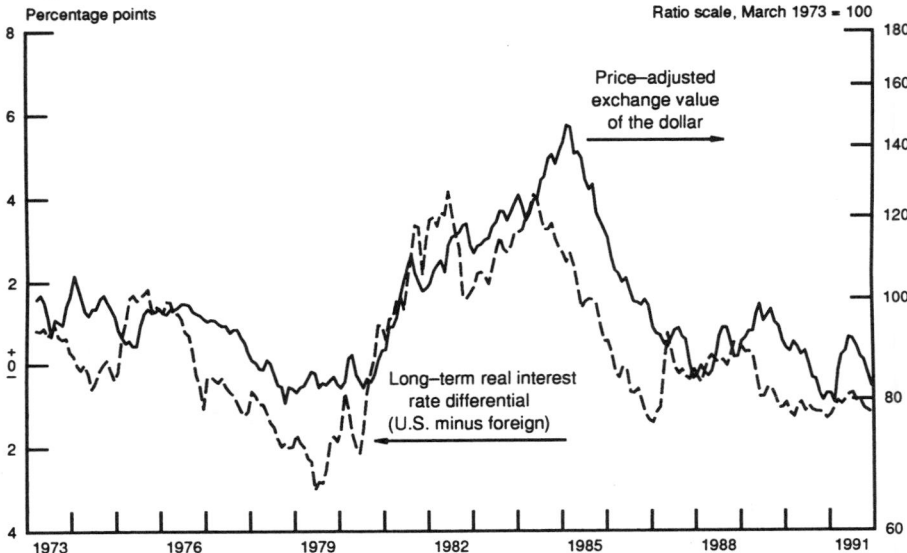

Note: The exchange value of the U.S. dollar is its weighted average exchange value against currencies of other G-10 countries using 1972-76 total trade weights adjusted by relative consumer prices.

The differential is the rate on long-term U.S. government bonds minus the rate on comparable foreign securities, both adjusted for expected inflation estimated by 36-month centered moving average of actual CPI inflation or by staff forecasts when needed.

Source: Federal Reserve Board.

that monetary factors or other macroeconomic fundamentals vary. The majority of short-term movements in exchange rates are apparently due to something else, something other than observable macroeconomic fundamentals. There is always the possibility that these movements are due to macroeconomic fundamentals that are not known to the economist-observer. But speculative bubbles are a prime suspect.[5]

Speculative Bubbles

Financial commentators have discussed the possibility of speculative bubbles ever since the classic historical episodes of the tulip bulb mania

---

5. Another suspect is possible frequent shifts in the equilibrium real exchange rate, attributable to changes in productivity or demand patterns. This possibility seems far-fetched, however, when one examines the evidence on real exchange rate variability over fixed-rate and floating-rate periods experienced by various countries at various times. As already noted, changes in the real exchange rate are much smaller during periods when the nominal exchange rate has been stabilized (e.g., Mussa 1990).

of the early 17th century and the South Sea Company bubble of the early 18th century.[6] In recent years, puzzling large movements in exchange rates have been identified as speculative bubbles by some. The final 20 percent appreciation of the dollar in the eight months preceding its peak in February 1985, for example, seems difficult to explain otherwise. Interest rates, and virtually all other standard observable macroeconomic variables, were moving in the wrong direction to explain the appreciation (figure 2.1). Such observers were led to the unorthodox conclusion that the market was not correctly valuing the dollar (see chapter 1, footnote 4).

A speculative bubble can be defined as an increase in the price resulting from an increase in demand that is not related to fundamentals or to expectations of fundamentals but that is rather a self-fulfilling response to expectations that the price will go up. Speculative bubbles are not necessarily inconsistent with rational expectations. If the price is going to continue to rise anyway, the rational speculator knows that he stands to lose money by not going along with the crowd. Even the knowledge that sooner or later the bubble will come to an end and the price will return to the level dictated by fundamentals is not sufficient to foreclose a speculative bubble because nobody knows when the crash will occur. Rational expectations imply only that, in each week, the rate of return to holding the asset in the event that the bubble continues is sufficient to offset the loss in the event that the bubble bursts during the coming week. From the viewpoint of individual investors, as long as the expected return for holding the asset is as great as the expected return in selling it, there is nothing inherently irrational about the speculative bubble.

The notion of rational speculative bubbles is important because it shows that exchange rates can be needlessly volatile, even if speculators behave optimally from their individual viewpoints. But there is something unsatisfying about the standard theory of rational speculative bubbles: it has nothing to say about when bubbles start or when they end.

Chartists and Fundamentalists

Stabilizing and Destabilizing Speculators

A speculative bubble could get started if an upward movement in the exchange rate, which might occur for reasons fully based in macroeconomic fundamentals, then causes investors to extrapolate. If "specula-

---

6. In these remarkable episodes, speculative trading frenzy bid to extreme heights the prices of improbable assets: tulip bulbs in the Netherlands, in the first case, and shares in a company formed in England for the purpose of trading along the Pacific Coast of South America, in the second. Twentieth-century candidates for speculative bubbles include the stock markets of the US 1920s and the Japanese 1980s.

tors" have bandwagon expectations, the mere fact that the exchange rate has been increasing in the recent past will cause them to expect further increases. If they act on this forecast, they will buy the foreign currency that they expect to appreciate, thereby driving up its price today. Because such behavior exaggerates existing swings in the exchange rate, it is called destabilizing speculation.

There is a temptation to think of overshooting as an example of destabilizing speculation and that investors, by freely buying and selling foreign exchange based on their expectations of changes in the exchange rate, make the exchange rate more variable than it would otherwise be. This would be a mistake, however. The overshooting model illustrates the general principle that expectations are stabilizing rather than destabilizing, so long as an increase in the level of the exchange rate causes investors to reduce their expectations as to its future rate of change. That is, if investors act on the basis of such expectations, they will buy currency when its value is low and sell when it is high. This will raise the currency's price when it would otherwise be low and lower the price when it would otherwise be high. This type of speculation works to moderate the fluctuations that would otherwise occur in the exchange rate.

Investors, or speculators, who buy low and sell high will also make a profit. This is why Milton Friedman (1953) argued that stabilizing speculators would prosper. Any speculators who were destabilizing would be buying high and selling low. They would lose money and thus eventually be driven out of business.

How do market participants actually form their expectations? In practice, as opposed to theory, they use a wide variety of approaches. As a consequence, they come up with a wide variety of forecasts at any one time. This dispersion of forecasts is evident in several surveys of market participants that are conducted regularly. The survey that was conducted in the 1980s by the *Economist*-affiliated *Financial Report* showed forecasts (at the six-month horizon) varying over a high-low range that averaged 15 percent. The survey that is currently conducted monthly by the *Currency Forecasters' Digest* shows an average range of 10 percent.[7] Ito (1990) also finds wide dispersion in forecasts made in Tokyo.

As distressing as it is for economists to admit, many professional exchange rate forecasters and traders do not base their forecasts on any model based on money supplies or other fundamental economic variables. "Technical analysts" instead forecast by using computer techniques, or hand-drawn graphs in the case of more old-fashioned "chart-

---

7. For the mark-dollar rate, also at the six-month horizon. This range is the difference between the average of the five lowest forecasts and the average of the five highest forecasts, as a percentage of the consensus forecast. The average of this range over the months from February 1990 to February 1992 was 9.9 percent.

ists," to try to uncover trends in the exchange rate. One of the most popular rules calls for buying a currency whenever the short-term moving average (the average over the preceding week, for example) rises above the longer-term moving average (over the preceding month), and selling whenever the reverse happens. The "momentum" models call for buying when the current price exceeds the price that existed, for example, five days ago. Such techniques, in effect, forecast by extrapolating past trends and thus generally fall into the category of expectations that are destabilizing if acted upon by investors. (There are probably as many methods of technical analysis as there are technical analysts, but most fit this description.)

Which kind of forecast tends to dominate in the marketplace—those of most technical analysts, who are subject to bandwagon expectations and are a destabilizing force, or those of adherents to the overshooting model, who are subject to regressive expectations and are a stabilizing force? Survey data suggest that the answer depends in part on the length of the forecast horizon. At horizons of six months or more (which is considered long-term in the foreign exchange market!), regressive expectations seem to dominate. For every 1 percent that the currency appreciates above its long-run average value, the median forecaster expects a depreciation of about 0.2 percent over the subsequent year.[8] At shorter horizons, however, bandwagon expectations seem to dominate. At horizons of one week or one month, survey respondents tend to extrapolate recent trends.[9] It is therefore worrisome that most trading in the foreign exchange market seems to be motivated by very short horizons.

1984–85: an Endogenous Speculative Bubble?

It does not take much to get a small speculative bubble started. In the neighborhood of the equilibrium exchange rate, those who base their forecasts on fundamentals have little reason to resist a small movement created by technical analysts who jump onto an incipient bandwagon. It is likely, however, that most speculative bubbles do not get very big before they burst. This is because the fundamentalists will begin to hold stronger expectations of future devaluation as the currency in question becomes more overvalued.

The interesting question is whether large speculative bubbles can occur. Many think that the final stages of the 1981–85 appreciation of the dollar was of this nature. One explanation of how a major speculative

---

8. This estimate is based on the *Financial Report* survey (Frankel and Froot 1987).

9. These estimates are based on the survey of Money Market Services, International; Frankel and Froot (1990a and b). See also Goodhart (1988), Schulmeister (1987), Schulmeister and Goldberg (1989, 117–64), and Taylor and Allen (1992).

bubble in the dollar might have begun in 1984 is that market investors had by then stopped listening to the forecasts issued by the fundamentalists because their predictions that the dollar would depreciate back to equilibrium had repeatedly failed to materialize over the preceding two years, and most investors were instead relying on the forecasts of the technical analysts. *Euromoney* magazine used to run an annual review of foreign exchange forecasting firms, covering between 10 and 27 services. In 1978–81, only one or two of the forecasting firms reported using models based on technical analysis. Most relied on models based on economic fundamentals. By 1984, however, models based on fundamentals had fallen into such disfavor that none of the forecasting firms that revealed their approach would admit to relying on them exclusively. Most said their forecasts were based only on technical analysis. If the weight assigned by the marketplace to the two competing schools of forecasting indeed shifted in this dramatic way in the mid-1980s, one can understand how investors could have gone on buying dollars notwithstanding the fundamentals models' predictions of a strong future depreciation.

For present purposes, the important point is that there are by now a number of reasons to believe that many movements in the exchange rate are not based in economic fundamentals. Even within the confines of the rational expectations hypothesis, the possibility of speculative bubbles has become very plausible, shaking the seemingly unshakable argument that destabilizing speculators would be driven out of the market.

More generally, the pillars of conventional exchange rate analysis— from the market efficiency hypothesis to the monetary models of exchange rate determination—have also been severely damaged by the econometric tests. It has gotten harder to claim that a freely floating exchange market necessarily functions in an optimal way. The question then arises: what, if anything, should be done about it?

3

Policy Issues

To identify imperfections in the free market, as summarized in the last chapter, is not the same thing as establishing a case for government intervention. Government intervention has many imperfections of its own. A host of issues concern the implementation of intervention policy and whether an activist policy would be desirable, even assuming it were effective.

Is an Independent Policy Tool Needed?

Would an independent tool to affect the exchange rate be desirable? The view that the government should leave exchange rates alone is not confined to those economists who regard exchange rate movements as inconsequential. The large majority, who agree that exchange rate movements have real effects on the trade deficit and other important variables, have many reasons for concluding that the government should refrain from interfering. One is the view that exchange rate movements are the natural result of changes in macroeconomic policy and may actually be desirable if one takes the policy—a budget deficit, for instance—as given.

The Exchange Rate as Symptom

In the case of the 1982–84 dollar appreciation, attributed to the widening federal budget deficit, the question was whether the dollar appreciation was desirable if one took the budget deficit as a given political constraint. Council of Economic Advisers Chairman Martin Feldstein argued that it was. The strong dollar acted as a "safety valve" to distribute the crowding-out effects of the budget deficit more evenly among sectors of the private economy. The Feldstein Doctrine (so christened by C. Fred Bergsten) held that even if policymakers were somehow able to force the dollar down without changing fiscal (or monetary) policy—for example, by sterilized foreign exchange intervention or capital controls—the favorable effects on the export and import-competing sectors would be more than offset by unfavorable effects: the lost capital inflow would result in real interest rates even higher than those prevailing at the time, which would hurt those sectors of the economy (such as capital goods) where demand is sensitive to the real interest rate. The result would be a "lopsided recovery" (Council of Economic Advisers 1984; Feldstein 1984).

Others refuse to take fiscal and monetary policy as given. They argue that exchange rate targets or other financial gimmickry can deflect political attention from budget deficits and other domestic objectives that ultimately may be more important than the exchange rate or the trade balance. A counterargument, which places more weight on the exchange-rate and trade-balance objectives, is based on the political-economy view that Congress tends to adopt damaging protectionist policies when a dollar appreciation increases the trade deficit. Bergsten (1982 and 1984a), for example, has argued that for such reasons the exchange rate objective should be given increased weight.

Another anti-intervention argument is that if central banks are encouraged to intervene in the foreign exchange market, they will gamble away the taxpayers' money, to little avail.[1] This argument is especially applicable when the authorities intervene to defend a commitment to a fixed exchange rate or the limit of a target zone. In such circumstances, speculators face a "one-sided bet": they stand to lose little if the currency they are selling short does not devalue and much to gain if it does. The central bank will be forced to absorb huge quantities of an unwanted currency or, where the weak currency is its own, to spend huge quantities of its valuable foreign exchange reserves. The September 1992 crisis in European financial markets was reminiscent of spectacularly failed attempts to defend the value of the pound in 1931 or the dollar in 1973. The Bundesbank alone spent $30 billion in September 1992 in an ultimately unsuccessful attempt to prop up the pound and lira, and another $27 billion in the successful attempt to prop up the French franc (*New York Times*, 2 October 1992; *Financial Times*, 16 November 1992).

---

1. This concern is common among the monetarists. In chapter 6, we review the record on how much money is lost or won through central bank intervention.

Analysts surmise that the total spent by all European central banks might have been as high as $100 billion. These figures do not represent a commensurate loss in resources on the part of the governments involved, since they acquired pounds and lira for their marks and dollars. But when the weaker currencies were finally devalued, the central banks suffered a capital loss in proportion.

A final viewpoint is that floating rates allow countries greater policy independence than do fixed rates or managed floating, even if they do not allow the complete insulation that they might if, as held under the old-fashioned view, they truly equilibrated the trade balance. It is argued that such decentralization of national policymaking is best because each country is the best judge of its own needs (Corden 1983).

Whether or not sterilized intervention offers an effective tool for influencing the exchange rate that is independent of monetary and fiscal policy, it may be dangerous for government officials to think that it does. Exchange rate movements are often signals of inappropriate monetary or fiscal policy. Government officials may be falsely lulled into believing that they can ignore such signals if they believe that they have an independent lever that can control the exchange rate.

A senior Fed official puts it as follows (Truman 1992, 11):

> If the authorities believe that intervention is always effective, they will be inclined to believe that more is better. The next step is that they will believe that intervention and something called "exchange rate policy" is a powerful, independent policy tool especially if it is coordinated or concerted. As a result the policy maker may be led to conclude, for example, that if a country has a large fiscal imbalance that is contributing to a large external imbalance, all that is necessary to correct the latter is to adjust exchange rates, while doing nothing about the former.

Subordinating Monetary Policy to an Exchange Rate Target

The preceding arguments apply even if sterilized intervention is effective. If it is not, then there are additional dangers to adopting official responsibility for an exchange rate target. If a government commitment to an exchange rate target ultimately means adopting a monetary policy that one otherwise would not choose, then the entire economy can be harmed. In 1990–92, many European countries, in order to fulfill their commitments under the European Exchange Rate Mechanism, raised interest rates to levels higher than they would have chosen if they were acting purely in response to their macroeconomic status. The result in the United Kingdom, for example, was a deep recession.

A possible American example arose on 19 October 1987. When US and other stock markets crashed (a 508-point fall in the case of the New York Exchange), one of the many possible causes that were identified had to do with exchange rate policy. The hypothesis is that the markets feared that the Fed would deliberately raise interest rates to try to keep the dollar from falling through a floor set by the G-7 at the Louvre the preceding February. This explanation was partly inspired by Chairman Alan Greenspan's move to raise interest rates earlier in the year.[2]

To complete the possible positions: some argue that a commitment to an exchange rate target is desirable precisely because it will require adjustment of macroeconomic policy. Committing countries to exchange rate targets maximizes the chance that monetary and fiscal policy will be appropriate. This argument is the mirror image to the argument, mentioned above, that allowing the full effect of the mix of monetary and fiscal policies to be reflected in a freely floating exchange rate maximizes the chance that those policies will be adjusted appropriately.

Many believe that the government should commit to some degree of stabilization of the exchange rate. We have already discussed in the preceding chapter the nominal anchor argument, that a commitment to a fixed exchange rate will increase the credibility of an anti-inflation policy. A target zone may be a more practical version of such a proposal. Part of the argument for making such a commitment is that, even though macroeconomic policies will ultimately have to be adjusted in order to keep the exchange rate within the band, such adjustment is desirable. Williamson (1985 and 1987) has argued, for example, that if target zones had been in place in the early 1980s, the Reagan administration would have been forced to abandon policies that were producing excessive budget deficits.[3]

How Foreign Exchange Intervention Policy Is Made

Exchange rate policy, like monetary and fiscal policy, is potentially vulnerable to populist pressures and other political considerations. Policymakers in the public eye—lacking forbearance, and sometimes lacking awareness—might succumb to the temptation to tinker with international financial gimmickry so as to seem to be addressing the exchange rate issue in place of making hard macroeconomic policy decisions.

---

2. Feldstein (1988) and Obstfeld (1990), as noted in chapter 1. But Greenspan's motivation was probably to earn his anti-inflation credentials in the eyes of the market soon after his appointment to replace Paul Volcker more than to meet any exchange rate commitment made by Baker at the Louvre. Five years later, there still existed some concerns that the Fed was withholding monetary ease to prop up the dollar (Feldstein and Feldstein 1992).

3. Feldstein, on the other hand, has countered that if a serious target zone had been in place in the early 1980s, the government would not have reacted to the dollar appreciation by cutting the budget deficit but would sooner have shifted to an inflationary monetary policy.

Sometimes policymakers will refuse to devalue a currency that needs to be devalued out of a stubborn unwillingness to admit publicly that their past policies have failed. Other times they will seek to devalue a currency that should not be in order to gain the short-term advantage of higher output and employment, figuring that the costs in terms of higher inflation will not show up until after the next election. For such reasons, we are skeptical of proposals to democratize the policymaking process for exchange rates and would, if anything, prefer to see more power concentrated with the responsible authorities, particularly with the Federal Reserve. The Fed tends to have more of the historical memory, technical expertise, and insulation from politics that are so lacking elsewhere.

The Roles of the Federal Reserve and the Treasury

In the United States the Treasury has primary responsibility for intervention while the Fed has official responsibility for monetary policy. Indeed, the Treasury in practice usually determines intervention in the foreign exchange market, even though the Federal Reserve Bank of New York is the agent that undertakes all intervention, at least in a mechanical sense, and even though the foreign exchange reserves that are used are the Fed's own as often as the Treasury's.[4] Decentralization of authority in this way makes little sense if one believes that foreign exchange intervention is merely one variety of monetary policy. But the division of responsibility has more of a possible rationale if one believes that sterilized intervention can have an effect.

Some history will illustrate the extent of harmony or disharmony that characterizes the relationship between the two bodies. In 1984 and 1985, Fed Chairman Volcker, concerned about the trade deficit, supported the idea of some amount of foreign exchange intervention to try to bring the dollar down. This put him in conflict with the Treasury, particularly with Regan and Sprinkel in 1984. There was little question of the Fed chairman trying to overcome Treasury objections to intervention; Volcker was well-advised to save most of his ammunition to protect Fed independence on monetary policy (and a bit to snipe at the fiscal policies that were at the root of the trade deficit). But Volcker clearly welcomed Baker's 1985 abandonment of the position that the strong dollar was a good

---

4. Over the years, some Treasury officials have taken the position that the secretary of the Treasury, as the chief financial officer of the government, has the ultimate legal authority over intervention, even when it is conducted with the Federal Reserve's own money. Fed officials such as Paul Volcker point out that such claims are not based in any legal statute such as the Federal Reserve Act, which gives the central bank its independence, but agree that the Fed has never challenged Treasury supremacy in this area in practice and is unlikely to do so in the future.

thing. He did not view the Plaza as putting undesirable constraints on monetary policy.

Soon after the Plaza, the positions had switched, with the Treasury in favor of further depreciation of the dollar and Volcker warning of the dangers of a speculative run. The Fed had no choice but to go along when the Treasury wanted to intervene. But during the remainder of the decade, the central bank played the traditional role of the party more concerned about the dangers of a free-fall of the currency and an increase in inflation. At times in 1986, Volcker found it convenient to point to the need to avoid a free-fall of the dollar as a way of defending against Reagan appointees to the board who favored easier money.

Chairman Greenspan in 1987 inherited Volcker's concern that a weak-dollar policy would be an inflationary policy, while Nicholas Brady in 1988 inherited Baker's concern that a strong-dollar policy would be bad for growth and bad for the trade balance. Indeed, these actors were playing out the age-old conflict between central bankers and treasury ministers over whether money should be tight. Vice Chairman Manuel Johnson had responsibility at the Fed for dealing with other countries' central banks. Johnson and David Mulford reportedly came into more open conflict over the dollar than did Greenspan and Brady. One story has it that after a stormy failure of Johnson and Mulford to iron out differences in 1989 (Redburn 1990, 63), Johnson in protest registered a technical objection to the way the Treasury was running exchange rate policy: a disproportionately large share of the intervention was being conducted with the Fed's reserves fund rather than with the Treasury's own Exchange Stabilization Fund. Later, in the aftermath of the Japanese stock market crash of early 1990, the Johnson-Mulford conflict resurfaced over whether the Fed or the Bank of Japan should be the one to ease. (Johnson resigned in mid-1990.)

Congressional Bids to Play a Larger Role

When the dollar was at its peak, a concerned Congress began to pass resolutions and consider bills that required specific action on exchange rate policy.[5] Of several bills submitted in mid-1985, a proposal by Senator Bill Bradley was the most specific. It would have required the creation of a "war chest" of intervention funds to be used according to the following rule: every time four consecutive quarters showed a current account deficit in excess of 1.5 percent of GNP and a dollar at least 15 percent above the level corresponding to current account balance, the Treasury was to be required to purchase at least $3 billion in foreign currency over the subsequent quarter. Needless to say, the Treasury

---

5. The following history draws heavily on Destler and Henning (1989, 99–111).

was disturbed by these open assaults on its right to make exchange rate policy. This threat from the Congress was one of the factors that contributed to Baker's reversal of policy in 1985.

Even after the Plaza, skeptical congressmen continued to press for systematic reform of exchange rate policy. More bills were proposed by others, including Representative Stan Lundine (D-NY), who, in the original version of his bill, proposed an explicit link between the exchange rate and negotiating authority for the Uruguay Round. The House Banking Committee in December 1985 passed a compromise bill that did not quantitatively mandate intervention as in the Bradley proposal but did require the secretary of the Treasury twice a year to report to Congress on exchange rates, among other provisions. As Congress debated various bills to deal with the still-widening trade deficit over the subsequent three years, with the twist of increasing emphasis on the East Asian newly industrializing economies (NIEs) rather than just Japan, proposals regarding exchange rates remained part of the debate.

The outcome, the Omnibus Trade and Competitiveness Act of 1988, included a large subsection on exchange rate policy. In four areas, it called for Treasury activism and, as in the House Banking Committee bill, required regular Treasury reports to the Congress (quoted from Destler and Henning 1989, 111–13): "An assessment of the impact of the exchange rate on the current account and trade balance, overall economic performance, competitive position, and indebtedness of the United States; recommendations for policy changes necessary to achieve a 'more appropriate and sustainable' current account balance; reporting of the results of bilateral negotiations with countries that manipulated their currencies; and analyses of exchange-market developments and their causes, including capital flows, and of intervention, among other things." In the biannual reports submitted subsequently, the Treasury understandably has evaded as much as possible the injunction to specify exchange rate and current account targets. But it did take up with relish the mandate regarding countries that "manipulate" their exchange rate, spending a high percentage of the reports on Korea and Taiwan, and later China.

Other Proposals for Institutional Reform

Most other countries, to a greater extent than the United States, vest responsibility for exchange rate policy and monetary policy with the same authority. But when it comes to international discussions, the US "schizophrenia" seems to prevail. The G-5 ministers, at the Plaza and subsequently, did not discuss sterilization of intervention, or even monetary policy, when deciding to take action to try to affect the exchange rate. Whether or not intervention in reality offers a tool for affecting the exchange rate that is independent of monetary policy, the policymaking apparatus is set up as if it does: exchange rate policy is discussed by the G-5 and G-7 finance ministers, while monetary policy is discussed by central bankers, for example, at G-10 meetings ten times a year at the Bank for International Settlements in Basel.

The decisions to depreciate the dollar at the Plaza and stabilize it at the Louvre, to judge from the communiqués as well as from informed reports of what went on inside the meetings, were made without much discussion of monetary policy. Dobson (1991, 59) reports that, in the pattern of G-7 meetings at the Treasury deputy level that has evolved in recent years, "Foreign exchange market developments . . . are reviewed separately from macroeconomic performance." Dobson (1991, 140) has proposed reform of the G-7 process to better integrate exchange rate policy with other macroeconomic considerations.

Although the G-7 meetings would probably benefit from the attendance of the central bankers, the latter are not entirely sure they want to be included. A system in which the politicians can be seen engaging in international economic diplomacy in the public eye, without binding the monetary authorities to the policies that would logically be required if the commitments to manage exchange rates were interpreted literally, is a system that has attractions for both sets of actors. Nevertheless, we support the recommendation for better integration of monetary and exchange rate policy in the G-7 process.

The leading recent proposal for systematic reform of the US institutional structure of exchange rate policymaking is that of Destler and Henning (1989). They argue that exchange rate policy is made by a very small circle of senior government officials in the Treasury and Fed, is dangerously divorced from fiscal and monetary policy, and is frequently unresponsive to the legitimate concerns of private economic actors. They recommend a broadening of the process, particularly through three important changes: the creation in both the House and Senate of new Select Oversight Committees on the Dollar and the National Economy; the establishment of a new private-sector Advisory Group on Exchange Rates to counsel the secretary of the Treasury; and more active involvement of agencies such as the Council of Economic Advisers, US Trade Representative, and Agriculture and Commerce Departments (Destler and Henning 1989, 145–164).[6]

Our view is that, under most circumstances, a broadening of the policy process in this way, in the sensitive and relatively technical area of exchange rates, could make things worse rather than better. We reach this belief notwithstanding the 1985 episode that Destler and Henning

---

6. One of their quite valid purposes in making the proposals was to make the exchange rate a deliberate policy instrument consistent with macroeconomic policy, rather than treating it as a residual.

have in mind, when the dollar had appreciated so far that some action such as foreign exchange intervention to try to bring it down was warranted. Since all the groups that Destler and Henning would like to bring in to the policymaking process were more worried about the dollar and the trade deficit at this time than was the Regan Treasury, it does indeed follow that exchange rate policy during the eight-month period of July 1984–February 1985 might have been better had their proposed institutional reforms already been in place. But next time, pressure on the designated authorities from the wider political process could be to move the exchange rate away from equilibrium rather than toward it.

4

Intervention Categorized and Defined

Foreign exchange market intervention is, most broadly defined, any transaction or announcement by an official agent of a government that is intended to influence the value of an exchange rate or the country's stock of foreign exchange reserves. In most countries, intervention operations are implemented by the monetary authority, although the decision to intervene can often also be made by authorities in the finance ministry or treasury department, depending on the country.

In practice, central banks define intervention more narrowly as any official sale or purchase of foreign assets against domestic assets in the foreign exchange market. This is the definition used by the major central banks in their daily coordination procedure. Even within this narrow definition of intervention policy, operations may take many forms. In this chapter we attempt to explain some mechanics and define various kinds of foreign exchange market intervention commonly undertaken by central banks.

Sterilized Versus Nonsterilized Intervention

Intervention operations aimed at decreasing the value of the domestic currency involve the official sale of the domestic currency in exchange for a foreign currency. If the central bank sells domestic currency that was not previously in circulation, the intervention operation will expand the domestic money base. Likewise, an intervention operation aimed at increasing the value of the domestic currency involves buying the domes-

Box 4.1 Glossary

Foreign exchange rate intervention an official sale or purchase of foreign assets against domestic assets in the foreign exchange market that is intended to influence the value of an exchange rate or the country's stock of foreign exchange reserves.

Nonsterilized intervention an intervention operation that involves a change in the domestic monetary base.

Sterilized intervention an intervention operation that is accompanied by an offsetting open-market operation that restores the domestic monetary base to its original size.

Signaling channel a hypothesized means by which a monetary authority can use intervention to convey information about future fundamentals to the market.

Portfolio-balance channel a hypothesized means by which a monetary authority can use intervention, which changes the relative supply of foreign and domestic assets, to increase the riskiness of investors' portfolios. If foreign and domestic assets are imperfect substitutes, then interventions will induce investors to demand a higher expected return on their portfolios, leading to a change in the exchange rate.

Public intervention an intervention operation of which the foreign exchange market is aware.

Secret intervention an intervention operation that is not discerned by the foreign exchange market, also termed discreet or stealth intervention.

Coordinated intervention simultaneous intervention operations by more than one central bank in support of (or against) the same currency.

Unilateral intervention an intervention operation that involves only one central bank.

Leaning-against-the-wind intervention an intervention operation that attempts to move an exchange rate in the opposite direction from its current trend.

Leaning-with-the-wind intervention an intervention operation that is motivated by a central bank's desire to support the current exchange rate trend.

Customer transactions foreign exchange purchases and sales between a central bank and a customer who would otherwise have undertaken the transaction in the exchange market.

tic currency in exchange for a foreign currency. If the central bank takes the domestic currency receipts out of circulation, the intervention operation will contract the domestic money base. Any intervention operation that involves a change in the domestic monetary base is called a *nonsterilized* intervention operation.

Nonsterilized intervention operations are analogous to domestic open-market operations, except that foreign rather than domestic assets are bought or sold. In monetary models of exchange rate determination (discussed in chapter 2), nonsterilized intervention will affect the exchange rate in proportion to the change in the relative supplies of domestic and foreign money, just as any other form of monetary policy does.

Sterilized intervention operations involve an offsetting domestic asset transaction that restores the monetary base to its original size. For example, an official nonsterilized sale of foreign assets on the open market would result in a reduction in the central bank's net foreign assets (NFA), and a contraction of the domestic monetary base (MB). This operation can be sterilized by an offsetting purchase of domestic assets that increases the central bank's net domestic assets (NDA) and returns the monetary base to its original level.

$$\Delta NFA + \Delta NDA = \Delta MB = 0 \qquad (3.1)$$

In theory, the process of sterilization is quite straightforward, but in practice it may be difficult for a central bank to offset fully the effects of a change in net foreign assets. The German Bundesbank considers sterilization a two-stage procedure (Dudler 1988). The first stage of sterilization involves offsetting the transitory change in the monetary base due to the intervention operation. The second stage of sterilization involves offsetting any permanent shift in the demand for foreign assets that may occur in reaction to an intervention operation.[1]

Countries that adhere to monetary targets are generally assumed to engage chiefly in sterilized intervention operations. The stated US policy is to sterilize its foreign exchange intervention operations always and immediately. Central banks such as the Bundesbank that operate under a dual exchange rate constraint—a fixed exchange rate against some currencies and a floating rate against others—can use the two markets to achieve full sterilization. The Bundesbank has on occasion intervened against the deutsche mark using the European Monetary System (EMS) currencies and in support of the deutsche mark using the dollar in order to sterilize its operations.

Whether or not to sterilize becomes a central issue when conflict arises for a country between internal and external balance, because monetary

---

1. Neumann and von Hagen (forthcoming) describe this two-stage process.

policies that are appropriate to achieve national objectives are at variance with exchange rate objectives. If sterilized intervention, which changes the relative supplies of foreign and domestic assets in private portfolios but leaves the monetary base unchanged, can influence the exchange rate, authorities have a second instrument with which to achieve internal and external targets simultaneously. In a world of N countries, N national policy goals, and N domestic policy tools, it is only by accident that exchange rate targets can be attained. Sterilized intervention, in theory, can provide the additional policy tool necessary for the resolution of internal and external balance conflicts. It is for this reason that much research has been devoted to examining the effectiveness of sterilized intervention operations in theory and practice.

There are two possible channels through which sterilized intervention can influence exchange rates: the portfolio balance channel and the signaling channel. Intervention can influence exchange rates through the portfolio channel, provided that domestic and foreign bonds are outside assets and that they are imperfect substitutes. Sterilized intervention can also influence the exchange rate in models where the monetary authority is assumed to have more information about relevant fundamentals than the market and can convey that information by signaling via intervention.

The Ricardian Equivalence Theorem—that government borrowing has no effect on the interest rate—holds when the public fully anticipates and internalizes the fact that current government debt will be serviced by future taxation. In this case the public saves more in anticipation of these future taxes, and net demand for government bonds increases to meet new supply. In such a world, government debt cannot be considered a true outside asset. Under these circumstances, sterilized intervention operations are simply swaps in the currency composition of inside assets, and these should have no effect on the foreign exchange market equilibrium.[2] Sterilized intervention will also have no influence on the exchange rate if domestic and foreign assets are perfect substitutes. If investors are completely indifferent as to whether they hold domestic or foreign assets, then changes in the relative supply of these assets should have no effect.

In portfolio-balance models of exchange rate determination, investors diversify their holdings among domestic and foreign assets as a function of both expected returns and the variance in returns. If intervention operations increase the supply of domestic relative to foreign assets held by the market, then investors will require a higher expected return on domestic assets to willingly hold the larger outstanding stock, leading to a depreciation of the domestic currency.[3]

---

2. Frankel (1979), Stockman (1979), and Obstfeld (1982) discuss this point.

3. The classic articles on portfolio balance models include Black (1973), Kouri and Porter (1974), Girton and Henderson (1977) and Branson (1979). The literature is reviewed, in the context of intervention, by Tryon (1983) and Henderson (1984).

Implications of Current Asset Supply Changes for Expectations

The second channel whereby intervention (whether sterilized or not) can influence exchange rates is termed the information or *signaling channel*. The signaling channel does not rely on the failure of Ricardian equivalence or the assumption that foreign and domestic assets are imperfect substitutes. Through the signaling channel, sterilized intervention can have an effect on exchange rates if it provides the market with relevant information previously not known or not fully incorporated in determining the current exchange rate. This channel for sterilized intervention is controversial. It relies on the existence of a difference between what is known by the monetary authority and what is known by market participants.

In order for sterilized intervention operations to influence exchange rates via the signaling channel, the monetary authority must both have inside information and have the incentive to reveal the information truthfully by way of their operations in the foreign exchange market.[4] Mussa (1981) suggests that sterilized intervention may be used by central banks to "buy credibility" for their future policy intentions. For example, a central bank that intends to contract the money supply in the future in order to reduce expectations of inflation may signal this intention by intervening in support of the domestic currency today. The intervention operation, a purchase of domestic assets with an offsetting sale of foreign assets, involves a commitment of central bank assets in support of the intended future monetary policy.

If market participants believe the signals provided by central bank intervention, they will influence exchange rates by betting with the central bank. For example, if intervention signals a change in future monetary policy, even though today's money supply has not changed, expectations of future monetary policy will change. In asset-pricing models of exchange rate determination, when the market revises its expectations of future money supplies, it also revises its expectations of the future spot exchange rate, which brings about a change in the current rate.

It is difficult to test the signaling channel. Observing what happens to the money supply *ex post*, in finite samples, would be a dubious way of approaching the question. At best, intervention is but one of many factors relevant for determining the future money supply; in finite samples, the relationship might not be detectable.

Public Versus Secret Intervention

Although practices differ across central banks as well as across time, most intervention operations are not publicly announced. Most foreign

---

4. See Dominguez (1992a) for further discussion of the signaling channel.

exchange transactions are anonymous; there is no central trading floor, and brokers are not obliged to reveal the identity of counterparties. It is somewhat puzzling that many central banks do not distinguish their foreign exchange transactions in the market with an accompanying public announcement. This is especially true given that the signaling channel relies on investors noticing the central bank's intervention signals.

Central bankers seem to value their ability to control which intervention operations are publicized and which are kept secret. Alternative terms for secret intervention include "discreet" intervention, the term typically used by the Fed, and "stealth" intervention, a term coined by the financial press. In practice, traders seem to be generally well-informed when central banks are in the market. But there are occasional interventions that the public does not discern. In chapter 5, we attempt to distinguish publicly known from secret interventions using reports of official intervention in the financial press.

In a recent report on US intervention policy, officials at the Fed explain, "Depending upon the degree of intervention visibility that is desired, we will either call banks and deal directly or operate through an agent in the brokers' market. Most operations are conduced in the brokers' market, though at the beginning of a major intervention episode we have sometimes chosen to deal directly with several banks simultaneously to achieve maximum visibility. Within the brokers' market we can be more or less aggressive, hitting existing quotes or leaving trailing quotes" (Smith and Madigan 1988).

At least six reasons have been offered to explain why central banks may want to keep their intervention operations secret. We recount them here, without regard to how convincing they may be. These explanations of central bank secrecy can, in turn, be grouped into three broad categories: reasons based on a central bank's convictions regarding the efficacy of intervention at a point in time, reasons based on the perceived depth or underlying volatility of the foreign exchange market at a point in time, and reasons based on portfolio adjustment.

The first category of reasons for secret intervention is based on the notion that central banks may not want intervention to have a major effect in certain periods. The central bank may not have its heart in intervention for various reasons. In a number of countries, decisions to intervene in the foreign exchange market may come from outside the central bank. In the United States, the Treasury Department has official jurisdiction over foreign exchange intervention policy. In practice, the Treasury Department and the Fed typically jointly decide when the United States should be in the market, but on occasion a decision may be made by Treasury over the objections of the Fed. Even though the Treasury can mandate intervention policy, it is the Federal Reserve Bank of New York that actually implements the policy. One can imagine circumstances in which the Fed might prefer to keep the intervention operation secret in order to minimize the effect in the market.

Many central bankers hold to the view that intervention can only have lasting effects in cases where supporting policy changes are forthcoming. Another instance in which a central bank may prefer to keep intervention operations secret is when monetary and fiscal policies are not consistent with intervention policy. Central bankers that care about their reputation for sending truthful signals regarding future policies will prefer to keep false signals quiet. Finally, foreign central banks may ask a central bank to enter into a coordinated intervention operation in support of a foreign exchange rate target. This may be another circumstance in which the central bank will agree to intervene for political reasons but prefer to keep the interventions secret for economic reasons.

Many central banks claim to use intervention policy to "calm disorderly markets." Disorderly markets are defined as markets in which bid-ask spreads are unusually large or price movements are unusually volatile. Disorderly conditions may be associated with markets in which investors seem to be joining a bandwagon for or against a currency whose exchange rate is not based on fundamentals. Central bankers sometimes use secret interventions in disorderly markets to provide a sense of two-way risk. (Skeptics may respond that this amounts to increasing the disorderliness of the markets!) Central banks may also use secret interventions to forestall a currency from breaking a so-called resistance level in cases where the market is perceived to be close to such a level. These operations are thought to be particularly important in light of the stop-loss program trading models that many currency traders use.

Secret interventions might be preferred to public interventions in times of market uncertainty if the central bank does not have a strong reputation for providing informative signals. However, the impact of secret intervention in this circumstance will depend on the depth of the market. It is said that if the market is unusually thin and disorderly, an intervention operation on the order of $200 million (the average size of US operations) may have the desired effect. On the other hand, if the market is deep and disorderly, a $200 million intervention operation will be swamped in the market. (The scale of intervention operations relative to the size of the foreign exchange market is discussed in detail in chapter 5.)

The final set of (more persuasive) reasons a central bank may prefer to keep intervention operations secret is in circumstances when it needs to adjust its own foreign exchange portfolio holdings. Central banks attempt to keep a rough target level of reserves denominated in different currencies in their portfolio to have available for future use. On occasion, central banks will need to increase their holdings of some currency denominations and decrease their holdings of other currency denominations for future intervention operations. In this circumstance, central banks may prefer that the market not confuse these portfolio adjustment transactions with transactions meant to influence the exchange rate. For the same reasons, central banks may also attempt to keep customer transactions (discussed below) secret.

Concerted Versus Unilateral Intervention[5]

Concerted or coordinated central bank interventions are simultaneous intervention operations by more than one central bank in support of (or against) the same currency. A more narrow definition, in keeping with standard definitions of coordination would exclude operations that individual central banks would have undertaken unilaterally regardless of the actions of other central banks (see Hamada 1976; Rogoff 1985; Wallich 1984).

The welfare gains to international economic policy coordination rest on the existence of spillover effects of each country's policies on other countries. For example, under floating exchange rates, contractionary monetary policy pursued by one country may hamper disinflationary efforts of other countries. The possibility of intended or unintended beggar-thy-neighbor practices provide governments incentives to coordinate macroeconomic policies. Foreign exchange intervention policy, if effective, will by definition cause spillovers because a change in the value of one currency changes the relative value of other currencies. Central banks, therefore, may find it in their interest to coordinate their intervention operations if they believe that the spillover effects on exchange rates are economically important.

The incentives for countries to coordinate nonsterilized intervention operations are identical to those for monetary policy coordination. A coordinated nonsterilized intervention operation, moreover, will in theory have the same influence on exchange rates as would a unilateral operation of the same size. The advantage of coordinating nonsterilized intervention operations is that it explicitly forces countries to coordinate their monetary policies in order to achieve exchange rate targets.

The efficacy (and spillover effects) of *coordinated sterilized* interventions on exchange rates are less straightforward. In portfolio-balance models of exchange rate determination, sterilized operations can influence exchange rates independently from monetary policy. In this context, countries can coordinate the pursuit of exchange rate targets without relinquishing sovereignty over monetary policy. Further, in portfolio-balance models, the size of the effect of a coordinated or unilateral sterilized intervention operation on the exchange rate, as was the case

---

5. This section draws heavily on Dominguez (1992b).

with nonsterilized operations, depends only on the size of the change in the supply of foreign assets relative to domestic assets held by the market.

The distinction between coordinated and unilateral interventions of the same size may matter when sterilized intervention operations influence the exchange rate through the signaling channel. Multiple signals will increase the total amount of inside information conveyed by intervention operations. Multiple *coordinated* signals, moreover, may strengthen investors' confidence that the signal is true.

In a world with more than one central bank and therefore multiple potential intervention signals, each individual central bank's ability to influence market expectations will depend not only on the relative size of its intervention operation, but on its reputation for truthful signals compared with other central banks.[6] Central banks may agree to coordinate intervention operations in order to piggyback off other central banks' reputations for providing informative signals. For example, a central bank that wants to reduce inflationary expectations can join in a coordinated intervention operation in support of its domestic currency to signal its intention to contract the domestic money base. If the coordinated intervention signal is believed and expectations of inflation do fall, however, the central bank may be tempted not to follow through with the promised contractionary monetary policy. The temptation to renege may be offset if the central bank knows that the market will eventually learn that the signal was false and thereafter bet against their future intervention signals. The information channel, however, may allow central banks with reputations for informative signals to coordinate effectively on exchange rate targets independently from monetary policy for short periods.

In fixed exchange rate systems, central banks are often obligated to coordinate intervention operations whenever exchange rates diverge too far from their central parities. In floating systems, the use of both unilateral and coordinated intervention policy is at the discretion of individual central banks.

Leaning Against the Wind Versus With the Wind

An intervention operation that attempts to move an exchange rate in the opposite direction from its current trend is termed "leaning against the wind." A strict definition of leaning against the wind is difficult because it depends on one's definition of the current trend. Exchange

---

6. See Dominguez (1990a) for further discussion of these issues.

rates have been extremely volatile, so that an intervention in support of a currency may look as if it is leaning against yesterday's trend but leaning *with* last week's trend.

Central banks that are motivated to intervene in the foreign exchange market mainly to calm disorderly markets are likely to lean against the wind. Implicit in this categorization of intervention is the notion that the central bank is attempting to move an exchange rate away from its recent trend. Interventions that are not motivated by a desire to change the direction of movement in the exchange rate but *ex post* have this effect should not be considered as leaning against the wind. For example, if a central bank intervenes in support of its domestic currency in the foreign exchange market in order to signal future contractionary monetary policy and the intervention causes a change in the direction of movement in the domestic currency, this should not be considered leaning against the wind.

Interventions that "lean with the wind" are defined as operations that are motivated by a central bank's desire to support the current exchange rate trend. The intervention operations that were part of the Plaza Agreement are generally considered leaning with the wind operations (Bergsten 1984b). The dollar had been moving in a downward direction during the spring of 1985 and the G-5 objective, announced at the Plaza, was to support the dollar on its downward path. There is some evidence that the dollar had begun to strengthen just before the Plaza Agreement, but the trend in the dollar was downward.

Transactions Undertaken by the Central Bank for Customers

Some definitions of intervention are broader than the narrow definition one usually thinks of—that is, transactions with the deliberate aim of affecting the value of the currency. Customer transactions include foreign exchange purchases and sales between a central bank and a customer who would otherwise have undertaken the transaction in the exchange market. These transactions are termed "passive" interventions because they are typically initiated by a customer rather than the central bank.

Customers of central banks include a central bank's own government when the government has receipts of payments in a foreign currency, as well as other central banks and foreign governments. A typical example of a customer transaction with a foreign government occurs when the government issues debt in the domestic currency. In this situation, the foreign government may request a direct conversion facility with the central bank. Another example of a common customer transaction is when central banks exchange currencies in order to provide one of them with the foreign currency needed to repay debt incurred in connection with earlier intervention.[7]

Although customer transactions are considered passive interventions, it is important to recognize that, since the timing of these transactions is under the discretion of the central bank, they can still serve to signal information to the market.

Transactions by Other Government Funds and Agencies

In most countries, the central bank implements intervention policy, but other government funds and agencies may finance intervention activities. For example, in the United States and Japan, the Treasury and the Ministry of Finance, respectively, have special accounts that are used to finance intervention operations.

When the US Treasury intervenes in foreign exchange markets, it acts through the Exchange Stabilization Fund (ESF). When the ESF sells foreign currencies, it deposits the dollar receipts at the Federal Reserve. The Treasury then issues a special nonmarketable security to the ESF, and the ESF pays for the security by having its balance at the Federal Reserve debited and the Treasury's balance credited by an equal amount. This set of transactions will contract the US monetary base. The Treasury offsets this by redepositing the funds with the commercial banking system, restoring the monetary base to its original level. In this way, the Treasury leaves monetary policy to the Fed.

In Japan, the Bank of Japan (BOJ) acts as the agent of the Ministry of Finance (MOF) under the Foreign Exchange Fund Special Account of the National Budget. Foreign exchange market intervention operations reallocate the liabilities of the BOJ between the Foreign Exchange Fund Special Account of the Central Government and the banking sector. When the BOJ intervenes in support of the dollar, the government's balance of foreign assets (typically dollars) increases while its (yen) deposits at the central bank decrease. At the same time, (yen) deposits of commercial banks at the central bank increase. As a consequence, the monetary base is increased. The BOJ can sterilize this increase by selling yen-denominated assets or by contracting domestic credit through its discount window operations.

In Germany, the Ministry of Finance has the authority to determine the country's exchange rate regime, including the fixing of exchange rate parities. But the Bundesbank has sole jurisdiction over monetary and exchange rate policy within a given exchange rate regime. Obligatory

---

7. See Adams and Henderson (1983) for further discussion of customer transactions.

and intramarginal Bundesbank interventions in the EMS are typically financed using the European Monetary Cooperation Fund (EMCF).[8] Non-EMS interventions in the foreign exchange market are financed using the Bundesbank's own foreign exchange portfolio.

Foreign- and Domestic-Currency Assets Sold by Other Countries

There are two situations that arise in which transactions by foreign central banks may have an influence on the domestic monetary base. However, in both cases, the domestic central bank can easily offset undesired changes in the domestic monetary base if it wishes, using open market operations or other forms of monetary policy.

The G-10 central banks have a daily exchange of information on intervention policy. When there are large movements in an exchange rate outside the domestic central bank's business hours, another central bank will be asked to intervene on its behalf. (Although the foreign exchange market is never closed, traders at the central banks rarely intervene after business hours.) The United States, for example, has intervened on behalf of the BOJ on occasion during US business hours. Depending on the particular arrangement negotiated between the two central banks, countries may need to sterilize the effect of these interventions on the domestic monetary base.

The second circumstance in which a country may need to sterilize the effects of another country's intervention operations occurs when a foreign central bank intervenes using the domestic currency. When foreign central banks purchase dollars, they may purchase dollar assets in the market or from the Federal Reserve, on either an outright basis or a repurchase basis. If the transaction involves the Federal Reserve, it will contract the monetary base. In this case, the Federal Reserve would need to engage in an open market sale of dollars to sterilize the foreign central bank's intervention operation.

Other Technical Issues of Definition

Official exchange market intervention takes place mainly in the spot exchange market. A study of intervention practices released by the Bank for International Settlements (1988) reports that authorities in most countries prefer using spot transactions because they are more easily detect-

---

8. EMS central banks can obtain strong-currency reserves for obligatory interventions supporting a weak currency from the EMCF. This leads to an increase in the net foreign asset position of the strong-currency central bank.

able when the authorities wish to convey a clear and precise message to the market. The US dollar is the main intervention currency, although use of the deutsche mark and the yen is increasing. The BIS study suggests that few recent official intervention operations are made in the forward exchange market.

Most central banks engage in foreign exchange swaps and repurchase agreements in order to adjust their own foreign exchange portfolios. These operations generally do not affect the central bank's total stock of net foreign assets and consequently should have few exchange rate implications. In a foreign exchange swap, the central bank combines a spot sale of foreign exchange to a commercial bank or another central bank with a forward repurchase, resulting in a temporary contraction in the monetary base. Foreign exchange repurchase agreements are loans to commercial banks or other central banks collateralized with foreign currency–denominated assets.

Prior to a large intervention episode, central banks may enter into swap arrangements with other central banks to acquire needed foreign currencies. These swap arrangements are typically reversed in small increments and secretly so as not to influence market expectations.

The value of a central bank's foreign exchange portfolio will change in reaction to interest earnings and exchange rate changes. Central banks generally hold their foreign currencies in the form of short-term foreign currency–denominated government securities. Valuation changes in a central bank's foreign exchange portfolio are not considered interventions, but they may affect the central bank's ability to engage in future intervention activities.

5

The Data on Intervention

The dearth of available official intervention data has long hindered empirical study of intervention policy. In this chapter we describe what data are available and present a preliminary depiction of what they say about when, why, and how central banks have implemented foreign exchange intervention policy in the 1980s.

Available, Unavailable, and Newly Available

Until recently, most central banks have not routinely made daily intervention data available to the public. Quarterly data on monetary authorities' international reserves are available both from central bank publications and the International Monetary Fund's *International Financial Statistics*. Quarterly changes in these data have commonly been used by researchers as proxies for intervention flows. These data, however, can differ significantly from actual official purchases of foreign exchange in the open market. The level of a country's reserves can change even if the central bank does not transact in the foreign exchange market. Reserves increase with interest accruals on official portfolio holdings and fluctuate with valuation changes on existing reserves. Reserve data also exclude some transactions that should be counted as intervention, such as the Japanese so-called hidden reserves, which are changes in official deposits of foreign exchange with Japanese commercial banks. A number of central banks also publish monthly series on foreign exchange reserves,[1] but these data suffer from the same limitations as do the quarterly data.

Apart from the fact that reserve data do not provide good approximations of official intervention activity, quarterly and monthly data obscure important daily information. Intervention operations are implemented on a minute-to-minute basis. It would be interesting to know at exactly what minute operations are performed, but at a minimum, net daily intervention information is necessary for study of intervention's effects. Data on daily official central bank purchases and sales in the foreign exchange market have rarely been made available to researchers outside the government.[2] At the Versailles Summit in 1982, the Group of Seven (G-7) central banks agreed to share daily intervention data with each other as part of a multicountry study of intervention policy.[3] The empirical results in the study, however, were presented in such a way so as not to compromise the confidentiality of the raw data. Despite numerous requests from researchers for the daily data, central banks have until recently maintained a policy of keeping intervention data confidential.

A number of central banks do publish summaries of their intervention policies. For example, the *Federal Reserve Bulletin* and the *Federal Reserve Bank of New York Quarterly Review* provide descriptions of US intervention operations in the previous quarter. Although these summaries frequently provide daily intervention magnitudes, they do not do so consistently. Moreover, in-house summaries of policy might be subject to selection bias with more details given on "successful" operations than for "unsuccessful" ones.

Why have central banks kept their intervention data secret? Although it is understandable that central banks may want to keep intervention operations secret in advance in order to be able to surprise the market, it is not clear why they also prefer to keep the data secret after the fact. Central bankers typically respond that they prefer to keep all operations secret for consistency, although they would have no problem releasing some of the data. For example, central banks at times need to transact in the foreign exchange market purely to rebalance their own foreign

---

1. For example, a monthly German series is published in the *Deutsche Bundesbank Monthly Review*, and a monthly Japanese series is published in the Bank of Japan's *Economic Statistics Monthly*.

2. Exceptions include Neumann (1984), Dominguez (1990a, 1992a, and 1993), Dominguez and Frankel (1993a and b), and Eijffinger and Gruijters (1991b), who were given access to Bundesbank intervention data. There are virtually no exceptions in the case of Federal Reserve data.

3. The results of this study are contained in the Jurgensen Report (1983) and summarized in Henderson and Sampson (1983). Three papers by members of the working group's research staff that use the confidential data were subsequently published separately: Loopesko (1984), Rogoff (1984), and Wonnacott (1982).

exchange portfolio, and they would rather that these transactions not be confused with transactions made for the purpose of influencing exchange rates.

Central bankers' preference for secrecy is all the more puzzling in the context of the signaling hypothesis described in chapter 4. How can intervention signal future monetary policy intentions if the market does not hear the signal? In practice, even though central banks do not publish intervention data, traders are well aware of central bank intervention activity most of the time. Evidence on this is presented in the next section of this chapter.

Theory suggests that full disclosure of intervention operations may not be an optimal policy.[4] If central bank announcements of policy intentions are not credible to the market because central banks have an incentive to renege on promises,[5] Cukierman and Meltzer (1986) suggest, a degree of policy ambiguity may be optimal. Intuitively, if the market cannot perfectly distinguish between the effects of intervention policy and other factors that move exchange rates (which the central banks do not control), ineffective intervention policy may be less likely to damage central bank credibility. That is, if intervention policy is sometimes ineffective due both to inconsistent central bank policy and other factors, the market is more likely to give the central bank the benefit of the doubt when they cannot distinguish the source of the problem.[6]

Whatever the rationale for keeping intervention data secret, US authorities have recently broken step with this practice. The US Treasury has agreed to change its long-standing policy and has allowed the Board of Governors of the Federal Reserve System to make its daily intervention data publicly available with a lag. At this time, none of the other G-7 central banks has a general policy of releasing its intervention data to the public. We are fortunate to have available for purposes of this study, in addition to the recently released Fed data, daily Bundesbank intervention data from 1982 through 1988 and daily Swiss National Bank (SNB) data through 1989.[7]

---

4. The practical reasons for why central banks prefer to keep intervention operations secret are discussed in chapter 4.

5. The classic example of this is the incentive central banks have to convince market participants that they will tighten monetary policy more than they intend in order to reduce expectations of inflation.

6. Canzoneri (1985) presents an alternative resolution to this time-inconsistency problem, which results in the market allocating full blame for ineffective policy on the central bank even when exchange rate movements are caused by other factors. For other possible theoretic explanations for central bank policy ambiguity, see Stein (1989) and Watanabe (1991).

7. The Swiss National Bank has always followed the practice of releasing its intervention data to the public. We would like to thank Jean-Pierre Roth for his help in obtaining the data.

The intervention data series measures consolidated daily official foreign exchange transactions in millions of dollars at current market values. Positive values denote purchases of dollars, and negative values denote official dollar sales. The Fed data distinguish between interventions against the mark and the yen and exclude so-called "passive" intervention operations. Passive interventions are Fed purchases and sales of foreign currency with customers who would otherwise have dealt with market agents.[8] The Bundesbank data exclude nondiscretionary interventions required by European Monetary System (EMS) rules. The Swiss data include transactions by the SNB and transactions by the Fed and the Bank for International Settlements (BIS) on the behalf of the SNB.

Do Market Participants Know When Central Banks Intervene?

Although central banks do not publish intervention operations on a daily basis,[9] daily intervention operations are frequently reported in newspapers and over the wire services. So although current official data are unavailable, there exist numerous unofficial sources of the data. How do traders and reporters learn about intervention operations? Although each central bank has its own particular set of practices, intervention operations generally take place in the broker market. If the Fed decides to intervene in support of the dollar, the Fed trader can either call a broker or deal directly with another trader at a commercial bank to place an order for dollars. If the Fed would like the market to know the source of the dollar purchase, the Fed trader will often call selected commercial banks with whom the Fed traditionally does business. Unless the Fed trader says otherwise, the bank traders will understand that not only does the Fed want to purchase dollars but that it would like the market to know this. This information is reportedly disseminated among other traders in the market within minutes of the original Fed call.

Given the speed at which information flows in the foreign exchange market, it is more remarkable when intervention operations are kept secret than when they are revealed. In the US case, the Fed is more likely to intervene secretly through the broker market, although it can also do so using a commercial bank with whom it does not traditionally do business. The Fed also on occasion intervenes secretly through the major banks with which it traditionally does business. In any case, if the Fed trader says that the intervention operation is to remain secret,

---

8. See chapter 4 and Adams and Henderson (1983) for more detailed discussion and definition of customer transactions.

9. The daily US data are now made available to researchers with a minimum of a one-year lag.

then the broker or bank trader has a strong incentive not to disclose the Fed's presence in the market if he or she ever wants to be privy to future intervention information and business.

What is the relative frequency of "secret" interventions? One can roughly infer which operations were secret by comparing the official data with published reports of intervention activity in the financial press. In the appendix, we list all the news of intervention activity (as well as more general exchange rate policy announcements) by central banks reported in the *Wall Street Journal,* the *Financial Times* (London) and *The New York Times* over the period 1982 through 1990. Although traders may sometimes know that central banks are intervening without its showing up in the financial press, this relatively conservative accounting for reported intervention reveals that the bulk of recent intervention is not secret.[10]

Tables 5.1 and 5.2 provide summary statistics on the number of total and reported intervention operations taken by the Fed, Bundesbank, and Swiss National Bank between 1982 and 1990. In table 5.1, major intervention episodes are listed chronologically. The first column lists the total number of days' duration in each of 12 intervention episodes. The second column lists the number of Fed intervention operations that took place during each of the intervention episodes. The third column lists the number of these operations that were reported in the financial press. The next three columns provide similar information for the Bundesbank and the Swiss National Bank, respectively. All SNB operations are publicly disclosed so that only the total number of interventions are listed. The final column lists the total number of coordinated interventions[11] between the Fed, Bundesbank, and the SNB over the first eight episodes.

The first thing to note from table 5.1 is that many of the operations prior to 1985 were not reported; out of 286 Bundesbank operations only 46 were reported. In early 1985 there were a number of reports that the Fed had been active in the market when in fact only the Bundesbank sold dollars. There are other reports where traders stated that they were surprised that central bank intervention had not occurred, but the Bundesbank and the Fed actually intervened on some of those occasions. The fraction and accuracy of reported operations and the fraction of those reports that were described as coordinated increased dramatically after the Plaza Agreement in September 1985 and continued to be high for the Fed throughout the rest of the sample period.[12] Bundesbank opera-

---

10. Klein (1992) has now studied this data, with similar results.

11. An operation was defined as coordinated if two or more of the central banks intervened on the same day and in the same direction.

12. The two exceptions to this generalization are the intervention operations that occurred between the Plaza and the Louvre, when few of the intervention operations were reported

tions were less frequently reported in 1988, the last year for which we have the official data.[13] It is presumably not coincidental that the fraction of intervention operations reported rose once the Fed became a major intervention player and the Group of Five (G-5) central banks publicly announced their intention to rely on intervention policy to influence exchange rates.

Table 5.2 presents data on the relationship between the magnitude of intervention operations and the percentage of operations that were reported. Both the Fed and Bundesbank data suggest that the larger the intervention operations, the more likely they will be reported. One hundred percent of all German dollar purchases equal to or greater than $250 million were reported, while 90 percent of analogous dollar sales were reported. The Fed data suggest that, on average, 80 percent of all intervention transactions greater than $150 million were reported.

When and Why Has the US Intervened?

As described in detail in chapter 1, the United States was largely absent from the foreign exchange market from 1981 to 1984. In early 1985 the United States reentered the market along with the other G-5 central banks to bring down the value of the dollar, although Fed operations were small in magnitude relative to the Bundesbank's.[14] It was not until the Plaza Agreement in September 1985 that the United States became a major intervention player. With a brief respite in 1986, the United States continued to use intervention policy actively over the next seven years. Figure 5.1 is a bar graph of Fed operations from 1984 through 1991. Dollar purchases by the Fed are denoted as positive values, and dollar sales are denoted as negative values in the figure. The average daily dollar purchase, on days that the Fed intervened, was $162 million, and the average daily dollar sale was $187 million. The largest US inter-

---

as coordinated, and the small-scale Fed interventions that occurred in the last intervention episode. As discussed in chapter 1, while the United States did not intervene in the foreign exchange market during 1986, officials at the US Treasury continued to "talk down" the dollar. At the same time, Japan and later Germany intervened, at times forcefully, resisting the appreciation of the yen and mark, respectively.

13. There are reasons to believe that our distinction between reported and secret intervention is more relevant for the Fed than for the Bundesbank. We have heard that Bundesbank intervention is for all practical purposes always discernible and that the only reason the historical data continue to be confidential is pressure from other European central banks that choose not to disclose their intervention data. If this is true, then it should not be surprising that fewer Bundesbank interventions are reported, as they would not be considered "news" in the same way as "truly secret" interventions by the Fed are.

14. Our figures show that, while the Bundesbank sold a total of $3.47 billion from January through March 1985, the Fed only sold $643 million over the same period.

Table 5.1 Interventions reported in the press, 1982–90 (number of operations)

Episode	Number of days in subperiod	Fed Total	Fed Reported	Bundesbank Total	Bundesbank Reported	SNB Total[b]	Coordinated[a] interventions
Nov 82–Dec 84	547	15	7	286	46	n.a.	13
Jan 85–Aug 85	170	8	6	24	13	0	7
Sep 85–Nov 85	63	22	22	23	23	0	15
Dec 85–Feb 87	315	1	1	15	11	2	2
Mar 87–Sep 87	150	32	20	13	8	11	15
Oct 87–Jan 88	85	27	23	24	20	16	18
Feb 88–Oct 88	196	31	27	61	38	12	27
Nov 88–Dec 88	44	13	9	11	2	2	2
Jan 89–Feb 89	42	15	14	n.a.	n.a.	8	n.a.
Mar 89–Oct 89	175	83	60	n.a.	n.a.	31	n.a.
Feb 90–Mar 90	32	13	10	n.a.	n.a.	n.a.	n.a.
May 90–Jul 90	36	17	3	n.a.	n.a.	n.a.	n.a.

SNB = Swiss National Bank
n.a. = not available

a. Number of coordinated intervention observations by the Fed, Bundesbank, and/or Swiss National Bank.
b. All intervention operations by the Swiss National Bank are publicly announced.

Source: US Federal Reserve Board; Deutsche Bundesbank; Swiss National Bank; and various issues of *Wall Street Journal*, *Financial Times* (London), and *The New York Times*.

Table 5.2   Intervention magnitudes and news reports, 1982–90[a] (number of observations, except where noted)

Intervention sales (millions of dollars)	Fed			Bundesbank			SNB[b]
	Total	Reported	Reported (percentages)	Total	Reported	Reported (percentages)	Total
> 250[c]	54	45	83	21	19	90	1
> 150[d]	30	25	83	26	14	54	1
> 100[e]	50	39	78	31	15	48	3
> 0[f]	57	41	72	319	75	24	46
Purchases (millions of dollars)							
> 250	19	15	79	7	7	100	0
> 150	16	13	81	11	8	73	0
> 100	17	10	59	9	6	67	6
> 0	39	18	46	33	17	52	28

SNB = Swiss National Bank

a. German data end in 1988; SNB data end in 1989.
b. All SNB operations are publicly announced.
c. Daily intervention sales of $250 million or greater.
d. Daily intervention sales of $150 million or greater, but less than $250 million.
e. Daily intervention sales of $100 million or greater, but less than $150 million.
f. Daily intervention sales of less than $100 million.

Source: US Federal Reserve Board; Deutsche Bundesbank; Swiss National Bank; and various issues of *Wall Street Journal, Financial Times* (London), and *The New York Times.*

Figure 5.1 Daily Fed intervention, 1984–91

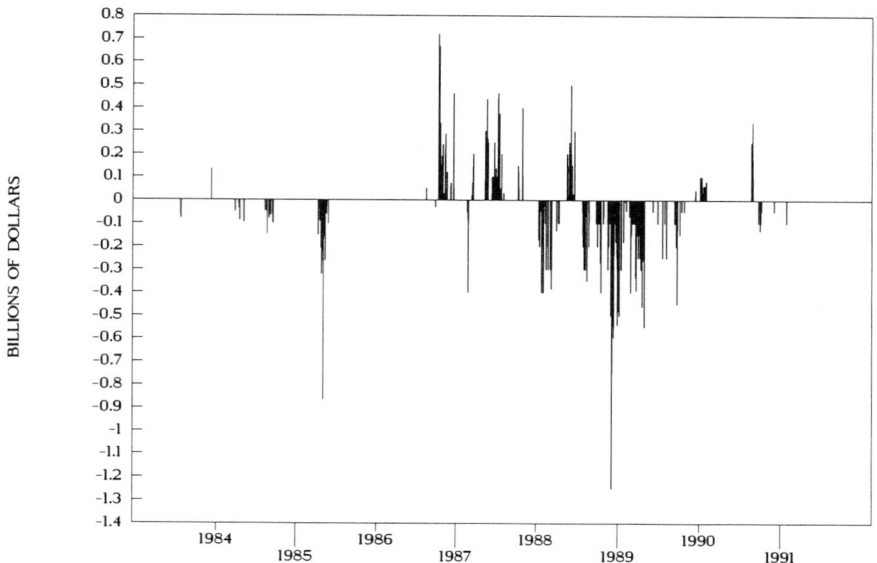

vention operation in one day in our sample period occurred on 18 May 1989, when the Fed sold $695 million against deutsche marks and $555 million against yen, for a total sale of $1,250 million. Interventions in February 1991 were also substantial.

Over the full period, 1982 through 1991, the Fed was a net seller of dollars. It sold a cumulative total of $35,080 million and purchased a cumulative total of $15,848 million between 1982 and 1991. The Fed's first dollar purchase after 1985 occurred on 28 January 1987; it continued to purchase dollars through 1987 until mid-1988, just before the Toronto Summit.[15] The US central bank was again a net purchaser of dollars before and after the US election in November 1988, after the G-7 meeting in mid-1990, and in early 1991. But the bulk of Fed interventions involved dollar sales, perhaps most dramatically in the wake of the Plaza Agreement in 1985 and again in late 1988 and throughout 1989.

Were Fed intervention operations predictable in the 1980s? Several recent studies attempt to estimate a US intervention reaction function in order to answer this question (Humpage 1990; Klein and Lewis 1991; Eijffinger and Gruijters 1991a). A general problem with this approach is that the words central banks use to explain their motives for intervention are rarely amenable to econometric modeling. The Fed claims to intervene

---

15. The Fed made one small dollar sale early in this period, $30 million on 11 March 1987, and sold dollars on four consecutive days in August 1987 for a total of $631 million.

for various reasons: to influence trend movements in exchange rates, to calm disorderly markets, to rebalance its foreign exchange reserve holdings, and, at times, simply to support fellow central banks in their exchange rate operations. The studies deal with this problem of defining intervention objectives by focusing on post-Louvre intervention operations. The Louvre Accord set out G-7 intervention rules, even if vague, that resemble a standard target-zone model. Although the studies find evidence in support of the hypothesis that central banks, including the Fed, intervened in a manner consistent with maintaining target zones for both the mark-dollar and yen-dollar exchange rates, they did not find evidence that it would have been possible to predict the timing of intervention operations.

The standard intervention reaction function models the hypothesis that current intervention is influenced by past changes in the spot exchange rate, deviations from the target exchange rate, and past intervention operations.

$$I_t = \beta_0 + \beta_1 \Delta s_t + \beta_2 (s_t - s_t^T) + \beta_3 I_{t-1} + \epsilon_t \qquad (5.1)$$

where I_t is current-period intervention, s_t is the log of the spot exchange rate, Δs_t is the one-day percentage change in the spot exchange rate, $s_t - s_{t-1}$, and s_t^T is the target exchange rate. A significant positive coefficient on the percentage change in the spot exchange rate (defined as domestic currency per foreign currency) would indicate that the central bank is leaning against the wind—i.e., pushing the exchange rate against the trend. A significant positive coefficient on the deviation from the target rate variable would indicate that the central bank is targeting the exchange rate. The past-intervention variable is included to serve as a proxy for other nonobservable factors that influence intervention decisions. This intervention reaction function can be estimated using daily data on intervention operations and spot exchange rates using the ordinary least squares method as long as intervention does not actually influence exchange rates. If intervention actually works, then we need to estimate the equation using instrumental variables.

Tables 5.3 and 5.4 present estimates of the standard intervention reaction function using daily Fed intervention operations as the dependent variable and the previous day's change in the dollar-mark exchange rate as the first explanatory variable. We also include the lagged percentage change in the exchange rate. We include two different variables to describe the target exchange rate. The Fed has never officially announced a target exchange rate since the collapse of the Bretton Woods system. However, Funabashi (1988) reports that the Fed, together with the other G-5 countries, agreed to a target central deutsche mark–dollar rate of 2.60 at the Plaza Hotel in September 1985. And again in February 1987, as part of the Louvre Accord, Funabashi (1988) reports that the Fed agreed to a mark-dollar target central exchange rate of 1.825. The Louvre

Table 5.3 Fed intervention reaction function estimates using Funabashi (1988) target exchange rates[a]

$$I_t^F = \beta_0 + \beta_1 \Delta s_t + \beta_2 \Delta s_{t-1} + \beta_3(s_t - s_t^T) + \beta_4 I_{t-1}^F + \beta_5 I_{t-1}^B + \epsilon_t$$

	Plaza	Louvre (1)	Louvre (2)	Louvre (3)
β_0	−33.21	10.19	−1.86	−13.04
s_e	11.41**	4.19*	4.46	5.58*
β_1	7.92	44.12	43.94	50.58
s_e	15.39	6.65**	76.70	112.35
β_2	−9.64	−7.59	−4.08	−7.45
s_e	14.43	7.14	8.28	11.29
β_3	9.38	6.85	12.45	4.59
s_e	4.23*	1.85**	2.67**	1.57**
β_4	0.24	0.30	0.43	0.52
s_e	0.10*	0.05**	0.05**	0.05**
β_5	0.74	0.41	n.a.	n.a.
s_e	1.17	0.06**		
R^2	0.25	0.42	0.41	0.36
Number of observations	68	478	738	900

Note: Where I_t is current-period intervention, s_t is the log of the spot exchange rate, Δs_t is the one-day percentage change in the spot exchange rate, $s_t - s_{t-1}$, and s_t^T is the target exchange rate.

n.a. = not available
s_e = standard error

a. Regressions estimated using instrumental variables. * denotes significance at the .05 level; ** denotes significance at the .01 level. Plaza subperiod begins in September 1985 and ends in December 1985. Louvre(1) subperiod begins in February 1987 and ends in December 1988; Louvre(2) ends in December 1989; Louvre(3) ends in December 1990.

Source: US Federal Reserve Board; Deutsche Bundesbank; DRI/McGraw-Hill, "Daily Exchange Rate Data (London Close)," DRIFACS database, Lexington (MA): Standard and Poor's Corporation; and Funabashi (1988).

target was reportedly adjusted downward in October 1987 to 1.70. The target was then returned to its original value in June 1988. Figure 5.2 presents a graph of the mark-dollar exchange rate and these target central rates reported in Funabashi (1988). An alternative target rate that has been used in the literature is the exchange rate dictated by purchasing-power parity (PPP). The PPP exchange rate is defined as the rate at which goods in one country sell for the same currency-adjusted price in the other country. Figure 5.3 presents another graph of the mark-dollar exchange rate, this time together with the PPP level of the exchange rate. The Funabashi and PPP targets are quite similar after 1988 but differ

Table 5.4   Fed intervention reaction function estimates using purchasing-power-parity target exchange rates[a]

$$I_t^F = \beta_0 + \beta_1 \Delta s_t + \beta_2 \Delta s_{t-1} + \beta_3(s_t - s_t^T) + \beta_4 I_{t-1}^F + \beta_5 I_{t-1}^B + \varepsilon_t$$

	1982–85	Plaza	Louvre(1)	Louvre(2)	Louvre(3)	Full
β_0	1.33	−36.19	12.05	−5.54	−14.71	9.19
s_e	2.72	15.08*	4.22**	4.88	5.47**	2.78**
β_1	−0.93	7.57	45.87	41.91	34.71	14.82
s_e	0.73	15.02	6.82**	81.26	117.67	2.68**
β_2	−0.92	−9.63	−9.03	−6.16	−7.73	−4.59
s_e	0.72	14.19	7.23	8.74	11.63	2.74
β_3	0.02	8.98	0.97	7.67	5.20	0.24
s_e	0.06	3.45*	0.88	1.39**	1.09**	0.08**
β_4	0.04	0.24	0.34	0.50	0.52	0.37
s_e	0.04	0.10*	0.05**	0.04**	0.04**	0.03**
β_5	0.006	0.72	0.42	n.a.	n.a.	0.31
s_e	0.01	1.16	0.06**			0.03**
R^2	0.07	0.27	0.40	0.39	0.35	0.33
OBS	729	68	478	738	900	1,023

Note: Where I_t is current-period intervention, s_t is the log of the spot exchange rate, Δs_t is the one-day percentage change in the spot exchange rate, $s_t - s_{t-1}$, and s_t^T is the target exchange rate.

n.a. = not available

s_e = standard error

a. Regressions estimated using instrumental variables. * denotes significance at the .05 level; ** denotes significance at the .01 level. 1982–85 begins in November 1982 and ends in August 1985. Plaza subperiod begins in September 1985 and ends in December 1985. Louvre(1) subperiod begins in February 1987 and ends in December 1988; Louvre(2) ends in December 1989; Louvre(3) ends in December 1990. Full period begins in September 1985 and ends in December 1988.

Source: US Federal Reserve Board; Deutsche Bundesbank; and DRI/McGraw-Hill, "Daily Exchange Rate Data (London Close)," DRIFACS database, Lexington (MA): Standard and Poor's Corporation.

widely in the Plaza period. We tried both measures of the target dollar exchange rate in the regressions.

The final explanatory variables included in the reaction function regressions are past Fed intervention operations and past Bundesbank intervention operations. The Bundesbank variable allows us to test whether Fed intervention decisions are influenced by the actions of another central bank. The regressions are estimated over various subperiods from 1982 through 1990.

Figure 5.2   G-5 targets and the mark-dollar rate, January 1985–December 1990

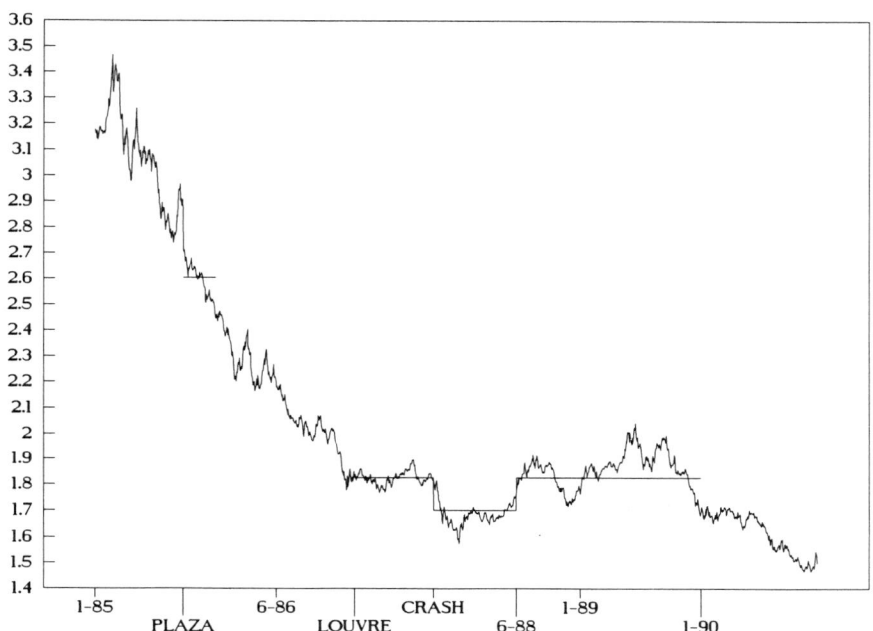

Figure 5.3   Purchasing power parity and the deutsche mark–dollar rate, January 1985–December 1990

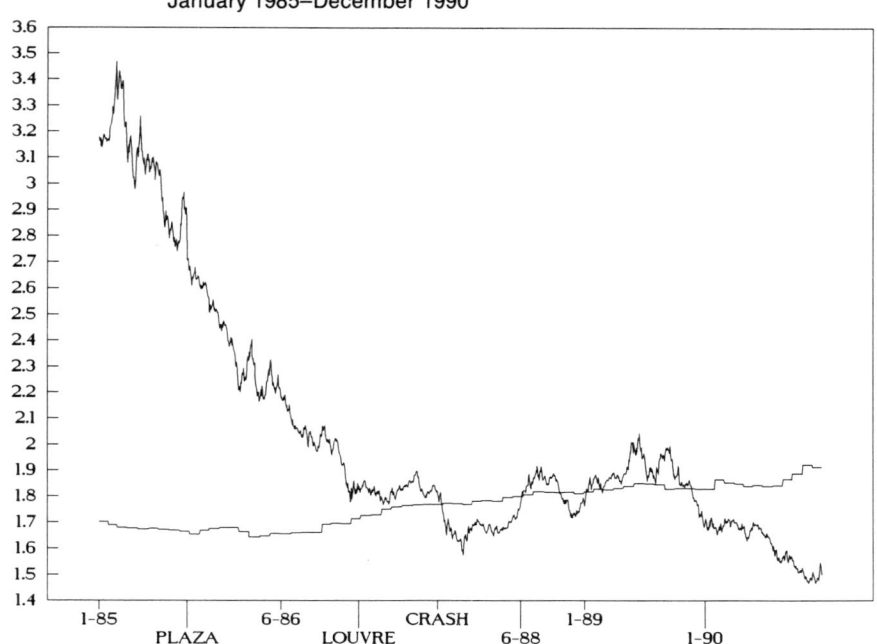

Table 5.3 presents the regression estimates using the Funabashi target exchange rates, and table 5.4 presents the regression estimates using the PPP exchange rate target. The results using the alternative targets are remarkably similar. We estimate the reaction functions over the Plaza and Louvre periods separately. The Bundesbank intervention data are only available through 1988, so the first post-Louvre subperiod is defined from February 1987 through December 1988. The second two post-Louvre subperiods end in 1989 and 1990, respectively. We estimate the reaction function using the PPP target also over an early subperiod that begins in 1982 and ends in August 1985 before the Plaza Agreement, and over the full post-Plaza period through 1988. The coefficient on the percentage change in the previous day's spot exchange rate is significant only in the first post-Louvre subperiod. The positive coefficient indicates that the Fed leaned against the wind in this period. The deviation from the Funabashi target exchange rate variable is consistently significant over all the subperiods. The deviation from the PPP target variable is significant in the first post-Plaza period, the second two post-Louvre periods, and the full post-Plaza period. The past Fed intervention variable is consistently significant, except in the pre-Plaza period. The past Bundesbank intervention variable is only significant in the post-Louvre subperiods. The R^2 statistics from the regressions indicate that Fed intervention was most predictable in the first post-Louvre subperiod and was least predictable in the pre-Plaza period.

The results presented in tables 5.3 and 5.4 suggest that over the period as a whole, Fed intervention was most likely to occur when the dollar wandered away from its target rate. There is little evidence that the Fed leaned against the wind except in the first two years following the Louvre Accord. Over the full period, Fed intervention was more likely to occur if intervention had occurred on the previous day. Unsurprisingly, Fed intervention was most predictable after the Louvre accord, when the central banks were quite specific about their objective to stabilize the dollar.

When and Why Have Other Major Countries Intervened?

The Bundesbank has maintained the most consistent presence of the G-7 countries in the foreign exchange markets. It intervened steadily before 1985, when the Fed was absent from the market. The German central bank may have been the major initial force in starting the dollar on its decline in early 1985 through both its own intervention operations and its view that the United States and Japan should join in coordinated

Figure 5.4 Daily Bundesbank intervention, 1984–88

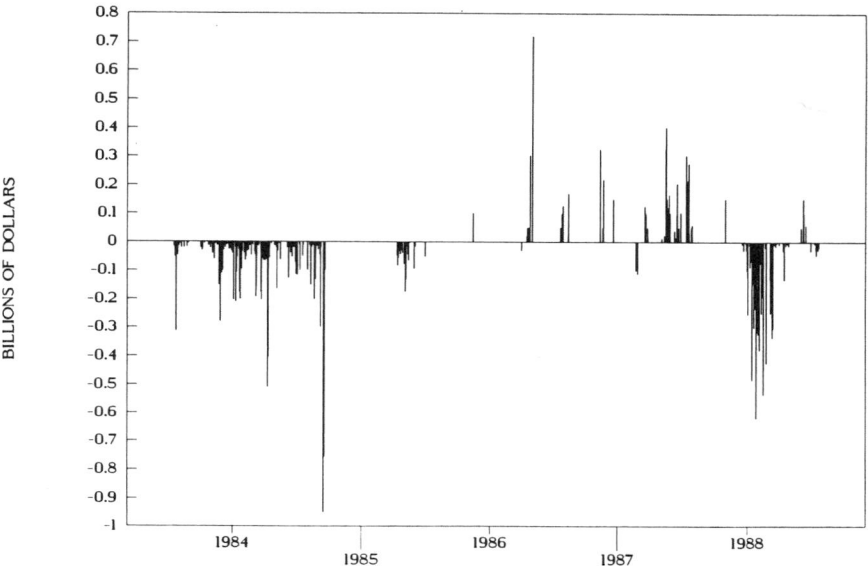

operations. Figure 5.4 is a bar graph of daily Bundesbank intervention from 1984 through 1988. If we exclude the period prior to 1985, when operations were generally small, the average daily dollar purchase on days that the Bundesbank intervened was $126 million, and the average dollar sale was $109 million. Over the full sample period, the Bundesbank, like the Fed, was a net seller of dollars. In 457 daily operations, the Bundesbank sold $26,230 million and purchased $6,963 million from 1982 through 1988. The burden of intervention was remarkably evenly shared by the Fed and the Bundesbank over this period; each sold on net just under $20 billion.

In a recent study of German and Japanese intervention policy from 1973 through 1987, Gaiotti, Giucca, and Micossi (1989, 24) find strong evidence of leaning-against-the-wind behavior by both banks. "The estimates provide evidence of an asymmetric behavior during dollar depreciations and appreciations; this asymmetry entails stronger resistance to appreciation of its currency by the Bank of Japan and stronger resistance to depreciation of its currency by the Bundesbank." The study also finds evidence that both central banks reacted to deviations in the *level* of the exchange rate from implicit targets for the real exchange rate.

Tables 5.5 and 5.6 present estimates of the standard intervention reaction function using daily Bundesbank intervention operations as the dependent variable and the same explanatory variables that we included in the Fed's reaction function regression. The two alternative target exchange rates, the Funabashi (1988) central rates and the PPP exchange

Table 5.5 Bundesbank intervention reaction function estimates using Funabashi (1988) target exchange rates[a]

$$I_t^B = \beta_0 + \beta_1 \Delta s_t + \beta_2 \Delta s_{t-1} + \beta_3(s_t - s_t^T) + \beta_4 I_{t-1}^B + \beta_5 I_{t-1}^F + \varepsilon_t$$

	Plaza	Louvre(1)
β_0	-8.37	-11.01
s_e	3.86*	3.63**
β_1	-2.41	14.25
s_e	6.91	7.32
β_2	-11.30	1.82
s_e	4.97*	7.26
β_3	3.23	1.36
s_e	1.43*	1.61
β_4	-0.01	0.24
s_e	0.11	0.05**
β_5	0.06	0.24
s_e	0.04	0.04**
R^2	0.27	0.28
Number of observations	68	478

Note: Where I_t is current-period intervention, s_t is the log of the spot exchange rate, Δs_t is the one-day percentage change in the spot exchange rate, $s_t - s_{t-1}$, and s_t^T is the target exchange rate.

s_e = standard error

a. Regressions estimated using instrumental variables. * denotes significance at the .05 level; ** denotes significance at the .01 level. Plaza subperiod begins in September 1985 and ends in December 1985. Louvre subperiod begins in February 1987 and ends in December 1988.

Source: US Federal Reserve Board; Deutsche Bundesbank; DRI/McGraw-Hill, "Daily Exchange Rate Data (London Close)," DRIFACS database, Lexington (MA): Standard and Poor's Corporation; and Funabashi (1988).

rate, are included in the regression estimates presented in tables 5.5 and 5.6, respectively. In the regressions over the Plaza Agreement period, the lagged percentage change in the spot rate is significant and negative in both tables. This suggests that the Bundesbank was leaning with the wind over this period—that is, moving with the exchange rate trend. The variable capturing the deviation from both the Funabashi and PPP target exchange rates is also significant and positive in the Plaza subperiod. In the post-Louvre Accord period, past interventions by the Fed and Bundesbank are significant in both tables. Only the PPP target is significant in the post-Louvre period, and there is no evidence of leaning against the wind, as we found for the Fed. In the early subperiod prior

Table 5.6 Bundesbank intervention reaction function estimates using purchasing-power-parity target exchange rates[a]

$$I_t^B = \beta_0 + \beta_1 \Delta s_t + \beta_2 \Delta s_{t-1} + \beta_3(s_t - s_t^T) + \beta_4 I_{t-1}^B + \beta_5 I_{t-1}^F + \varepsilon_t$$

	1982–85	Plaza	Louvre(1)	Full
β_0	15.75	30.62	−11.26	−4.22
s_e	11.95	15.87*	3.61**	2.85
β_1	8.63	−2.38	13.89	4.02
s_e	3.97*	6.95	7.31	3.26
β_2	1.79	−11.28	1.88	0.37
s_e	4.04	5.02*	7.25	3.28
β_3	0.67	3.12	1.80	0.07
s_e	0.27*	1.29*	0.79*	0.09
β_4	0.35	−0.02	0.22	0.33
s_e	0.04**	0.11	0.05**	0.03**
β_5	0.37	0.05	0.24	0.23
s_e	0.19*	0.04	0.04**	0.03**
R^2	0.20	0.26	0.29	0.24
Number of observations	729	68	478	1,023

Note: Where I_t is current-period intervention, s_t is the log of the spot exchange rate, Δs_t is the one-day percentage change in the spot exchange rate, $s_t - s_{t-1}$, and s_t^T is the target exchange rate.

s_e = standard error

a. Regressions estimated using instrumental variables. * denotes significance at the .05 level; ** denotes significance at the .01 level. 1982-85 begins in November 1982 and ends in August 1985. Plaza subperiod begins in September 1985 and ends in December 1985. Louvre subperiod begins in February 1987 and ends in December 1988. Full period begins in September 1985 and ends in December 1988.

Source: US Federal Reserve Board; Deutsche Bundesbank; and DRI/McGraw-Hill, "Daily Exchange Rate Data (London Close),"DRIFACS database, Lexington (MA): Standard and Poor's Corporation.

to the Plaza Agreement, however, we find evidence of leaning against the wind, targeting (to the PPP exchange rate), and influence of past interventions by both the Fed and the Bundesbank. Overall, the regression results suggest that the Bundesbank changed its intervention behavior over the different subperiods. But, the R^2 statistic suggests that consistently only about one-quarter of the variation in Bundesbank intervention is predictable.

Although we do not have access to official daily Japanese intervention operations, evidence from the graphs in Catte, Galli, and Rebecchini (1992a), newspaper reports, and total reserve shifts suggest that the Bank

Figure 5.5 Daily Swiss National Bank intervention, 1984–89

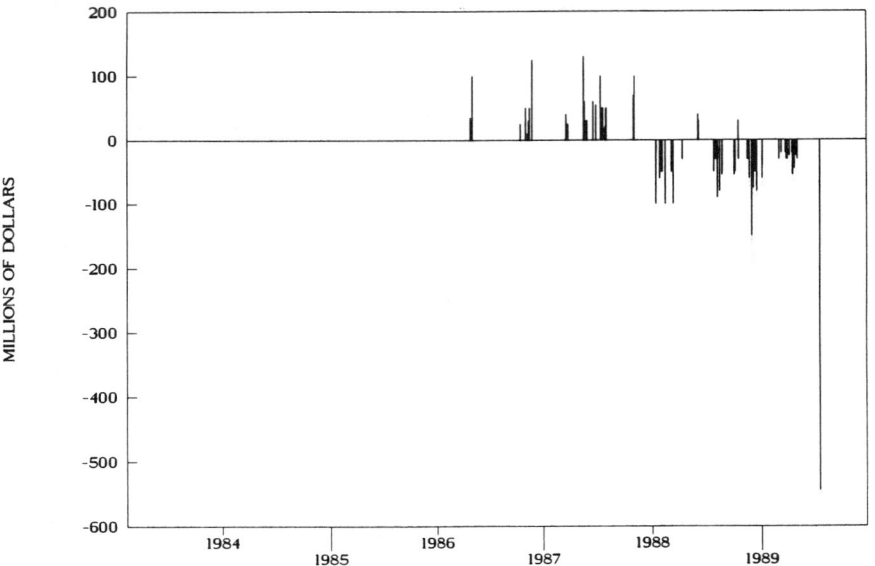

of Japan (BOJ) was a larger presence in the foreign exchange market than were the Fed and Bundesbank over this period. The Bank of Japan was involved in both sets of coordinated G-5 intervention operations in 1985. In early 1986, however, it began to intervene unilaterally and in support of, rather than against, the dollar. By late 1986 the Bundesbank joined the Japanese in support of the dollar, and in early 1987 the Fed also joined forces. The BOJ reportedly bought $1.7 billion against yen on 24 March 1987 and another $2 billion on 27 March 1987.[16] In total, during the first quarter of 1987, Funabashi (1988) reports, the BOJ purchased $16 billion against yen. In early August 1987, for the first time since the Plaza, the BOJ and the Fed engaged in a yen-supporting intervention operation in order to maintain the Louvre yen-dollar target. The BOJ joined forces again with the Fed and the Bundesbank in the aftermath of the stock market crash, during the "bear-trap" (or bear squeeze) operation, and in numerous coordinated and unilateral operations in 1988, 1989, and 1990.[17]

Figure 5.5 is a bar graph of the Swiss National Bank's intervention operations from 1984 through 1989. It was not involved in the coordinated operations in 1985 to bring the dollar down and, except for one

---

16. *Nihon Keizai Shimbun.*

17. Further detail on BOJ intervention operations is given in Dominguez (1990b), Gaiotti, Giucca, and Micossi (1989), and Catte, Galli, and Rebecchini (1992a and b). See figures 1.1 and 1.3 for the years 1989 and 1991. The BOJ generally sold dollars during this period.

large operation in 1989,[18] has been in the market both infrequently and for small amounts relative to the G-3 countries. The average daily SNB dollar purchase on days in which the Swiss intervened over this period was $52 million, and the average dollar sale was $58 million. In total, the SNB sold $3 billion and purchased $1,760 million. In a study of SNB intervention policy from 1974 through 1984, Gartner (1987) finds evidence both that the SNB leaned against the wind and that it uses intervention to target the Swiss franc exchange rate.

The Tendency to Sterilize

When central banks intervene, they buy (or sell) foreign assets with domestic assets, if not sterilized, the intervention will result in an increase (or decrease) in the domestic money base. For example, when the Fed intervenes against the dollar, the Fed's portfolio of foreign assets (typically deutsche mark- and yen-denominated assets) increases, and its dollar deposits decrease. At the same time, dollar deposits of commercial banks at the Fed increase. As a consequence, the US monetary base (commercial bank deposits at the Fed plus currency in circulation) is increased. The Fed can sterilize this increase by selling the appropriate number of dollar-denominated assets in open-market operations.

The Federal Reserve Bank of New York is reported to fully and automatically sterilize its intervention operations on a daily basis. In practice, the foreign exchange trading room immediately reports its dollar sales to the open market trading room, which then buys that many fewer bonds so that the daily money supply is unaffected.

Like the Fed, the Bundesbank and the BOJ both claim to sterilize their foreign exchange intervention operations routinely as a technical matter. Nevertheless, the general view is that both banks have at times allowed intervention operations to influence monetary aggregates. The degree of monetary accommodation is limited to the extent that they both target their money supply growth. A recent study by Takagi (1990, 22–23) finds that the BOJ almost completely sterilized reserve movements for the period 1973–89 taken as a whole. However, over the post-1986 period, "only about 50 percent of reserve inflows was sterilized." Takagi argues that domestic rather than international considerations may explain the Japanese monetary authorities' reluctance to sterilize its recent dollar purchases completely. Further, Takagi argues, financial market liberalization and the consequent increase in the money multiplier "allowed them to tolerate the rapid monetary expansion without sacrificing price stability." It is not clear, therefore, whether the monetary expansion that

---

18. The SNB sold $545 million on 27 December 1989.

occurred in Japan after 1986 was the cause or the result of intervention policy decisions.

Gaiotti, Giucca, and Micossi (1989), using Obstfeld's (1983) model of the Bundesbank's monetary policy reaction function, find a sterilization coefficient in the range of .5 to .8 for Germany for the period 1973 through 1987. The study, moreover, finds evidence that the degree of German sterilization has fluctuated widely. They suggest that while the degree of German sterilization was low in 1985 and 1986, this was due to the fact that external and domestic objectives coincided. Some observers have noted, on a longer term basis, a larger correlation of cumulated intervention and the monetary base.[19] If the exchange rate is one objective of Bundesbank monetary policy, then it is difficult, even at a conceptual level, to distinguish intervention and monetary policies. von Hagen (1989) attempts to address these complications by estimating the degrees of both short-run and long-run sterilization and separating periods when the Bundesbank was able to use interventions in the EMS to offset dollar interventions. He finds almost perfect short-run sterilization, but the degree of long-run sterilization depends on the possibility of offsetting interventions. When the mark was weak within the EMS and strong against the dollar, long-run sterilization was perfect. When the mark's stance in both markets was the same, about 40 percent of the dollar market interventions and 50 percent of EMS interventions had permanent effects on the German monetary base.

The SNB does not claim to sterilize its intervention operations and indeed relies almost exclusively on intervention operations to control the growth of its monetary aggregates.[20]

The Scale of Intervention

The scale of central bank intervention operations has been large in the post-1985 period relative to that in the early 1980s but small relative to the overall size of the foreign exchange market. Bordo and Schwartz (1990, 11) state, "If one judges by trading volume, it is difficult to believe that in most of the period since 1985 it has been large enough to do more than nudge exchange rates. . . . If one judges by the stock of internationally traded assets denominated in U.S. dollars and other major currencies—amounting to trillions of dollars—it is even more difficult to believe."

Every three years, the Federal Reserve, Bank of England, and Bank of Japan conduct a survey of banks and other foreign exchange traders

---

19. McKinnon (1984).

20. Edison (1993) provides summaries of other studies that estimate the degree of sterilization of intervention operations by various central banks.

to gauge the market. The most recent survey, conducted during April 1992, found that the volume of trading in the US market averaged $192 billion a day, up 49 percent over 1989. The volume of trading in London averaged $303 billion, up 62 percent, and in Tokyo $128 billion, up 11 percent. Adding in other markets, the worldwide total is thought to be about $1,000 billion a day.[21] This figure dwarfs the average size of intervention operations, which is less than $200 million per day.

Hung (1991, 11), however, suggests that central banks "can conceivably manipulate the exchange rate by entering a relatively thin and uncertain market." She suggests that the size of intervention over a very short period (an hour or so) can be sufficiently large relative to total private transactions, even if over the course of a full day intervention is relatively small.[22] Of course, the observed flow through the market in a given hour is irrelevant if there exist billions of dollars more in portfolios waiting to pounce on any deviation between the market rate and the "true value" that investors believe the currency should hold. All depends on whether investors hold firm expectations or whether they easily revise expectations in response to current developments, including central bank intervention. Along these lines, Mulford (1991, 17) suggests of intervention operations that "[a]lthough the amounts of money involved in sending a message like that or a signal are very small in relation to the total market, such action can have an influence well beyond its magnitude because the market watches carefully."

Figures 5.6 through 5.13 are stacked bar graphs of actual daily intervention activity by the Fed, Bundesbank, and SNB from 1985 to 1991. The figures show that there is wide variation in the daily magnitudes of intervention, with the largest operations occurring in 1985 and 1989. It is interesting to note that total intervention activity was relatively small during the post-Louvre period and during the so-called bear trap relative to the less publicized dollar sales operations in mid-1988, which were much larger in magnitude.

The Relationship between Intervention and Exchange Rates

Figures 5.14 and 5.15 present daily mark-dollar and yen-dollar exchange rates, respectively, from 1984 through 1991. Two patterns are worth noting: both exchange rates fall dramatically in 1985 and 1986, and both are relatively stable throughout the rest of the period. Is there any evi-

---

21. The figure is net of all double-counting and is corrected for omissions and gaps in reporting.

22. Peter Kenen has also stressed this point.

Figure 5.6 Fed and Bundesbank intervention, January 1985–March 1985

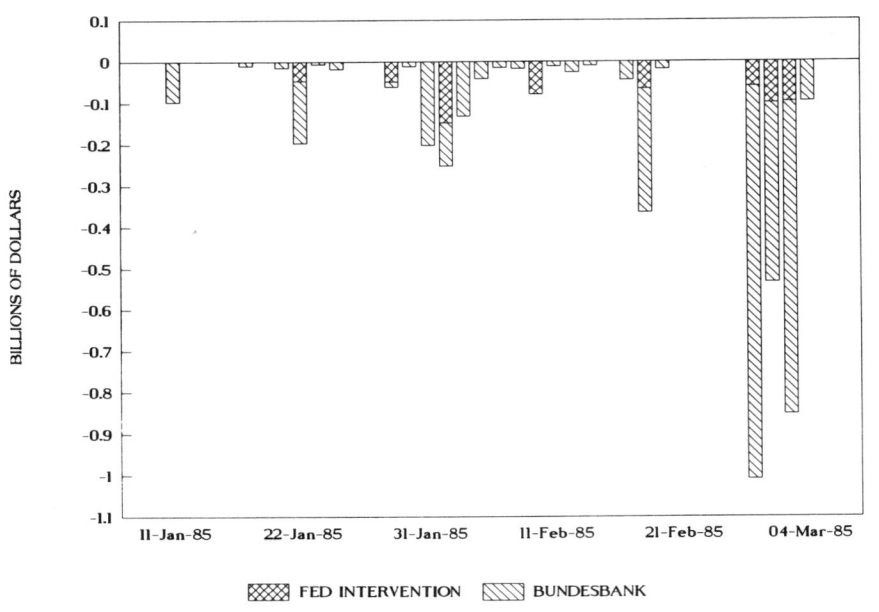

Figure 5.7 Fed and Bundesbank intervention, September 1985–November 1985 (Plaza)

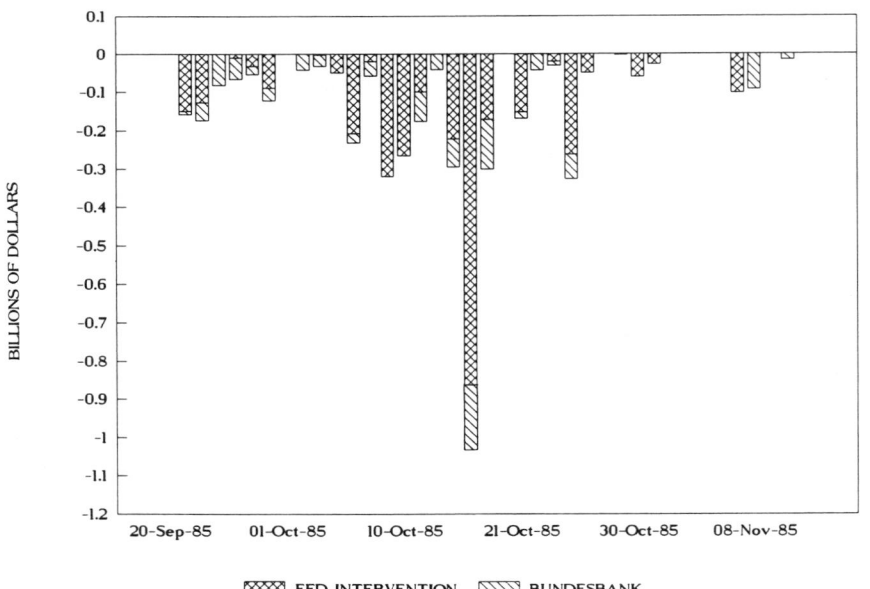

Figure 5.8 Fed and Bundesbank, and SNB intervention, March 1987–June 1987 (Louvre)

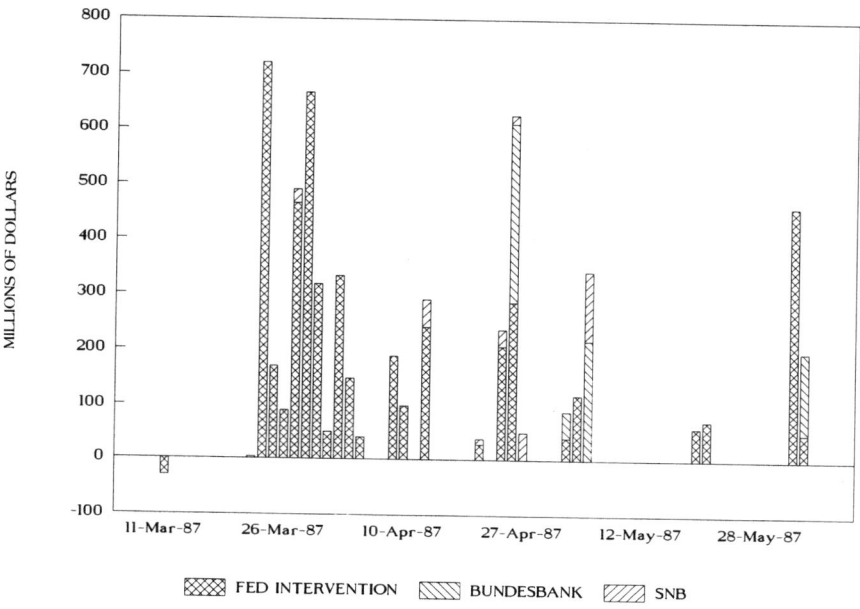

Figure 5.9 Fed, Bundesbank, and SNB intervention, October 1987–January 1988 (Crash and bear squeeze)

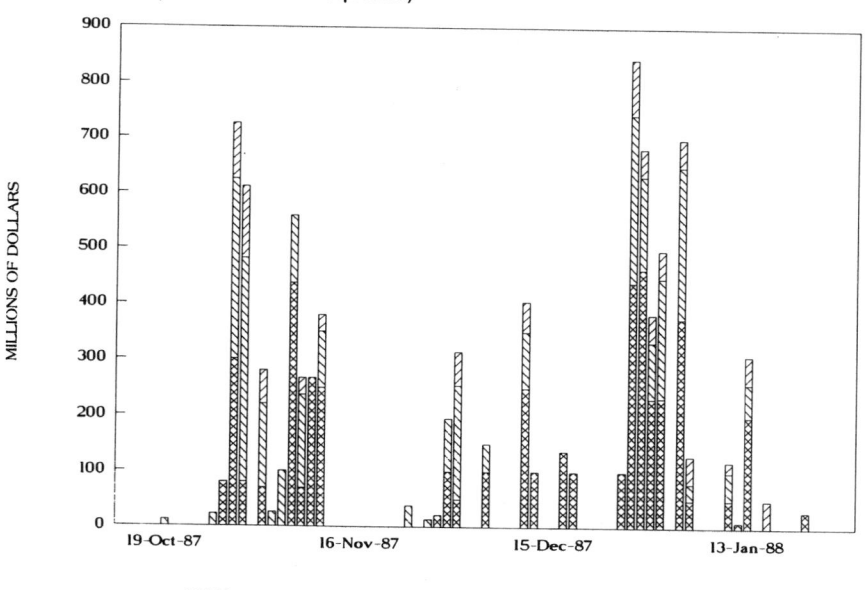

Figure 5.10 Fed, Bundesbank, and SNB intervention, May 1988–December 1988

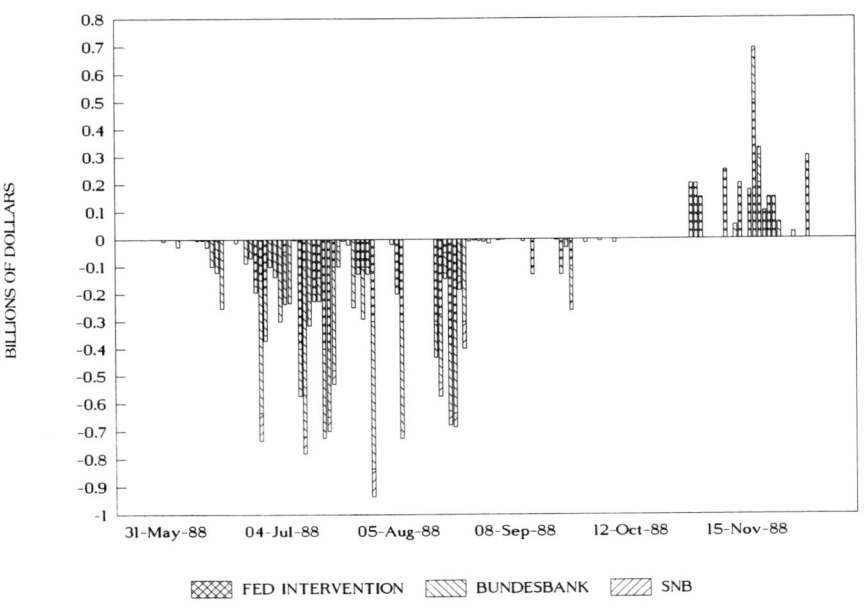

Figure 5.11 Fed and SNB intervention, 1989

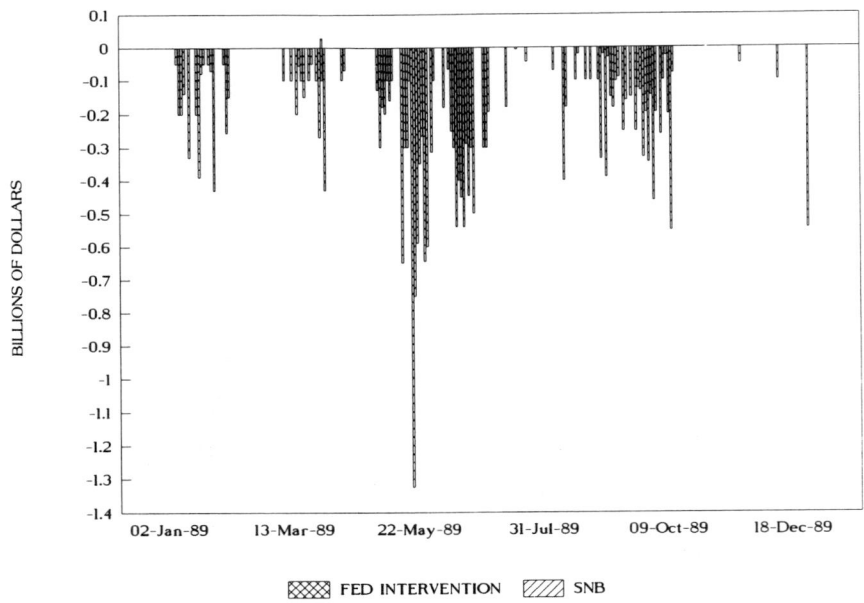

Figure 5.12 Fed intervention, 1990

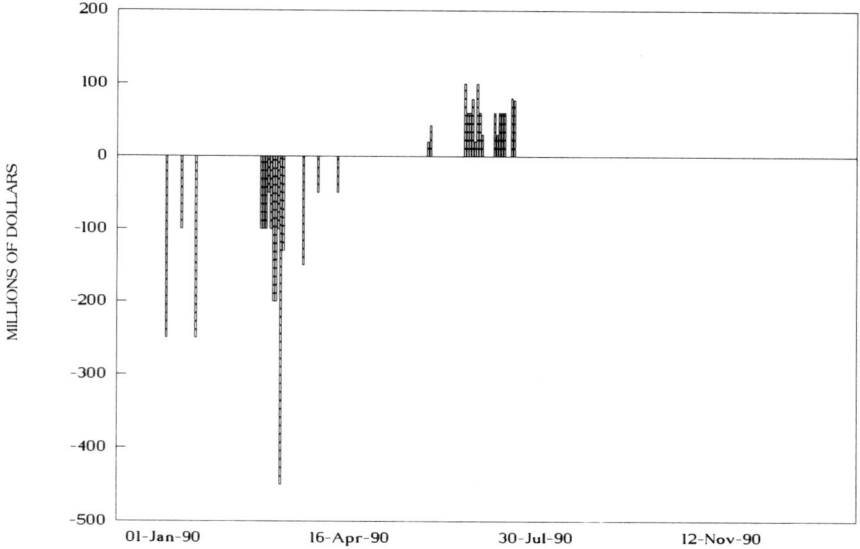

Figure 5.13 Fed intervention, 1991

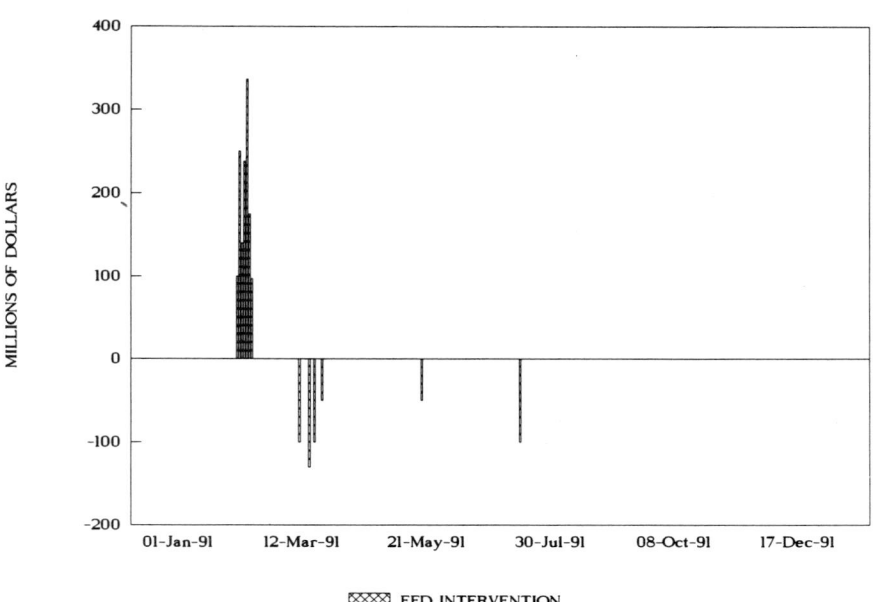

⊠ FED INTERVENTION

Figure 5.14 Daily mark-dollar exchange rate (London close)

Figure 5.15 Daily yen-dollar exchange rate (London close)

dence that intervention activity by central banks had anything to do with these exchange rate patterns?

We take our first look at the central question of this study, the effectiveness of intervention, by means of a simple table. Table 5.7 presents data on the relationship between the number and magnitudes of intervention operations and movements in the mark-dollar rate over 11 episodes of intervention activity. The first column lists the percentage change in the exchange rate in the month preceding the intervention episode, and the second column lists the value of the mark-dollar rate on the day before the intervention episode begins. The next three columns in the table present the total value of dollars bought or sold in each episode by the Fed, Bundesbank, and SNB, respectively. The sixth column lists the total number of days over which the central banks intervened, and the next column lists the percentage change in the exchange rate during the period of intervention. The final column lists the percentage change in the exchange rate in the month following the intervention episode. The most striking pattern to note from table 5.7 is that, generally, in the month following the end of an intervention episode, the mark-dollar exchange rate moved in a manner consistent with the intervention operations. When intervention operations were in support of the dollar, the dollar appreciated against the mark in the month following the end of the operations. Likewise, when central banks sold dollars, the dollar depreciated against the mark in the month following the end of the intervention operations.

From the first column we learn that in six out of eleven episodes, during the month prior to the start of intervention, the mark-dollar rate was moving in the opposite direction to subsequent intervention. The seventh column shows that in ten out of eleven episodes, during the period of intervention, the mark-dollar rate moved in the opposite direction to intervention operations. But the key information is in the final column: in ten of the eleven episodes, in the month following the end of the intervention operations, the mark-dollar rate moved in the same direction as the operations.

The information summarized in table 5.7 is presented visually in figures 5.16 through 5.23. Figures 5.16 through 5.21 show the mark-dollar exchange rate starting one month before the beginning of an episode of intervention and ending one month after the last intervention operation in the episode.[23] The symbols on the graphs represent days on which the Fed, Bundesbank, SNB, or a combination of the banks intervened

---

23. Intervention episodes were defined as a bunching of intervention operations that involved more than one central bank. In some cases, small unilateral intervention operations occurred during the month before or after the defined intervention episode. These magnitudes are not included in the statistics in table 5.7, but they do show up in figures 5.16 through 5.23.

Table 5.7 Intervention and exchange rate changes

Episode	Percentage change in DM/$ over preceding month[a]	Level of DM/$ before intervention	Amount of intervention (millions of dollars)[c]			Number of days of intervention during episode[d]	Percentage change in DM/$ during period[b] of intervention	Percentage change in DM/$ over subsequent month[e]
			Fed	Bundesbank	SNB			
11 Jan 85–4 Mar 85	2.3	3.152	−643	−3,470	0	25	6.9	−8.3
23 Sep 85–12 Nov 85	4.5	2.910	−3,301	−1,123	0	29	−8.6	−3.5
11 Mar 87–3 Jun 87	1.3	1.858	4,840	744	305	25	−3.6	0.80
19 Oct 87–21 Jan 88	−0.5	1.801	4,600	3,130	935	34	−6.2	2.0
31 May 88–7 Oct 88	2.5	1.714	−5,066	−7,851	−730	62	7.6	−3.7
31 Oct 88–2 Dec 88	−5.8	1.774	2,600	359	70	15	−1.96	3.0
8 Dec 88–6 Feb 89	−1.3	1.748	−2,230	−174	−415	22	7.8	−0.86
8 Mar 89–12 Oct 89	−0.86	1.856	−19,676	n.a.	−1,280	86	2.9	−1.5
23 Feb 90–9 Apr 90	−1.1	1.669	−1,780	n.a.	n.a.	13	0.81	−1.96
29 May 90–17 Jul 90	−0.16	1.681	1,000	n.a.	n.a.	17	−1.69	−5.07
4 Feb 91–12 Feb 91	−2.59	1.468	1,336	n.a.	n.a.	7	−0.74	7.98

SNB = Swiss National Bank

n.a. = not available

a. Percentage change in DM/$ rate in month prior to first day of intervention; $(\ln S_{t-21} - \ln S_{t-1})$ where S is the DM/$ rate and t is the first day of official intervention in the episode; positive sign denotes dollar appreciation, and negative sign denotes dollar depreciation.

b. $(\ln S_t - \ln S_{t+k})$ where $t+k$ is the last day of intervention in the episode.

c. Positive values represent operations in support of the dollar, and negative values represent operations aimed at reducing the value of the dollar

d. Number of days on which one or more central banks (Fed, Bundesbank and/or SNB) intervened during the episode

e. $(\ln S_{t+k+1} - \ln S_{t+k+21})$

Source: US Federal Reserve Board; Deutsche Bundesbank; Swiss National Bank; and DRI/McGraw-Hill, "Daily Exchange Rate Data (London Close),"DRIFACS database, Lexington (MA): Standard and Poor's Corporation.

Figure 5.16 Intervention and the mark-dollar exchange rate, December 1984–April 1985

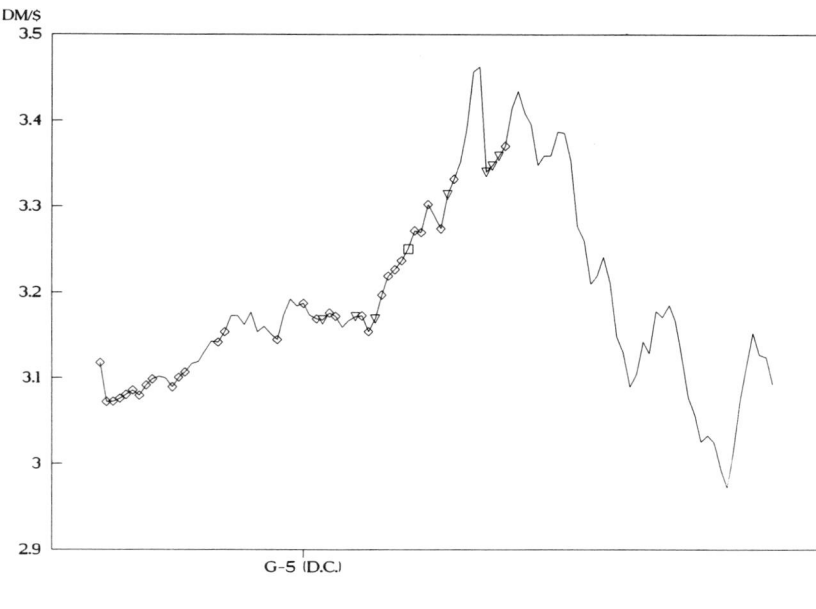

□ FED INTERVENTION   ◇ BUNDESBANK   ▽ COORDINATED

Figure 5.17 Intervention and the mark-dollar exchange rate, August 1985–December 1985

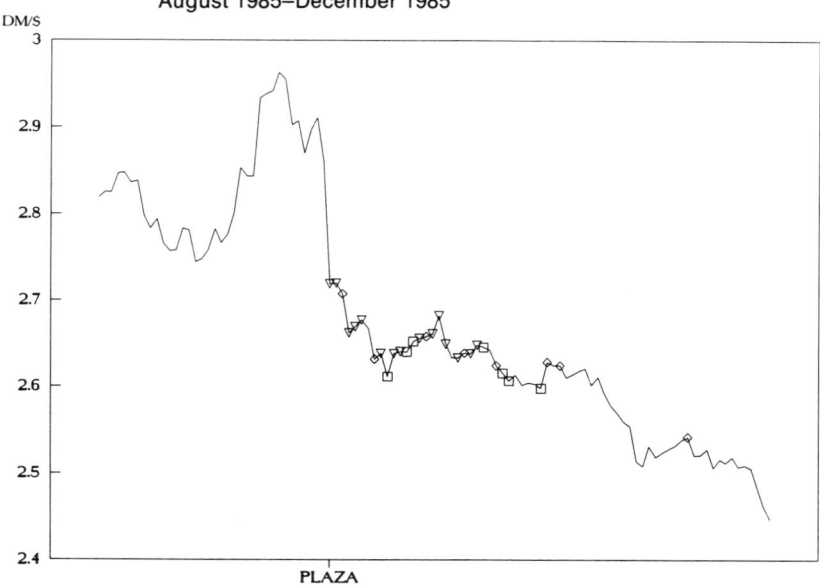

□ FED INTERVENTION   ◇ BUNDESBANK   ▽ COORDINATED

Figure 5.18 Intervention and the mark-dollar exchange rate, February 1987–June 1987

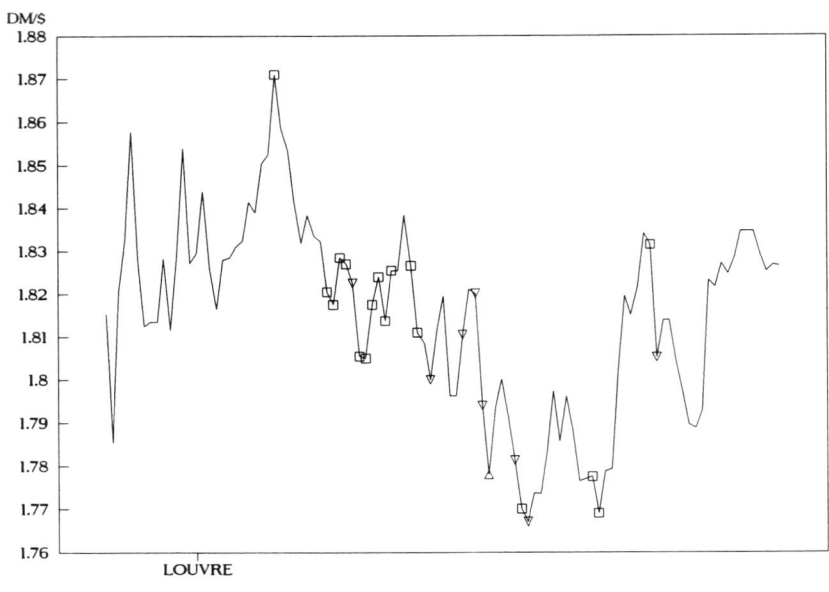

LOUVRE

□ FED INTERVENTION ◇ BUNDESBANK △ SNB ▽ COORDINATED

Figure 5.19 Intervention and the mark-dollar exchange rate, October 1987–February 1988

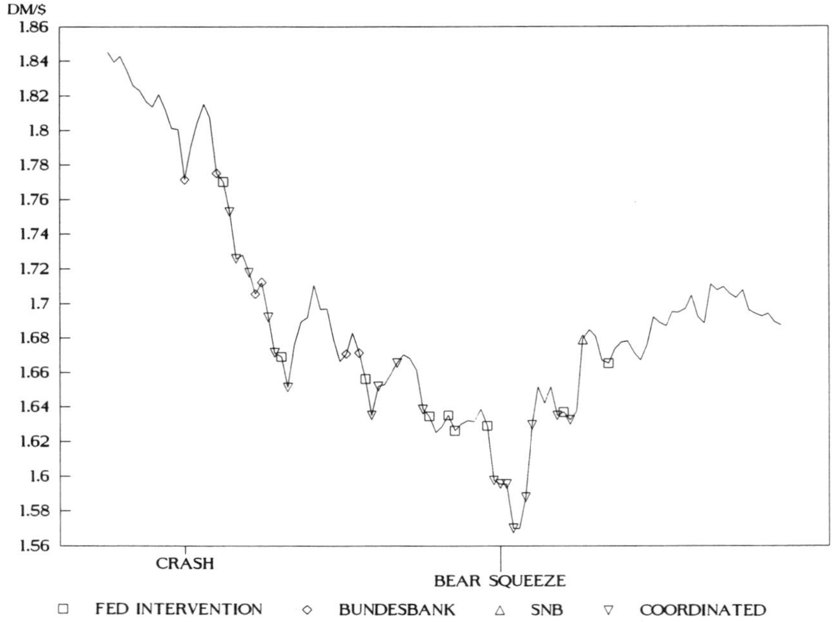

CRASH

BEAR SQUEEZE

□ FED INTERVENTION ◇ BUNDESBANK △ SNB ▽ COORDINATED

Figure 5.20 Intervention and the mark-dollar exchange rate, May–October 1988 ($ sales), October–December 1988 ($ purchases)

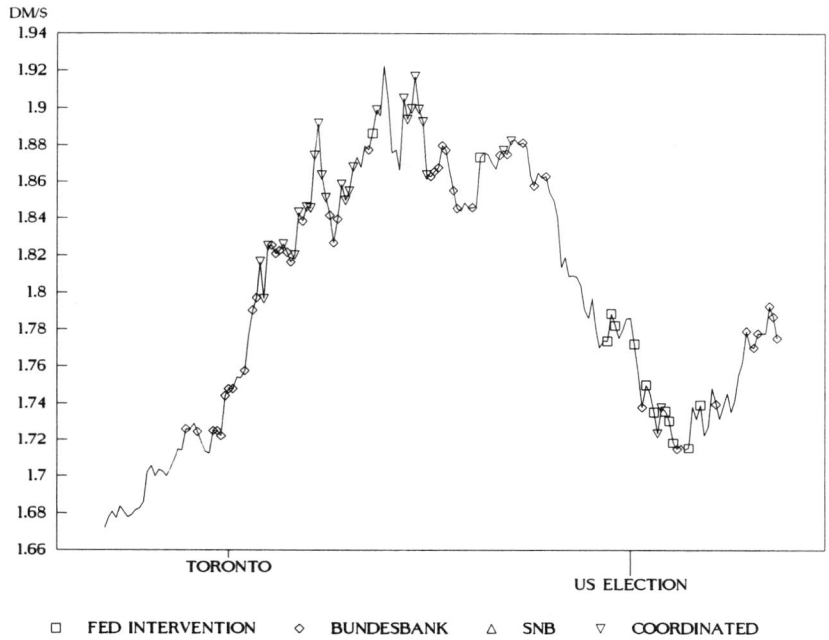

Figure 5.21 Intervention and the mark-dollar exchange rate, 1989

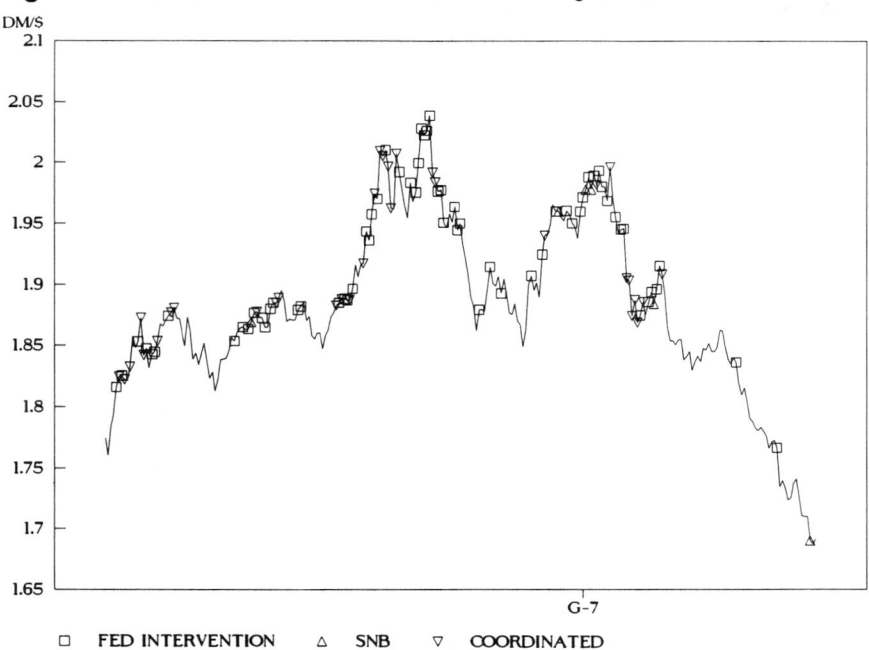

Figure 5.22 Intervention and the mark-dollar exchange rate, 1990

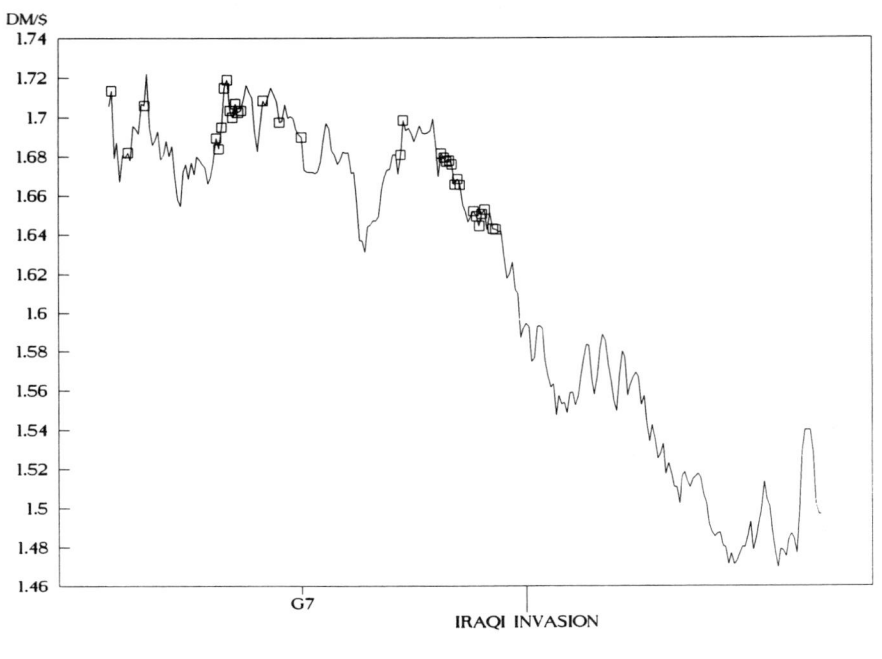

○ FED INTERVENTION

Figure 5.23 Intervention and the mark-dollar exchange rate, 1991

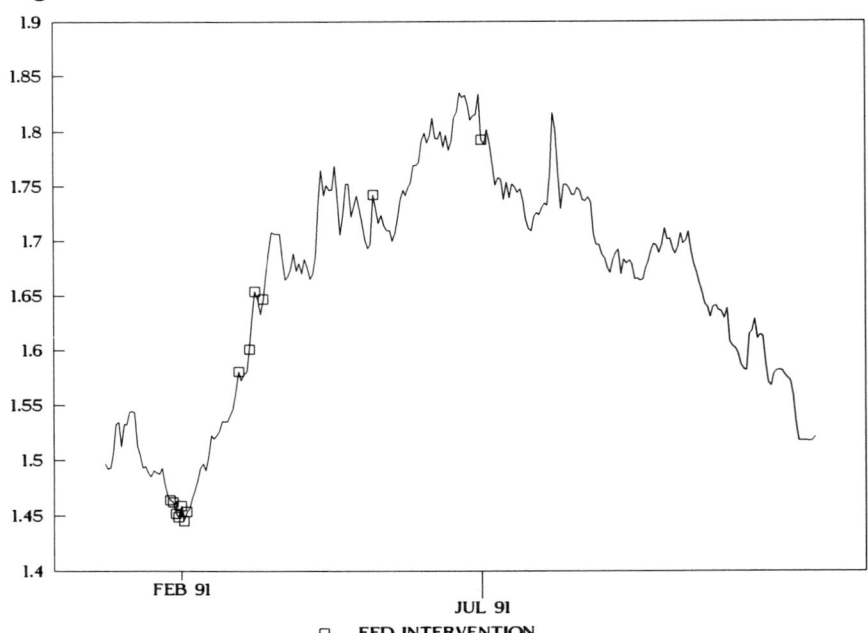

○ FED INTERVENTION

in the foreign exchange market. Figures 5.22 and 5.23 present the mark-dollar exchange rate and Fed intervention in 1990 and 1991. Perhaps the two most dramatic of these figures are 5.17 and 5.19. Figure 5.17 shows the mark-dollar rate before, during, and after the Plaza Agreement in September 1985. The figure shows that the dollar had begun to rise (after falling precipitously earlier in the year, shown in figure 5.16) just before the central banks began intervention operations. The dollar then continued on its downward path both during and after the intervention episode ended. Figure 5.19 shows the mark-dollar rate for the period starting a month before the global stock market crash and ending a month after the so-called bear trap, or bear squeeze. The dollar fell in the month before the crash and continued on a downward path until after the bear trap. Even a month after the end of the intervention episode, the dollar was still below where it had started in October 1987, but the dollar rose steadily in the months to follow, so much so that the central banks began to sell dollars in May 1988 (shown in figures 5.10 and 5.20) to bring the dollar back down.

The data in table 5.7 and the figures suggest that, in most of the episodes, the dollar exchange rate eventually moved in a direction consistent with intervention policy. This supports the conclusion reached by Catte, Galli, and Rebecchini (1992a and b) in a recent study of the daily intervention data between 1985 and 1991. They claim that of 17 episodes of coordinated intervention, all were successful at moving the exchange rate in the desired direction (which was usually to reverse the preceding trend in the dollar). Of these, nine episodes are labeled "definitely successful" and another eight "temporarily successful." Furthermore, they find that out of ten major exchange rate turning points during this period, nine coincided exactly with episodes of concerted intervention.[24] Their study probably claims a bit too much. The variable length of the "success criterion" leads to problems of subjectivity. It is likely that more episodes are classified as successes than should be,[25] though even on a more conservative accounting, the success rate is impressive. The question calls for more systematic statistical analysis.

---

24. Ironically, the one major turning point that the authors do not classify as coinciding with major coordinated intervention is July 1991, a date that we would consider an example of successful intervention by the US and German authorities, even though it does not meet the Italian authors' criteria for coordination.

25. Truman (1992). The exchange rate comes close to following a random walk. It is a property of a random walk that one can usually find a movement in either direction, positive or negative, if one is free to vary the number of days elapsed.

6

Assessing Intervention's Effectiveness

In this chapter we briefly describe what the academic literature has had to say about the impact of intervention policy.[1] As we described in chapter 3, daily intervention data has only recently been released by the Fed and is generally not available from other central banks. Consequently, most empirical studies of the efficacy of intervention operations use changes in international reserves to serve as a proxy for intervention data. One notable exception to this is the Jurgensen report. In 1982 the Group of Seven (G-7), during its economic summit at Versailles, commissioned a comprehensive study of intervention policy. The research departments of each of the G-7 central banks were asked to examine their own intervention policies using daily intervention data. The working group report, known as the Jurgensen report, was completed in 1983 and presented to the G-7 leaders at the Williamsburg summit. The report drew no firm conclusions but suggested that the effects of sterilized interventions by each of the G-7 countries on exchange rates was, at most, small and transitory during 1973–81.[2]

Estimating Effects of Asset Supplies on the Exchange Rate

The portfolio-balance theory says that investors diversify their holdings among domestic and foreign assets based on both expected returns and

---

1. See Edison (1993) for a thorough survey of recent literature on intervention.

2. Henderson and Sampson (1983) summarize the intervention research done at the Fed for the G-7 working group.

the variance in returns. According to the theory, intervention operations that change the composition of outside assets can influence the exchange rate because they lead investors to rebalance their portfolios. A sterilized central bank intervention operation changes only the composition of foreign and domestic assets outstanding. The portfolio balance theory says that as long as foreign and domestic assets are imperfect substitutes for each other in investors' portfolios, a change in their relative outstanding supply will require a change in expected relative returns. For example, a sterilized, dollar-supporting intervention operation increases the relative supply of outstanding foreign assets. In this case, the portfolio-balance theory predicts that investors will require a higher expected return on foreign assets to hold willingly the larger outstanding stock, leading to a depreciation of the foreign currency.

Three difficulties arise in setting up an appropriate test of the portfolio-balance theory. The first two difficulties involve data availability: measuring expected rates of return and measuring asset supplies. The expected rate of return on a portfolio that contains domestic and foreign assets depends on the interest earnings on both kinds of assets and the expected change in the exchange rate. Interest rate data are readily available, but exchange rate expectations data are not. Some early tests in the literature assumed away this problem by setting expected depreciation equal to zero and simply looking for a relationship between the level of the exchange rate and the supplies of domestic and foreign assets (e.g., Branson, Halttunen, and Masson 1977). An alternative way to deal with the problem of measuring exchange rate expectations is to invoke rational expectations. If investors are rational, then *ex post* changes in the exchange rate will provide an unbiased measure of expected depreciation.[3]

The second data difficulty involves measuring asset supplies. Total asset supply data are notoriously difficult to obtain. Data on individual assets is typically unavailable, forcing researchers to use aggregated data. The degree of measurement error in these data is likely to be quite high.

The third, and potentially most serious, difficulty that arises with tests of the portfolio-balance theory involves an econometric problem: simultaneity bias. This problem arises because exchange rates and asset supplies may be simultaneously determined. In this case, it is inappropriate to use the level of the exchange rate as the dependent variable. Studies that do not take account of simultaneity bias generally report that the coefficients on asset supplies are statistically significant but incorrectly signed. In other words, these studies find an apparent perverse relationship between the exchange rate and the supply of domestic

---

3. See Dooley and Isard (1983) and Frankel (1982a). This approach was adopted by Rogoff (1984), Boothe et al. (1985), Danker et al. (1987), and others.

and foreign assets. The explanation is that asset supplies respond to exchange rate swings. A depreciation of the domestic currency relative to the foreign currency may engender a change in the supply of domestic assets relative to foreign assets through current account balances or through endogenous intervention. This relationship obscures the effect of intervention on the market exchange rate.

Estimating Effects of Intervention on the Risk Premium

To avoid the simultaneity problem that arises when we test whether changes in asset supplies influence exchange rates, a number of studies take the "rational expectations approach": they use *ex post* excess returns as the dependent variable. This approach examines whether changes in asset supplies help to explain the expected or predictable component of *ex post* excess returns in the foreign exchange market. *Ex post* excess returns are defined as the realized profit a trader would make simultaneously borrowing in one currency and lending in another.[4]

Regardless of how the portfolio-balance tests are specified, studies using data from the 1970s find little evidence of portfolio-balance effects. Dooley and Isard (1982 and 1983), Frankel (1982a), and Rogoff (1984) regress *ex post* returns on a constant and on asset supplies; they find no evidence of a relationship between asset supplies and the expected risk premium. A second set of tests attempt to increase the power of the portfolio-balance tests by taking into account that investors also care about the variance of returns. Frankel (1982b), Frankel and Engel (1984), Lewis (1988), Engel and Rodrigues (1989), and Giovannini and Jorion (1989) impose the constraint that the coefficient on asset supplies is inversely proportionate to the variance of the return differential. These studies also find no evidence of portfolio-balance effects. In both sets of

---

4. Over the period t to $t + k$, the *ex post* excess return, $e_{t,k}$, is calculated as:

$$e_{t,k} = (1 + i_{t,k}) \left(\frac{S_{t,k}}{S_t}\right) \qquad (7.1)$$

where $i_{t,k}$ is the k-period-ahead domestic interest rate, $i_{t,k}^*$ is the k-period-ahead foreign interest rate, S_t is the spot rate, and $S_{t,k}$ is the k-period-ahead spot exchange rate. If the foreign exchange market is unbiased and efficient, then *ex post* excess returns can further be decomposed into an expected risk premium on domestic assets and a spot rate forecast error, which will be uncorrelated with asset supplies in period t.

$$e_{t,k} = rp_{t,k} + \epsilon_{t,k} \qquad (7.2)$$

where $rp_{t,k} = i_{t,k} - i_{t,k}^* + \Delta s_{t,k}$, $\Delta s_{t,k}$ is the k-period-ahead change in the log of the spot exchange rate, and $\epsilon_{t,k}$ is the spot rate forecast error. An alternative measure of the expected risk premium uses survey data on exchange rate expectations rather than *ex post* changes in the exchange rate.

studies, asset supplies are computed to include not only foreign exchange intervention, but also government budget deficits and other forms of asset creation that usually dwarf intervention in magnitude.

A few studies that focus more narrowly on daily changes in asset supplies through foreign exchange intervention do find an effect on the *ex post* excess return. Loopesko (1984) examines data in the late 1970s, and Dominguez (1990a and b) and Catte, Galli, and Rebecchini (1992a) examine data in the mid-1980s. Dominguez and Frankel (1993a) also find that daily, weekly, and cumulative intervention influences the expected differential in rates of return in 1980s data. (We discuss these results in further detail in chapter 7.) The cumulative measure of intervention more closely approximates the definition of relative stock supplies of outside assets described in the portfolio-balance theory. Black (1993) uses the net stock of foreign assets rather than total stocks of outside assets in his tests and, likewise, finds a statistically significant portfolio-balance effect in the mid-1980s data.[5]

Other Approaches

Profitability of Intervention

In "The Case for Flexible Exchange Rates," Milton Friedman (1953, 188) outlined his views on when official exchange rate intervention is appropriate:

> A positive disadvantage of government speculation is the danger that government authorities operating under strong political pressures will try to peg the exchange rate, thereby converting a flexible exchange rate system into a system of rigid rates subject to change from time to time by official action. . . . It also may be that government officials may have access to information that cannot readily be made available, for security or similar reasons, to private speculators. In any event, it would do little harm for a government agency to speculate in the exchange market provided it held to the objective of smoothing out temporary fluctuations and not interfering with fundamental adjustments.

Friedman goes on to suggest that we can distinguish periods in which the central bank appropriately used intervention by examining the profitability of those operations. The implication is that if intervention is to be stabilizing, then the central bank must be buying when the currency value is low and selling when it is high (this assumes the central

---

5. Ghosh (1992) tests the monetary model of exchange rate determination but uses the portfolio-balance model as the alternative hypothesis. He finds that although the portfolio-balance channel is statistically significant in monthly data from 1979 to 1988, the effect is not quantitatively important.

bank truly has superior information), in which case it should make profits in the market.

This Friedman hypothesis is not without flaws, both in theory and in practice. Counterexamples are possible. Profitable intervention may have no effect on exchange rates. Central banks may have superior information that allows them to buy low and sell high, but these profitable transactions may not lead to an exchange rate change. Conversely, an inept central bank could initiate a speculative bubble without losing any money. This suggests that the profitability criterion does not tell us everything about the efficacy of intervention.

Apart from the conceptual problems with the Friedman criteria, it is difficult to implement a meaningful test of profitability. Profit calculations are extremely sensitive to the time period over which they are measured and the method by which interest earnings are measured. A study by Taylor (1982) finds strong evidence that central banks lost large sums of money from 1973 through 1979. Jacobson (1983) extends Taylor's sample through 1981 and includes interest earnings. He finds that the United States made large intervention profits. Leahy (1989) improves on Jacobson's method of calculating interest earnings, extends the sample period through 1985, and also finds that the United States made intervention profits.

A sample period that included the purchases of marks and yen in 1985, when the dollar was at its peak, and sales in 1987 would presumably also show profits.

Effects of Intervention on Exchange Rate Variance

Most of the studies of intervention examine its effects on the level of the exchange rate. However, intervention may also influence the variance of exchange rate changes. Indeed, the motivation of "calming disorderly markets" explicitly suggests that central bank intervention can reduce the variability of exchange rates. Alternatively, intervention policy might increase uncertainty in the market and might lead to an increase in exchange rate volatility.

The hypothesis that intervention policy increases (or decreases) the variance of exchange rates is especially interesting because exchange rates have displayed a surprisingly high degree of time-conditional volatility. That is, studies have found that the variance of exchange rate changes is predictable on the basis of past variance. Periods of turbulence in exchange markets tend to be followed by periods of high volatility, and periods of calm tend to be followed by periods of low volatility in rates.

Is there evidence that intervention policy can explain the time dependence in exchange rate volatility? Dominguez (1993) tests this proposition using a generalized autoregressive conditional heteroskedasticity model. In the post–Louvre Accord period, publicly known Fed and Bundesbank intervention appears to have decreased daily volatility. Further, it appears that intervention need not be public for it to influence the conditional variance of exchange rate changes. Secret intervention operations by both the Fed and the Bundesbank generally increased exchange rate volatility in the 1980s.

Baillie and Humpage (1992) and Mundaca (1989) also use generalized autoregressive conditional heteroskedasticity models to estimate the effects of intervention on the exchange rate. In both studies the authors assume that the exchange rate is in a target zone (the dollar-mark and dollar-yen rates in the Baillie and Humpage study and the Norwegian exchange rate in the Mundaca study). Baillie and Humpage do not find evidence that intervention policy effectively contained the dollar-mark or dollar-yen rates in a target zone. Mundaca finds evidence that Norwegian intervention was most effective at reducing exchange rate volatility when it occurred within the band rather than at the edges of the band.

The studies that have examined the effects of intervention on exchange rate volatility define volatility over a day. Central bankers may hope to stabilize exchange rates over a longer horizon. It may be that intervention smooths daily movements of exchange rates but increases the variability of weekly or monthly movements. This is the subject of ongoing research.

Signaling

In chapter 4 we described how intervention may influence the exchange rate through two channels: the portfolio channel and the signaling channel. In the signaling channel, intervention serves as a means by which the central bank conveys its inside information to the market. If the market believes that the information is relevant, it will act on the information, and in so doing, affect the exchange rate.

There are few empirical examinations of the signaling channel. Studies of the signaling channel fall into two categories: studies that examine whether intervention is a leading indicator of monetary policy changes and studies that examine whether intervention influences exchange rate expectations.

Dominguez (1992a) examines whether US intervention policy communicated information useful for predicting future monetary policies between 1977 and 1981. In the period from the Fed's monetary-targeting shift in October 1979 through the following spring, there is a significant positive relationship between money surprises (defined as Fed announcements of the M-1 money supply less survey forecasts of M1) and Fed interventions in support of the dollar. This relationship, however, does not appear to have held up over the bulk of the period examined.

Klein and Rosengren (1991) examine the relationship between reports of intervention in the newspaper and monetary policy. They find little evidence of a systematic relationship between reports of intervention and contemporaneous 5-day, 10-day, and 15-day ahead changes in interest rates. Kaminsky and Lewis (1993) examine actual US intervention, together with a number of US monetary policy variables from 1985 to 1990, and strongly reject the hypothesis that intervention provides no information about future monetary policy. But they find that subsequent monetary policy changes are frequently in the opposite direction to what was signaled. Ghosh (1992) tests whether the information in intervention helps forecast future monetary policy and finds that knowledge of changes in official international reserves (used as a proxy for intervention policy) does improve predictions of future monetary policy.

In Dominguez and Frankel (1993b) we test the signaling hypothesis by examining whether intervention influences exchange rate expectations. We find evidence of a strong positive relationship between reported interventions and expectations measured by exchange rate survey data. We discuss our methodology and provide additional tests of this relationship in chapter 7.

Estimating How Expectations Are Formed[6]

There is reason to think that *ex post* changes in the exchange rate are a particularly bad measure of what investors expected *ex ante*. Independent estimates of market forecasts of exchange rates, drawn from survey data, suggest that expected depreciation varies closely with the forward discount, while *ex post* changes in the exchange rate do not and tend if anything to lie in precisely the opposite direction (Frankel and Froot 1990b).

In our tests of both the portfolio-balance and signaling channels, presented in chapter 7, we use survey data to measure exchange rate expectations. Although some readers will not require justification for using survey data, such data have often been dismissed by economists who claim that surveys are not representative of the agents who drive the market. A common example cited is that of a market with only a few rational agents but whose actions ensure rationality at the margin despite the irrationality of the majority (Mishkin 1981). The rationality-on-the-margin argument may bear relevance. However, no one has been able to provide convincing theoretical evidence of how such a marginal condition might apply. Indeed, newer work concludes that only under a very restricted set of conditions is rationality of some but not all agents

---

6. This section draws heavily from chapter 1 in Dominguez (1992a).

sufficient to ensure rationality in the market overall (e.g., Akerlof and Yellen 1985; Haltiwanger and Waldman 1985).

Surveys of large samples of respondents, along the lines of the Livingston series,[7] may bias the tests improperly toward rejection of rationality (in the sense of examining reported forecasts of irrelevant actors). One way around the problem is to use surveys of professional forecasters. Since the success and indeed livelihood of a professional forecaster is presumably a function of accuracy, the use of professional forecasters as representative agents will ensure that those examined are those most likely to have the most relevant expectations. The performance of professional forecasters therefore may be taken to define an upper bound on the expectational accuracy of agents in the economy as a whole.

The survey data that we will use in our empirical tests are provided by Money Market Services International (MMS). The methodology and respondent sample for the MMS survey inspire unusual confidence. The 30 respondents are professional exchange rate forecasters; most work in foreign currency trading divisions of major commercial banks. The standard arguments against surveys—in particular, that they do not adequately reflect the decisive players in the market—are less problematic with this sample than in most surveys. There is equal reason to have confidence in the survey's design and execution. Unlike many surveys, which are administered through the mail, the MMS survey is conducted by telephone (and more recently by fax) each Wednesday afternoon eastern standard time (EST). Such accurate timing minimizes the problem of different information sets across forecasters.

---

7. Numerous papers have examined this biannual data set on inflation forecasts compiled by Joseph Livingston of the *Philadelphia Inquirer*. See, for example, Carlson (1977) for tests of unbiasedness and efficiency.

7

Intervention in the 1980s: The Results

In chapters 1 and 5, we described the intervention policies the major industrial countries followed in the 1980s and corresponding movements in exchange rates over the period. The data suggested that exchange rates have generally moved in a manner consistent with intervention policies. In chapter 6 we described the difficulties involved in formally testing the effects of intervention on exchange rates. We also reviewed the previous statistical studies that attempt to measure these effects. The conventional wisdom, drawn from these studies, is that intervention has few (if any) independent effects. In this chapter we present our own econometric evidence on the effects of Fed and Bundesbank intervention policy on the dollar-mark exchange rate from 1982 through 1990. We have already described the circumstances under which intervention *might* have an effect. Now we will examine whether recent foreign exchange intervention actually worked.

The Effect of News[1]

Reports of a particular event through the media—newspaper, wire service, on-line computer service, radio, or television—often have a greater impact in the financial markets than the event itself. The value of the dollar increases, for example, when there are news reports of strong economic growth in the US economy or of improvement in the trade

---

1. This section draws heavily on Dominguez and Frankel (1993b).

balance (Hardouvelis 1988; Hogan, Melvin, and Roberts 1991; Klein, Mizrach, and Murphy 1991). Researchers have in many contexts found it useful to relate financial market prices to news reports. Studies of the impact of public announcements on prices of shares in particular corporations are known as "event studies." Other examples include the effect of money supply announcements on stock prices, commodity prices, and foreign exchange prices.

One advantage of this approach is that, when the market price is observed immediately before the news is released and then immediately after, fewer extraneous factors intervene in determining the change in market price than would be the case when changes are observed on a weekly or monthly basis. Another advantage is that news reports tend to focus on economic developments—whether changes in GNP, money supplies, or whatever else—that were not widely expected. It is precisely the unexpected component of such developments that matters to financial markets, the expected component having in most cases already been "discounted," or built into the existing market price. So, for example, if the domestic money supply is widely known to have been increasing rapidly over several quarters in response to high demand for the domestic currency, news reports will call attention only to information suggesting increases in the money supply beyond what was previously expected. This helps (but does not entirely) remove the systematic component of the money supply and produces better estimates of the effect on the marketplace. In other words, news reports, by "purging" the change in the money supply of the systematic component that could have been predicted by investors, allow us to observe only the unexpected component of effects, which are less plagued by problems arising from the fact that exchange rates and asset supplies are determined simultaneously, as discussed in chapter 6.

Our News Variables

We define "news" in our empirical work as all reports of official exchange rate policy that are published in one of three newspapers: the *Wall Street Journal*, the *Financial Times* (London), and *The New York Times*. A brief description of each news report is included in the appendix. We separate this exchange rate policy news into two categories. The first category, *NEWS*, includes official exchange rate policy announcements but excludes those that involve intervention operations. An example of a policy announcement appears on 15 July 1985: the *Wall Street Journal* reports, "Baker said that the Reagan administration isn't unhappy about the drop in the dollar." $NEWS_t$ is set equal to $+1$ if there were central bank announcements in support of the dollar (including, for example, announcements of G-7 meetings to deal with dollar weakness), -1 if there were official announcements against the dollar, and 0 if there were no such announcements.

The second category of news, *REPINT*, includes reports of unilateral Fed and Bundesbank intervention operations and reports of coordinated intervention operations. $REPINT_t$ is set equal to $+1$ if there were reports of central bank intervention in support of the dollar, -1 if there were reports of intervention against the dollar, and 0 if there were no such reports.

Official intervention operations that are not reported in the financial press are considered secret interventions, denoted *SECINT*. $SECINT_t$ is set equal to $+1$ if there were no reports of intervention when a central bank in fact intervened in support of the dollar, -1 if interventions against the dollar were not reported, and 0 for days in which there were no secret interventions. We expect the two news variables, $NEWS_t$ and $REPINT_t$, to have a negative effect on expectations of the dollar-mark rate. If nonreported intervention is truly secret, we expect that $SECINT_t$ will have no effect on exchange rate expectations.

On the Spot Rate

We estimate the effects of newspaper reports concerning official exchange rate policies on daily changes in the exchange rate from 1985 through 1990. We examine two subperiods. The first subperiod covers the Plaza period, January 1985 through January 1987. The second covers the Louvre period, February 1987 through December 1988. Official policy is believed to have changed from a focus on reducing the value of the dollar in the early period to a focus on stabilizing dollar exchange rates in the post-Louvre period. We end our second subperiod in 1988 because the Bundesbank data is only available through 1988. We also provide estimates over the full period and estimates for Fed intervention over the post–Louvre Accord period through 1990.

This section describes some preliminary tests. (The more formal tests come later in the chapter.) Table 7.1 presents estimates from a regression of the change in the spot rate (over the period in which news occurs) against the news variables and secret intervention.

$$(s_t - s_{t-j}) = \gamma_0 + \gamma_1 NEWS_t + \gamma_2 REPINT_t + \gamma_3 SECINT_t + \eta_t \qquad (7.1)$$

where the dependent variable $(s_t - s_{t-j})$ is the daily percentage change in the dollar-mark spot exchange rate, and η_t is the error term. Although the low R-squareds suggest that a small proportion of the variation in exchange rate changes is explained by the news variables, in all the subperiods the coefficient on exchange rate announcements, $NEWS_t$, is statistically significant and correctly signed. Official announcements in support of the dollar are positively associated with dollar appreciation over the next day.

Table 7.1 Effects of news and reported and secret interventions on daily changes in the spot rate, 1985–90[a]

$$(s_t - s_{t-j}) = \gamma_0 + \gamma_1 NEWS_t + \gamma_2 REPINT_t + \gamma_3 SECINT_t + \eta_t$$

	Plaza Jan 85–Jan 87 (OBS = 532, j = 1)	Louvre Feb 87–Dec 88 (OBS = 464, j = 1)	Full period Jan 85–Dec 88 (OBS = 996, j = 1)	Fed only Feb 87–Dec 90[b] (OBS = 957, j = 1)
γ_0	0.113	0.028	0.084	0.050
S_e	0.037**	0.027	0.023**	0.052
γ_1	−0.693	−0.402	−0.588	−0.296
S_e	0.091**	0.079**	0.062**	0.133*
γ_2	0.180	0.306	0.239	0.285
S_e	0.126	0.065**	0.066**	0.067**
γ_3	−0.500	0.427	0.197	0.317
S_e	0.351	0.143**	0.155	0.079**
D.W.[c]	2.08	2.08	2.07	2.36
R^2	0.10	0.11	0.09	0.14

S_e = standard error

a. s_t is the dollar/mark spot exchange rate; $NEWS_t$ is a (1,0,-1) dummy variable for official exchange rate announcements (excluding interventions); $REPINT_t$ is a (1,0,-1) dummy variable for reported interventions; $SECINT_t$ is a (1,0,-1) dummy variable for secret interventions. * denotes significance at the 95% level; ** denotes significance at the 99% level.
b. Regression includes only reported and secret Fed intervention variables.
c. D.W. is the Durbin-Watson statistic, and R^2 is the coefficient of determination.

Source: US Federal Reserve Board; Deutsche Bundesbank; DRI/McGraw-Hill, "Daily Exchange Rate Data (London Close)," DRIFACS database, Lexington (MA): Standard and Poor's Corporation; and various issues of *Financial Times* (London), *Wall Street Journal*, and *The New York Times*.

The coefficient on reported intervention, $REPINT_t$, appears statistically significant in all but the Plaza period but is always incorrectly signed. We suspect that this is another instance of the familiar problem of reverse causality or simultaneity discussed in chapter 6: appreciation causes central banks to sell dollars. We understand this factor: the central banks were leaning against the wind on a daily basis in the post-Louvre period. Recall that we found correlations of the same sign in our central bank reaction functions presented in chapter 5. But here it is obscuring the effect of intervention on the exchange rate. Secret interventions also appear to be statistically significant and incorrectly signed in the post-Louvre period, reflecting leaning against the wind even more strongly.

In a second set of tests (table 7.2) we regress the change in the spot exchange rate over the period in which news occurs on the announcement variable and intervention magnitudes, distinguished according to whether intervention was reported. It must be admitted that there is no

Table 7.2 Effects of news and intervention magnitudes on daily changes in the spot rate[a]

$$(s_t - s_{t-j}) = \phi_0 + \phi_1 NEWS_t + \phi_2 REPINT_t + \phi_3 |REPINT|_t^* I_t$$
$$+ \phi_4 SECINT_t + \phi_5 |SECINT|_t^* I_t + \nu_t$$

	Plaza Jan 85–Jan 87 (OBS = 532, j = 1)	Louvre Feb 87–Dec 88 (OBS = 464, j = 1)	Full period Jan 85–Dec 88 (OBS = 996, j = 1)	Fed only Feb 87–Dec 90[b] (OBS = 957, j = 1)
ϕ_0	0.112	0.019	0.080	0.060
S_e	0.037**	0.027	0.023**	0.051
ϕ_1	−0.695	−0.380	−0.584	−0.297
S_e	0.091**	0.078**	0.062**	0.132*
ϕ_2	0.296	0.079	0.186	0.113
S_e	0.154†	0.100	0.093*	0.107
ϕ_3	−0.683	0.823	0.240	0.724
S_e	0.501	0.272**	0.267	0.351*
ϕ_4	−0.372	0.111	−0.049	0.170
S_e	0.395	0.177	0.189	0.134
ϕ_5	0.843	1.605	1.347	1.389
S_e	1.611	0.519**	0.592*	1.028
D.W.[c]	2.09	2.11	2.09	2.37
R^2	0.11	0.15	0.10	0.16

S_e = standard error

a. s_t is the dollar/mark spot exchange rate; $NEWS_t$ is a (1,0,-1) dummy variable for official exchange rate announcements (excluding interventions); $REPINT_t$ is a (1,0,-1) dummy variable for reported interventions; $SECINT_t$ is a (1,0,-1) dummy variable for secret interventions; I_t is official intervention. The coefficients on $|REPINT|_t^* I_t$ and $|SECINT|_t^* I_t$ (ϕ_3 and ϕ_5) and their corresponding standard errors are multiplied by 10^4 for readability. † denotes significance at the 90% level; * denotes significance at the 95% level; ** denotes significance at the 99% level.
b. Regression includes only reported and secret Fed intervention variables.
c. D.W. is the Durbin-Watson statistic, and R^2 is the coefficient of determination.

Source: US Federal Reserve Board; Deutsche Bundesbank; DRI/McGraw-Hill, "Daily Exchange Rate Data (London Close),"DRIFACS database, Lexington (MA): Standard and Poor's Corporation; and various issues of *Financial Times* (London), and various issues of *Wall Street Journal*, and *The New York Times*.

reason to think these regressions will be less subject to simultaneity bias than those on the simple intervention dummy variables.

$$(s_t - s_{t-j}) = \phi_0 + \phi_1 NEWS_t + \phi_2 REPINT_t + \phi_3 |REPINT|_t \cdot I_t$$
$$+ \phi_4 SECINT_t + \phi_5 |SECINT|_t \cdot I_t + \nu_t \tag{7.2}$$

The daily intervention variable, denoted as I_t in the regression equation, is official central bank net purchases or sales of dollars in the foreign exchange market. Again, we find that the variable that captures official announcements of exchange rate policy is always significant and correctly signed. The variable that captures reports of central bank intervention is significant but incorrectly signed in both the Plaza period and over the full sample period. The coefficient on the amount of reported intervention is insignificant in these regressions. However, in the Louvre period, the opposite is true. The coefficient on the amount of reported intervention is significant, while the coefficient on the report of intervention is insignificant. In this period, the coefficient on the amount of secret intervention is also significant. From these regressions it is difficult to interpret whether it is simply the report of intervention or the amount of intervention that provides information to the market.

In table 7.3 we test whether it matters how frequently central banks use intervention policy. Is intervention most effective when sparingly used and unexpected, as some observers of recent history suggest? We divide intervention operations into two categories: initial interventions and subsequent interventions. An initial intervention is defined as one that occurs after at least five consecutive days of no intervention. Subsequent interventions are interventions that occur as part of a sequence of interventions.[2]

$$(s_t - s_{t-j}) = \beta_0 + \beta_1 NEWS_t + \beta_2 REPINT_t {*} INIT_t$$
$$+ \beta_3 REPINT_t {*} SUBS_t + \beta_4 SECINT_t + \epsilon_t \qquad (7.3)$$

The coefficient on official exchange rate announcements is once again highly significant and correctly signed in both subperiods and in the full period. Neither initial nor subsequent reported interventions are significant in the Plaza period (this is consistent with our findings in table 7.1). Initial intervention, however, is highly significant in both the Louvre period and the full period. Subsequent intervention is also significant in the Louvre period, but the size of the coefficient is much smaller than the size of the coefficient on initial intervention. Over the full period, subsequent intervention is statistically insignificant. These results provide evidence that the information that initial interventions provide the market is indeed greater than that for subsequent interventions. The initial signal seems to be more important than subsequent (backup) signals.

In table 7.4 we test the hypothesis that coordinated interventions are more effective than unilateral interventions of the same size. As we discussed in chapter 4, it may be that coordinated signals have a more than proportionate influence because they send a more powerful signal to the market. Reported coordinated interventions (*REPCOORD*) are

---

2. This hypothesis has been tested by Humpage (1989).

Table 7.3 Effects of intervention frequency on daily changes in the spot rate[a]

$$(s_t - s_{t-j}) = \beta_0 + \beta_1 NEWS_t + \beta_2 REPINT_t * INIT_t + \beta_3 REPINT_t * SUBS_t + \beta_4 SECINT_t + \epsilon_t$$

	Plaza Jan 85–Jan 87 (OBS=532, j=1)	Louvre Feb 87–Dec 88 (OBS=464, j=1)	Full period Jan 85–Dec 88 (OBS=996, j=1)	Fed only Feb 87–Dec 90[b] (OBS=957, j=1)
β_0	0.111	0.023	0.077	0.051
S_e	0.037**	0.027	0.023**	0.052
β_1	−0.695	−0.408	−0.592	−0.286
S_e	0.091**	0.077**	0.062**	0.132*
β_2	0.455	0.829	0.727	0.672
S_e	0.298	0.125**	0.136**	0.201**
β_3	0.119	0.127	0.096	0.243
S_e	0.140	0.074†	0.074	0.069**
β_4	−0.473	0.417	0.205	0.316
S_e	0.351	0.139**	0.154	0.079**
D.W.[c]	2.08	2.13	2.07	2.34
R^2	0.11	0.15	0.11	0.15

S_e = standard error
a. s_t is the dollar/mark spot exchange rate; $NEWS_t$ is a (1,0,-1) dummy variable for official exchange rate announcements (excluding interventions); $REPINT_t$ is a (1,0,-1) dummy variable for reported interventions; $INIT_t$ is a (1,0) dummy variable distinguishing initial interventions; $SUBS_t$ is a (1,0) dummy variable distinguishing subsequent interventions; $SECINT_t$ is a (1,0,-1) dummy variable for secret interventions. † denotes significance at the 90% level; * denotes significance at the 95% level; ** denotes significance at the 99% level.
b. Regression includes only Fed intervention variables.
c. D.W. is the Durbin-Watson statistic, and R^2 is the coefficient of determination.

Source: US Federal Reserve Board; Deutsche Bundesbank; DRI/McGraw-Hill, "Daily Exchange Rate Data (London Close), DRIFACS database, Lexington (MA): Standard and Poor's Corporation; and various issues of *Financial Times* (London), *Wall Street Journal*, and *The New York Times*.

defined as those days on which it was reported that more than one central bank intervened in support of (or against) the same currency.

$$(s_t - s_{t-j}) = \theta_0 + \theta_1 NEWS_t + \theta_2 REPCOORD_t + \theta_3 REPFED_t + \theta_4 REPBUND_t + \theta_5 SECINT_t + \mu_t \qquad (7.4)$$

Reported unilateral interventions are defined as those days on which it was reported that only the Fed or the Bundesbank (*REPFED* or *REPBUND*) were in the market. The results in table 7.4 indicate that official announcements of exchange rate policy continue to be significant and correctly signed. The coefficients on both coordinated and unilateral intervention are generally significant in the Louvre period. However,

Table 7.4 Effects of coordinated and unilateral interventions on daily changes in the spot rate[a]

$$(s_t - s_{t-j}) = \theta_0 + \theta_1 NEWS_t + \theta_2 REPCOORD_t + \theta_3 REPFED_t + \theta_4 REPBUND_t + \theta_5 SECINT_t + \mu_t$$

	Plaza Jan 85–Jan 87 (OBS = 532, j = 1)	Louvre Feb 87–Dec 88 (OBS = 464, j = 1)	Full period Jan 85–Dec 88 (OBS = 996, j = 1)
θ_0	0.105	0.020	0.084
s_e	0.037**	0.028	0.024**
θ_1	−0.693	−0.399	−0.588
s_e	0.091**	0.078**	0.062**
θ_2	−0.133	0.484	0.277
s_e	0.213	0.098**	0.103*
θ_3	0.170	0.279	0.235
s_e	0.301	0.108**	0.121†
θ_4	0.401	−0.012	0.194
s_e	0.177*	0.142	0.117
θ_5	−0.581	0.430	0.202
s_e	0.353	0.143**	0.156
D.W.[b]	2.11	2.07	2.08
R^2	0.11	0.13	0.09

S_e = standard error

a. s_t is the dollar/mark spot exchange rate; $NEWS_t$ is a (1,0,-1) dummy variable for official exchange rate announcements (excluding interventions); $REPCOORD_t$ is a (1,0, -1) dummy variable for reported coordinated interventions; $REPFED_t$ is a (1,0,-1) dummy variable for reported unilateral Fed interventions; $REPBUND_t$ is a (1,0,-1) dummy variable for reported unilateral Bundesbank interventions; $SECINT_t$ is a (1,0,-1) dummy variable for secret interventions. † denotes significance at the 90% level; * denotes significance at the 95% level; ** denotes significance at the 99% level.
b. D.W. is the Durbin-Watson statistic, and R^2 is the coefficient of determination.

Source: US Federal Reserve Board; Deutsche Bundesbank; DRI/McGraw-Hill, "Daily Exchange Rate Data (London Close),"DRIFACS database, Lexington (MA): Standard and Poor's Corporation; and various issues of *Financial Times* (London), *Wall Street Journal*, and *The New York Times*.

the coefficient on reported coordinated intervention is larger than that on reported unilateral Fed intervention when both are statistically significant. The evidence suggests again that reported interventions in the Louvre period were leaning against the wind and that reports of coordinated interventions seem to have a more powerful influence on the market than reports of unilateral intervention.

In tables 7.5 through 7.7 we estimate the effects of newspaper reports concerning official exchange rate policies on weekly changes in the exchange rate over two periods: 1982 through 1984, and 1985 through

Table 7.5 Effects of news and reported and secret interventions on weekly changes in the spot rate[a]

$$(s_t - s_{t-j}) = \gamma_0 + \gamma_1 NEWS_t + \gamma_2 REPINT_t + \gamma_3 SECINT_t + \eta_t$$

	Pre-Plaza period Nov 82–Oct 84 (OBS = 54, j = 14)	Post-Plaza period Oct 84–Dec 88 (OBS = 185, j = 7)
γ_0	0.001	0.003
s_e	0.005	0.001**
γ_1	−0.011	−0.008
s_e	0.011	0.003**
γ_2	0.011	−0.004
s_e	0.007	0.002*
γ_3	0.006	0.003
s_e	0.004	0.004
ρ^b	0.181	−0.013
s_e	0.143	0.076
D.W[c]	1.94	2.01
R^2	0.14	0.06

S_e = standard error

a. s_t is the dollar/mark spot exchange rate; $NEWS_t$ is a (1,0,-1) dummy variable for official exchange rate announcements (excluding interventions); $REPINT_t$ is a (1,0,-1) dummy variable for reported interventions; $SECINT_t$ is a (1,0,-1) dummy variable for secret interventions. * denotes significance at the 95% level; * denotes significance at the 95% level; ** denotes significance at the 99% level.
b. ρ is the estimated first lag correlation coefficient.
c. D.W. is the Durbin-Watson statistic, and R^2 is the coefficient of determination.

Source: US Federal Reserve Board; Deutsche Bundesbank; DRI/McGraw-Hill, "Daily Exchange Rate Data (London Close)," DRIFACS database, Lexington (MA): Standard and Poor's Corporation; and various issues of *Financial Times* (London), *Wall Street Journal*, and *The New York Times*.

1988. We split the sample in 1985 for the reasons explained in chapter 1: we think the key shift in US willingness to intervene dates from January 1985. We examine weekly changes in exchange rates in order to compare these results with the effects on exchange rate expectations as measured by survey data. The expectations data, introduced below, are only available on a biweekly basis from 1982 through 1984 and on a weekly basis after 1985.

In table 7.5 we estimate equation (7.1) using weekly rather daily changes in the exchange rate. As was the case in the daily change regressions, the low R-squareds suggest that a relatively small proportion of the variation in exchange rate changes is explained by the news variables. In the early subperiod, none of the explanatory variables is statistically significant. In the latter subperiod, however, both $NEWS_t$ and $REPINT_t$

are statistically significant and correctly signed. Official announcements and reports of intervention in support of the dollar during a given week are positively associated with dollar appreciation over the week. These results suggest that while central banks may have been leaning against the wind on the basis of daily changes, this was not the case over the course of a week. Assuming that there is no feedback effect of exchange rates on intervention, reports of intervention in support of the dollar are associated with an estimated appreciation of 0.4 percent.[3] The dummy variable that captures secret intervention, $SECINT_t$, is statistically insignificant over the two subperiods, as expected.

In tables 7.6a, 7.6b, and 7.6c we use weekly changes in the exchange rate over the three sample periods. The intervention variable is measured in three ways in these regressions. "One-day" intervention is Fed and Bundesbank purchases of dollars on day $t - 1$. "Two-week" or "one-week" intervention is cumulated between day $t - j$ and day $t - 1$, so that it measures total Fed and Bundesbank dollar purchases since day $t - j$. "Cumulative" intervention is cumulated from the beginning of the sample period and therefore measures the relative stock supplies of outside assets denominated in dollar and mark currencies. There is little evidence that any of our news variables or intervention magnitudes influence exchange rates over the early subperiod. Over the latter subperiod, the evidence is mixed, as was the case with the daily regressions, but the results suggest that the report of intervention taking place may be more important to the market than the actual magnitude of the operation.

The results from tables 7.1 through 7.6 suggest that publicly known official exchange rate policy influenced exchange rates during 1985–88. There is no evidence of such an effect for 1982–84, when the United States did not actively use intervention policy. We find that both initial interventions and coordinated interventions had large effects and that intervention magnitudes seem to be less important than reports of intervention.

---

3. If one were to accept the argument that the news reports reflect purely unexpected information regarding intervention and are thereby exogenous, then one would interpret the table 7.5 results as reduced-form estimation of the complete effect on the exchange rate. Below, we will argue that if interest rates were held constant, reports of intervention would have an expectations effect, plus a portfolio-balance effect. They are estimated using simultaneous equations techniques on a complete two-equation system. One could interpret the simple spot rate reduced-form effect, estimated in table 7.5 at 0.4 percent, as being considerably smaller than the complete effect calculated from the two-equation system estimated below because in practice interest rates are not held constant and in fact respond to an increase in demand for domestic assets by declining and thereby absorbing much of the impact. Or it may be that news reports of intervention are not exogenous, and the differences in estimates come because those reported in this section are subject to simultaneity bias.

Table 7.6a Effects of news and intervention magnitudes on weekly changes in the spot rate, November 1982–October 1984 (OBS = 54, j = 14)[a]

$$(s_t - s_{t-j}) = \phi_0 + \phi_1 NEWS_t + \phi_2 REPINT_t + \phi_3 |REPINT|_t^* I_t + \phi_4 SECINT_t + \phi_5 |SECINT|_t^* I_t + v_t$$

	One-day intervention[b]	Two-week intervention[c]	Cumulative intervention[d]
ϕ_0	0.002	0.003	0.002
s_e	0.004	0.004	0.004
ϕ_1	−0.011	−0.014	−0.008
s_e	0.011	0.010	0.011
ϕ_2	0.005	0.008	0.024
s_e	0.007	0.009	0.012†
ϕ_3	2.278	0.084	−0.013
s_e	1.171†	0.112	0.012
ϕ_4	0.005	0.002	0.003
s_e	0.004	0.005	0.005
ϕ_5	1.082	0.294	0.009
s_e	0.771	0.150†	0.008
ρ^e	0.114	0.108	0.148
s_e	0.151	0.150	0.148
D.W.[f]	2.01	1.99	1.97
R^2	0.22	0.20	0.18

S_e = standard error

a. s_t is the dollar/mark spot exchange rate; $NEWS_t$ is a (1,0,-1) dummy variable for official exchange rate announcements (excluding interventions); $REPINT_t$ is a (1,0,-1) dummy variable for reported interventions; $SECINT_t$ is a (1,0,-1) dummy variable for secret interventions; I_t is official intervention. † denotes significance at the 90% level. The coefficients on $|REPINT|_t^* I_t$ and $|SECINT|_t^* I_t$ (ϕ_3 and ϕ_5) and their corresponding standard errors are multiplied by 10^4 for readability.
b. Intervention variable is measured at the end-of-day prior to the survey.
c. Intervention variable is an accumulated measure between survey forecasts.
d. Intervention variable is an accumulated measure from the beginning of the sample period.
e. ρ is the estimated first lag correlation coefficient.
f. D.W. is the Durbin-Watson statistic; R^2 is the coefficient of determination.

Source: US Federal Reserve Board; Deutsche Bundesbank; DRI/McGraw-Hill, "Daily Exchange Rate Data (London Close)," DRIFACS database, Lexington (MA): Standard and Poor's Corporation; and various issues of *Financial Times* (London), *Wall Street Journal*, and *The New York Times*.

Table 7.6b Effects of news and intervention magnitudes on weekly changes in the spot rate, October 1984–December 1988 (OBS = 185, j = 7)[a]

$$(s_t - s_{t-j}) = \phi_0 + \phi_1 NEWS_t + \phi_2 REPINT_t + \phi_3|REPINT|_t^*I_t + \phi_4 SECINT_t + \phi_5|SECINT|_t^*I_t + v_t$$

	One-day intervention[b]	One-week intervention[c]	Cumulative intervention[d]
ϕ_0	0.003	0.003	0.003
s_e	0.001**	0.001**	0.001**
ϕ_1	−0.008	−0.008	−0.008
s_e	0.003**	0.003**	0.003**
ϕ_2	−0.007	−0.009	0.012
s_e	0.002**	0.003**	0.006†
ϕ_3	0.355	0.084	−0.094
s_e	0.109**	0.031**	0.035**
ϕ_4	0.001	−0.001	0.001
s_e	0.003	0.004	0.002
ϕ_5	0.483	0.148	−0.065
s_e	0.335	0.091	0.102
ρ^e	−0.071	−0.012	−0.036
s_e	0.077	0.076	0.076
D.W.[f]	2.01	2.01	2.00
R^2	0.12	0.11	0.10

S_e = standard error

a. s_t is the dollar/mark spot exchange rate; $NEWS_t$ is a (1,0,-1) dummy variable for official exchange rate announcements (excluding interventions); $REPINT_t$ is a (1,0,-1) dummy variable for reported interventions; $SECINT_t$ is a (1,0,-1) dummy variable for secret interventions; I_t is official intervention. † denotes significance at the 90% level. ** denotes significance at the 99% level. The coefficients on $|REPINT|_t^*I_t$ and $|SECINT|_t^*I_t$ (ϕ_3 and ϕ_5) and their corresponding standard errors are multiplied by 10^4 for readability.

b. Intervention variable is measured at the end-of-day prior to the survey.

c. Intervention variable is an accumulated measure between survey forecasts.

d. Intervention variable is an accumulated measure from the beginning of the sample period.

e. ρ is the estimated first lag correlation coefficient.

f. D.W. is the Durbin-Watson statistic, and R^2 is the coefficient of determination.

Source: US Federal Reserve Board; Deutsche Bundesbank; DRI/McGraw-Hill, "Daily Exchange Rate Data (London Close)," DRIFACS database, Lexington (MA): Standard and Poor's Corporation; and various issues of *Financial Times* (London), *Wall Street Journal*, and *The New York Times*.

Table 7.6c Effects of news and intervention magnitudes on weekly changes in the spot rate, November 1982–December 1988 (OBS = 240, j = 14 & 7)[a]

$$(s_t - s_{t-j}) = \phi_0 + \phi_1 NEWS_t + \phi_2 REPINT_t + \phi_3 |REPINT|_t^* I_t + \phi_4 SECINT_t + \phi_5 |SECINT|_t^* I_t + v_t$$

	One-day intervention[b]	14- & 7-day intervention[c]	Cumulative intervention[d]
ϕ_0	0.002	0.002	0.003
s_e	0.001	0.001*	0.001*
ϕ_1	−0.008	−0.009	−0.008
s_e	0.003**	0.003**	0.003**
ϕ_2	−0.004	−0.006	0.018
s_e	0.002*	0.003**	0.005**
ϕ_3	0.305	0.086	−0.012
s_e	0.112**	0.031**	0.003**
ϕ_4	0.004	0.002	0.007
s_e	0.003†	0.003	0.003*
ϕ_5	0.489	0.177	−0.001
s_e	0.311	0.077*	0.003
ρ^e	0.009	0.034	0.015
s_e	0.067	0.067	0.066
D.W.[f]	2.01	2.00	2.01
R^2	0.10	0.11	0.12

S_e = standard error

a. s_t is the dollar/mark spot exchange rate; $NEWS_t$ is a (1,0,-1) dummy variable for official exchange rate announcements (excluding interventions); $REPINT_t$ is a (1,0,-1) dummy variable for reported interventions; $SECINT_t$ is a (1,0,-1) dummy variable for secret interventions; I_t is official intervention. † denotes significance at the 90% level. * denotes significance at the 95% level. ** denotes significance at the 99% level. The coefficients on $|REPINT|_t^* I_t$ and $|SECINT|_t^* I_t$ (ϕ_3 and ϕ_5) and their corresponding standard errors are multiplied by 10^4 for readability. b. Intervention variable is measured at the end-of-day prior to the survey.
c. Intervention variable is an accumulated measure between survey forecasts.
d. Intervention variable is an accumulated measure from the beginning of the sample period.
e. ρ is the estimated first lag correlation coefficient.
f. D.W. is the Durbin-Watson statistic, and R^2 is the coefficient of determination.

Source: US Federal Reserve Board; Deutsche Bundesbank; DRI/McGraw-Hill, "Daily Exchange Rate Data (London Close)," DRIFACS database, Lexington (MA): Standard and Poor's Corporation; and various issues of *Financial Times* (London), *Wall Street Journal*, and *The New York Times*.

Effects on Expectations

The next question is how much of intervention policy's influence on the exchange rate is the "news" effect and how much is the effect of actual official purchases and sales of foreign currency occurring at the same time? It is clear that news has an effect to the extent that it causes investors to revise their expectations of future rates of return. They buy or sell foreign currency in response to the change in expected returns and thereby drive up or down the current price of foreign exchange. A prime example of this expectations effect is the possible signaling effect, described in chapter 4: market participants may interpret a news report of intervention by the authorities in support of the currency as revealing that the central bank is likely to tighten monetary policy, thereby inducing them to bid up the value of the currency today in anticipation of future appreciation.

One would like to be able to test more specifically than was the case in tables 7.1 and 7.6 whether exchange rate policy reports affect the market through expectations of changes in the exchange rate. It is always difficult to measure the expectations of investors because we cannot peer inside their minds. The forward exchange rate is sometimes used as a measure of what the typical market participant expects the future exchange rate to be. The problem with this is that (as noted in chapters 2 and 6), if investors are risk-averse, then the forward rate will not reflect the expected future spot rate. Rather, the expected future spot rate will fall short of the forward rate by an exchange risk premium that compensates investors for the risk of taking a position in uncertain foreign currency. (The risk premium on foreign currency can as easily be negative if the domestic currency is perceived as riskier than the foreign currency.)

There are measures of market participants' exchange rate expectations that are immune from the possible complications of an exchange risk premium: namely, survey data on the forecasts of bankers, foreign exchange traders, and other major players in the market regarding the future exchange rate.[4] The use of such data was pioneered by Dominguez (1986), Frankel and Froot (1987), Froot and Frankel (1989), and Ito (1990). Data used in this study come from biweekly and weekly surveys conducted by MMS International, Belmont, California. From 1982 through October 1984, MMS surveyed traders biweekly for their two-week and three-month ahead forecasts of four currencies against the dollar: the mark, pound, Swiss franc, and yen. Starting in late October 1984, MMS began to survey traders weekly for their one-week and one-month ahead forecasts of the same four currencies against the dollar. MMS provided

---

4. Survey data were discussed in some detail in chapter 6.

us the median response to each survey taken during 1984–88 for this study.

We combine the survey data on investor expectations of exchange rates with our news and intervention data to test whether the market effect of exchange rate policy operates through expectations. Our expectations equation is:

$$(\hat{s}^e_{t,k} - \hat{s}^e_{t-j,k}) = \alpha_0 + \alpha_1(s_t - s_{t-j}) + \alpha_2(s_t - \hat{s}^e_{t-j,k}) +$$
$$\alpha_3 \text{NEWS}_t + \alpha_4 \text{REPINT}_t + \alpha_5 \text{SECINT}_t + \epsilon_t \qquad (7.5)$$

where $(\hat{s}^e_{t,k} - \hat{s}^e_{t-j,k})$ is the revision in the log of the MMS survey prediction of the k-period ahead dollar-mark spot rate from time $t - j$ to time t, s_{t-j} is the log of the spot rate on the day of the last MMS survey, and ϵ_t is the error term.[5]

Early research using such survey data found evidence that respondents form their expectations partly by using various rules of thumb. The expected spot rate has been found, in general, to fluctuate roughly one-for-one in proportion to the most recent realized spot rate. But other factors enter the equation as well. By including some of these other variables in our equation for changes in exchange rate expectations, we can hope to get better statistical estimates, even though ultimately we are primarily interested in just the coefficients on exchange rate policy news. Frankel and Froot (1987) considered three possible alternative candidates for the other factor: the lagged spot rate, in which case the specification is extrapolative expectations; the lagged expectation, in which case the specification is adaptive expectations; and a long-run equilibrium measured by purchasing-power parity, in which case the specification is regressive expectations. In each case, the variable in question entered with statistical significance.

Here we allow for both extrapolative and adaptive expectations. At the four-week horizon, respondents have been observed to put negative weight on the lagged spot rate and more-than-unit weight on the contemporaneous spot rate, so that they are extrapolating the recent trend to get their forecast.[6] Our extrapolative parameter is α_1. Bandwagon expectations are the special case $\alpha_1 > 0$ and $\alpha_2 = 1$. Previous work has also found evidence that respondents form their predictions adaptively,

---

5. This equation does not suffer from the overlapping observation problem familiar from studies of bias in spot rate forecasts because the dependent variable is the change in expectations, not the prediction error.

6. Frankel and Froot (1990b). Models based on technical analysis (which often essentially extrapolate past trends) are more widely used by professional forecasting services, especially at short horizons, than models based on macroeconomic fundamentals (which could be viewed as regressive expectations). Of 27 foreign exchange forecasting services reviewed by *Euromoney* magazine in 1988, 12 used only technical models, only 1 relied exclusively on fundamentals models, and 12 used a combination of the two techniques.

Table 7.7a Effects of news and reported and secret interventions on investors' biweekly, three-month-ahead exchange rate expectations, November 1982–October 1984[a]
(OBS = 54, k = 90, j = 14)

$$(\hat{S}^e_{t,k} - \hat{S}^e_{t-j,k}) = \alpha_0 + \alpha_1(S_t - S_{t-j}) + \alpha_2(S_t - \hat{S}^e_{t-j,k}) +$$

$$\alpha_3 NEWS_t + \alpha_4 REPINT_t + \alpha_5 SECINT_t + \varepsilon_t$$

α_0	0.006 (0.004)
α_1	0.491 (0.197)*
α_2	0.522 (0.153)**
α_3	−0.001 (0.007)
α_4	0.001 (0.005)
α_5	−0.003 (0.003)
$\chi^2(1)$	9.646**
$\chi^2(2)$	62.261**
D.W.	2.01
R^2	0.74

a. $(\hat{S}^e_{t,k} - \hat{S}^e_{t-j,k})$ is the revision in the log of the MMS survey prediction of the k-period ahead dollar/mark spot rate from time $t-j$ to time t; s_t is the dollar/mark spot exchange rate; $NEWS_t$ is a (1,0,-1) dummy variable for official exchange rate announcements (excluding interventions); $REPINT_t$ is a (1,0,-1) dummy variable for reported interventions; $SECINT_t$ is a (1,0,-1) dummy variable for secret interventions. Standard errors are in parentheses. * denotes significance at the 95% level; ** denotes significance at the 99% level. The $\chi^2(1)$ statistic pertains to the hypothesis that $\alpha_2 = 1$ (expectations are not adaptive); and $\chi^2(2)$ pertains to the hypothesis that $\alpha_1 = \alpha_2 = 0$ (expectations are not extrapolative, but are completely adaptive).

Source: Money Market Services International, "Foreign Exchange Rate Survey Data," Belmont, CA; US Federal Reserve Board; Deutsche Bundesbank; DRI/McGraw-Hill, "Daily Exchange Rate Data (London Close),"DRIFACS database, Lexington (MA): Standard and Poor's Corporation; and various issues of *Financial Times, Wall Street Journal,* and *The New York Times.*

putting positive weight on the lagged survey prediction. Our speed of adaptation parameter is $(1 - \alpha_2)$. Adaptive expectations are the special case $\alpha_1 = 0$ and $\alpha_2 < 1$. Static expectations are the special case $\alpha_1 = 0$, $\alpha_2 = 1$. Expectations are stabilizing overall if $\alpha_1 + \alpha_2 < 1$, and destabilizing overall if $\alpha_1 + \alpha_2 > 1$. There is danger of simultaneity bias in that the current spot rate is certainly an important determinant of current expectations of the future spot rate.

Table 7.7a presents the expectations equation regression results for the early sample period. News reports appear to have had no effect on expectations in the early period, 1982 through 1984. However, the estimates for the same regression over the 1985–88 subperiod, presented in table 7.7b, indicate a marked change in regime. The coefficients on the news variables appear with the correct sign and are statistically significant in all the regressions for the latter sample: newspaper reports of exchange rate policy announcements and central bank intervention in support of the dollar tend to lower expectations of the future dollar-mark exchange rate. The average effect of reported intervention on the one-month ahead expectations of the dollar-mark exchange rate was .4 percent.[7] The effect of other official announcements was over twice as large, at .9 percent. The effect of exchange rate policy news on exchange rate expectations is remarkably similar to its effect on the contemporaneous spot rate itself (shown in table 7.5).

In Table 7.7b, the coefficient on the lagged spot rate, $-\alpha_1$, and the coefficient on the lagged expectation, $(1 - \alpha_2)$, are each statistically different from both zero and one. In other words, there is evidence of extrapolative behavior *and* gradual adaptation. Expectations are overall neither stabilizing nor destabilizing.

Table 7.7c presents the expectations equation over the full sample period. The estimates are generally similar to those reported in table 7.7b for the period 1985–88. These results suggest that over the full period, exchange rate policy announcements and reports of intervention changed investors expectations of exchange rates in the intended direction. US and German policy to support the dollar led investors to revise their expectations of the future value of the dollar upward. Over the full period, the net effect of speculation was neither stabilizing nor destabilizing.

Estimation of the Risk Premium Effect

If the effect of reported intervention on the expected exchange rate is on the order of .4 percent, how big is the effect on today's spot exchange rate? The estimated spot rate effects described at the beginning of this chapter were subject to simultaneity bias. Therefore, in order to gauge the effect on the current spot rate, we must consider a second relationship that connects the current spot rate and the expected future rate, which holds simultaneously with the expectations relationship we described in the previous section. That second relationship is the risk premium equation discussed in chapter 6. Whether investors demand greater shares of dollar assets or deutsche mark assets depends, among other things, on the expected returns on those assets. If the mark is expected to depreciate and the expected depreciation is not offset by a differential

---

7. Hung (1991) tests a similar equation, showing the effect of news and actual intervention on the change in the spot rate *measured relative to the previous MMS forecast of the spot rate*. She finds that every net purchase of $1 billion increased the yen-dollar rate by 5 percent over the period April 1984 to December 1986. The effect was smaller during the Louvre period January 1987 to December 1989.

Table 7.7b   Effects of news and reported and secret interventions on investors' weekly one-month-ahead exchange rate expectations, October 1984–December 1988[a]

(OBS = 186, k = 30, j = 7)

$$(\hat{s}^e_{t,k} - \hat{s}^e_{t-j,k}) = \alpha_0 + \alpha_1(s_t - s_{t-j}) + \alpha_2(s_t - \hat{s}^e_{t-j,k}) +$$

$$\alpha_3 NEWS_t + \alpha_4 REPINT_t + \alpha_5 SECINT_t + \varepsilon_t$$

α_0	0.006 (0.001)**
α_1	0.309 (0.095)**
α_2	0.707 (0.075)**
α_3	−0.009 (0.002)**
α_4	−0.004 (0.002)*
α_5	0.005 (0.003)
$\chi^2(1)$	15.318**
$\chi^2(2)$	139.367**
D.W.	2.07
R^2	0.68

a. $(\hat{s}^e_{t,k} - \hat{s}^e_{t-j,k})$ is the revision in the log of the MMS survey prediction of the k-period ahead dollar/mark spot rate from time $t-j$ to time t; s_t is the dollar/mark spot exchange rate; $NEWS_t$ is a (1,0,-1) dummy variable for official exchange rate announcements (excluding interventions); $REPINT_t$ is a (1,0,-1) dummy variable for reported interventions; $SECINT_t$ is a (1,0,-1) dummy variable for secret interventions. Standard errors are in parentheses. * denotes significance at the 95% level; ** denotes significance at the 99% level. The $\chi^2(1)$ statistic pertains to the hypothesis that $\alpha_2 = 1$ (expectations are not adaptive); and $\chi^2(2)$ pertains to the hypothesis that $\alpha_1 = \alpha_2 = 0$ (expectations are not extrapolative, but are completely adaptive).

Source: Money Market Services International, "Foreign Exchange Rate Survey Data," Belmont, CA; US Federal Reserve Board; Deutsche Bundesbank; DRI/McGraw-Hill, "Daily Exchange Rate Data (London Close)," DRIFACS database, Lexington (MA): Standard and Poor's Corporation; and various issues of *Financial Times* (London), *Wall Street Journal*, and *The New York Times*.

in interest rates, then the expected rate of return on dollars exceeds the expected rate of return on marks. Investors will respond by immediately demanding more dollar assets, thereby driving up the price of the dollar.

Estimating the risk premium effect will help us answer two questions (aside from circumventing potential simultaneity bias problems). First, it can tell us something important regarding actual intervention, as distinct from reported intervention: do sterilized purchases or sales of foreign currency have any effect? We can test this by looking for an effect of intervention on the risk premium. If investors treat mark assets and dollar assets as perfect substitutes, then sterilized intervention has no effect. In this case, the effect will be zero. Second, if we reject this null case, estimating the risk premium will help us, when there is news of intervention that changes expected rates of return, discern the effect on

Table 7.7c Effects of news and reported and secret interventions on investors' pooled exchange rate expectations over the full sample period, November 1982–December 1988[a] (OBS = 240, k = 90 & 30, j = 14 & 7)

$$(\hat{s}^e_{t,k} - \hat{s}^e_{t-j,k}) = \alpha_0 + \alpha_1(s_t - s_{t-j}) + \alpha_2(s_t - \hat{s}^e_{t-j,k}) +$$
$$\alpha_3 NEWS_t + \alpha_4 REPINT_t + \alpha_5 SECINT_t + \varepsilon_t$$

α_0	0.006 (0.001)**
α_1	0.386 (0.082)**
α_2	0.621 (0.061)**
α_3	−0.009 (0.002)**
α_4	−0.004 (0.001)**
α_5	−0.001 (0.002)
$\chi^2(1)$	38.338**
$\chi^2(2)$	200.474**
D.W.	2.07
R^2	0.68

a. $(\hat{s}^e_{t,k} - \hat{s}^e_{t-j,k})$ is the revision in the log of the MMS survey prediction of the k-period ahead dollar/mark spot rate from time $t-j$ to time t; s_t is the dollar/mark spot exchange rate; $NEWS_t$ is a (1,0,-1) dummy variable for official exchange rate announcements (excluding interventions); $REPINT_t$ is a (1,0,-1) dummy variable for reported interventions; $SECINT_t$ is a (1,0,-1) dummy variable for secret interventions. Standard errors are in parentheses. ** denotes significance at the 99% level. The $\chi^2(1)$ statistic pertains to the hypothesis that $\alpha_2 = 1$ (expectations are not adaptive); and $\chi^2(2)$ pertains to the hypothesis that $\alpha_1 = \alpha_2 = 0$ (expectations are not extrapolative, but are completely adaptive).

Source: Money Market Services International, "Foreign Exchange Rate Survey Data," Belmont, CA; US Federal Reserve Board; Deutsche Bundesbank; DRI/McGraw-Hill, "Daily Exchange Rate Data (London Close)," DRIFACS database, Lexington (MA): Standard and Poor's Corporation; and various issues of *Financial Times* (London), *Wall Street Journal*, and *The New York Times*.

the demand for marks versus dollars. This will in turn indicate the effect on the exchange rate.

The magnitude of the effect of news on the exchange rate depends very much on interest rates. If the US interest rate changes by the same amount as the expected rate of depreciation, then there will be no effect on the risk premium, on the portfolio demand for mark versus dollar assets, nor on the exchange rate. In general, one would not expect the interest rate to respond enough to absorb the impact fully. But in the absence of a complete model of financial markets, including other aspects of central bank policy, it is impossible to say how much of the response to expected depreciation will be absorbed by the interest rate and how much by the exchange rate. We will follow the strategy of holding interest rates constant when considering the effect of changes in expectations.

The risk premium equation we consider is a version of the one discussed in chapter 6:

$$i_{t,k}^{DM} - i_{t,k}^{\$} + \Delta \hat{s}_{t,k}^{e} = \beta_0 + \beta_1 v_1 + \beta_2 v_t x_t + u_{t,k} \qquad (7.6)$$

where $i_{t,k}$ is the k-period ahead Euromark interest rate, $i_{t,k}^{\$}$ is the k-period ahead Eurodollar interest rate, $\Delta \hat{s}_{t,k}^{e}$ is the expected change in the spot rate between period t and $t+k$ measured by the survey data, v_t is the daily variance of exchange rate changes between period t and $t+k$, x_t is the portfolio share that is allocated to mark assets, and $u_{t,k}$ is the error term meant to reflect any measurement error in the data.

If investors' asset demands depend on any factors other than those included here (expected returns and variances), then the existence in the equation of an error term that is correlated with portfolio shares will probably introduce simultaneity bias.[8] We report both ordinary-least-squares and instrumental-variable estimates of the risk premium equation in Dominguez and Frankel (1993a) but omit the tables here in the interest of brevity.

We measure intervention in a number of ways. Unilateral operations by the Fed and Bundesbank are included both separately and combined with coordinated operations. Intervention is also measured in terms of both stocks and flows.[9] Intervention is included with the constraint that comes from the optimal diversification theory (where the variance and intervention enter multiplicatively) and separately. Over the early sample period, November 1982 through October 1984, we find that the coefficient on the intervention variable is statistically significant and of the correct sign only when intervention is defined as a stock—that is, intervention is cumulated from the beginning of the sample period. However, from January 1985 to December 1988, when intervention activity became more popular among the central banks, and over the full sample period, the coefficient on intervention is always statistically significant, regardless of how it is measured. Further, coordinated interventions by the two central banks had a larger statistical effect than unilateral Fed intervention and about the same effect as unilateral Bundesbank intervention. The effect of cumulated intervention is statistically significant, whether

---

8. Similarly, if there is measurement error in the asset supplies, which is quite possible, there will again be a bias in the coefficient estimate. The only plausible conditions under which there could conceivably be no simultaneity problem is if the regression error consists solely of measurement error in the survey data *and* that error is uncorrelated with the variables on the right-hand side of the equation.

9. Conventional theory strictly suggests that only the stock of intervention should influence the risk premium. But the flow of intervention should also matter if the *change* in stocks held depends on the desired stock, which in turn depends on the risk premium; if we invert a simple stock adjustment model of this sort, we find that the risk premium depends on the flow of intervention.

the equation is estimated using ordinary-least-squares or simultaneous-equation techniques.[10]

We conclude from these results that intervention has an effect, even if sterilized. If mark and dollar assets were perfect substitutes, then the coefficient on intervention should be zero: changes in asset supplies would have no effect on the risk premium. But this is not, in fact, the case. The existence of an effect for sterilized intervention is one of our most important findings, countering many past studies that have not found evidence of this effect.

A Quantitative Summary of the Estimated Effects[11]

In the first two sections of this chapter, we described regression results that suggest that intervention operations can influence the exchange rate both through the news effect and through a portfolio effect. Is the relationship between intervention and exchange rates simply a minor statistical phenomenon, or is there evidence that intervention can have a quantitatively significant effect on exchange rates? To answer this question, it is helpful to draw on some of our sample parameter estimates and use these to calculate the quantitative effects of intervention operations on the dollar–deutsche mark exchange rate. For these calculations, we maintain the rather strict assumption that interest rates are held constant in order to gauge the upper-bound effect of intervention on exchange rates. We conclude this section with a discussion of how the results might differ if we allow interest rates to absorb some of intervention's effects. We also assume in our calculations that expectations are neither extrapolative nor adaptive. Recall that our regression results reported in table 7.7c suggest that over the full period the net effect of speculation was neither stabilizing nor destabilizing. Again, we will conclude by discussing how our results could be modified if we relax this assumption.

Let us start with the case where intervention is secret but not sterilized. If market participants are not aware that an intervention operation has taken place, then the operation cannot directly influence expected asset returns and thus cannot have an effect on the risk premium. If the risk premium does not change, then equation (7.6) indicates that x_t does not change.

---

10. When the intervention variable is measured on a daily flow basis, or cumulated only over the preceding week rather than from the beginning of the sample period, the effect is statistically significant in the simultaneous-equation tests, but not under OLS.

11. This section draws heavily on Dominguez and Frankel (1993b).

The portfolio share that is allocated to mark assets, x_t, is defined as $S_t M_t / W_t$, where S_t is the spot mark-dollar exchange rate, M_t is the total quantity of mark assets in investors' portfolios (denominated in marks), and W_t is total wealth (denominated in dollars). Analogously, the portfolio share that is allocated to dollar assets, $1 - x_t$, is defined as D_t / W_t, where D_t is the total quantity of dollar assets held in investors' portfolios, and $S_t M_t + D_t = W_t S_t$, the spot exchange rate, is thus equal to:

$$S_t = \frac{D_t}{M_t} \frac{x_t}{1 - x_t} \tag{7.7}$$

From this expression for S_t, it is evident that the effect of intervention (even if secret) on the exchange rate is in proportion to the supply of mark assets in investors' portfolios.

What is the effect of \$100 million of secret and nonsterilized intervention? If the Bundesbank intervenes secretly in support of the dollar by purchasing \$100 million for marks, then the total effect on the dollar-mark exchange rate will be \$100 million divided by the total reserve money supplied to the banking system by the Bundesbank, in dollar terms. At the end of 1988, total Bundesbank reserve money equaled DM221.1 billion, or translated into dollars, \$124.19 billion. Therefore, the effect of a \$100 million secret, nonsterilized Bundesbank intervention is only .081 percent, even in an environment where nonsterilized intervention is the only kind that matters. In an environment where sterilized operations also matter, the effect of secret intervention would be even smaller because the denominator would include the total supply of mark-denominated bonds.

The next case to consider is one in which intervention is reported but never in fact transpires. In other words, we consider the pure effect of intervention news. In this case, the risk premium will be affected. More specifically, the risk premium will change by the coefficient of reported intervention in the expectations equation (7.5) when estimated simultaneously with the risk premium equation (7.6). Such a change in the risk premium will have a large effect on the demand for mark versus dollar assets.

In order to calculate the effect of a report of intervention on the exchange rate we need to return to equation (7.7). The log form of the equation is:

$$\log S_t = \log\left(\frac{D_t}{M_t}\right) + \log(x_t) - \log(1 - x_t) \tag{7.8}$$

The effect of reported intervention on the spot exchange rate can be calculated using equation (7.8) and the knowledge that the portfolio share allocated to mark assets, x_t, is a function of the risk premium, rp_t, which is in turn a function of expected depreciation, $\Delta \hat{s}^e_{t,k}$, which is in turn a function of the news variables $REPINT_t$ and $NEWS_t$.[12] The change in the portfolio share allocated to mark assets due to a change in the risk premium is the parameter estimate on intervention, $(v_t\beta_2)^{-1}$, from equation (7.6). If we rearrange equations (7.5) and (7.6), hold interest rates constant, and assume that expectations are neither extrapolative nor adaptive (set $\alpha_1 = 1$ and $\alpha_2 = 0$), we see that the effect of reported intervention on the risk premium is equal to its effect on expected depreciation, which is the parameter estimate on $REPINT$, α_4, from equation (7.5).

The coefficient estimate on reported intervention, $REPINT$, does not vary much whether estimated in our simultaneous system or simply by ordinary least squares (OLS). Recall that our OLS estimate reported in table 7.7b indicates that news of intervention in support of the dollar is on average associated with an 0.4 percent expected appreciation of the dollar. The parameter estimate on cumulative Fed and Bundesbank intervention in equation (7.6) from table 2 in Dominguez and Frankel (1993a) is 18,081. The other two parameter values we need in order to calculate the effect of pure intervention news on the exchange rate are the portfolio share allocated to mark assets, x_t, and the variance of exchange rate changes, v_t. We take the portfolio share that is allocated to mark assets to be a half, $x = .5$, and we measure the variance term as the average value of v_t over the latter subperiod, or .00005803. Using these parameter values, the effect of an intervention report on the exchange rate is 1.5 percent.[13] If we measure x_t at the end of the sample period (.112),[14] the effect is over twice as large.

The final case to consider is the one both where intervention news is reported and where an intervention operation actually takes place. The total effect of reported intervention is the sum of the small effect described in our first case and the larger news effect described in our second case. If we stick with our example of a nonsterilized Bundesbank purchase of $100 million against the mark but now allow the intervention operation to be publicly known, then the full estimated effect on the exchange rate will be 1.581 percent.

Intuition suggests that a 2 percent effect of intervention on exchange rates is rather high. But remember that embedded in our calculations is the assumption that interest rates are constant. Even if the intervention operation is sterilized, it is likely that interest rates will absorb some of the impact of the change in asset demand. Returning to our Bundesbank example, interest rates in both Germany and the United States are likely

---

12. See equation (7.6); the derivation is provided in Dominguez and Frankel (1993a).

13. $[1/x + 1/(1 - x)]\alpha_4/(v_t\beta_2) = [1/.5 + 1/.5](.004)/(1.049) = .015$

14. Total debt issued by the German government divided by the total of German and US debt was .112 at the end of 1988.

to absorb some of the decreased demand for mark assets. The German interest rate is likely to rise and the US rate to fall in reaction to the dollar support operation. If this is the case, the dollar appreciation is likely to be smaller than would be the case if interest rates did not change.

The second maintained assumption in our calculations is that expectations are neither extrapolative nor adaptive. Although our estimates over the full sample period do not indicate a tendency toward either of these extremes, over shorter subsamples, estimates do suggest that one sort of behavior or the other is operative. The estimates in Frankel and Froot (1990a) indicate that expectations are extrapolative at short-term horizons and eventually turn regressive at longer horizons. If market expectations are extrapolative, then the short-run effects of intervention would be smaller that those reported here. But the long-run effects become magnified. Leaning into the wind could have an extra effect over time by starting a snowball effect, as speculators jump on the bandwagon (Bergsten 1984b).

8

Implications for Policy

In this study we have challenged the conventional view that foreign exchange intervention can move the exchange rate if and only if it changes the money supply, regardless of other circumstances (and that it does so in proportion to that change). We have argued that the key consideration is whether foreign exchange traders react to intervention by revising their forecasts of future exchange rates. If they react by changing their forecasts, they will act to change present exchange rates; if they do not, then the mere change in current asset supplies is unlikely to have a substantial effect, regardless of whether the intervention is sterilized or not—that is, regardless of whether it is the supply of bonds or the supply of money that is changed.

The traditional version of the signaling hypothesis is one example of how expectations act to determine the exchange rate: if intervention in support of a currency is interpreted as new information that monetary policy will be more restrictive in the near future, then it will work to appreciate the currency today. Intervention has been found to improve forecasts of monetary policy (Dominguez 1992a; Ghosh 1992; Kaminsky and Lewis 1993). But there is little evidence that central bankers *consistently* seek to communicate their monetary policy initiatives through intervention.

The signaling hypothesis is not the only theory that can explain how intervention could affect expectations. One possibility is that investors come to expect monetization of an intervention operation in the distant future, even if the authorities are not deliberately signaling monetary ease in the short term. Another possibility is that even sterilized intervention will have an effect through the portfolio-balance channel: if investors do not view domestic and foreign bonds as perfect substitutes—and we have offered new evidence that they may not—then sustained additions to the supply of bonds will have an effect even if they are never monetized, and investors will take this into account in forming their expectations. Yet another possibility is that known intervention can work by pricking an existing speculative bubble. This last possibility may be the most promising for would-be interveners: if a speculative bubble like that of 1984–85 is the circumstance in which intervention has the greatest effect on the market, it is also the circumstance in which such a policy lever is most desired.

The question of how intervention works—and our evidence suggests that it can work—is an issue that is not of purely academic interest. If, as our results suggest, intervention has an important effect on the exchange rate only when it influences expectations, this implies that the intervention must be publicly known in order to be effective. It follows that, contrary to much actual practice, the authorities should make their intervention activities public.

The extra punch packed by public intervention is evident on three levels. First, our results in chapter 7 show that the effect of US intervention is much greater when the New York Federal Reserve Bank lets the market know it is intervening. Second, the results reported in tables 7.1 through 7.7 suggest that official announcements regarding exchange rate policy have far more impact than intervention information that is quietly disseminated. To take the most widely cited example, the announcement of the Plaza Agreement in 1985 immediately knocked more than 4 percent off the value of the dollar. To take another example (which is too recent to be included in the data set on which our econometric results are based), the decision by Treasury officials to announce to the press the July 1991 "ambush" to reverse the preceding dollar appreciation appears likely to have contributed to the success of the intervention.

Finally, finance theory—in the form, for example, of the target zone model originated by Paul Krugman (1991)—suggests that when the authorities are prepared to intervene at a particular upper or lower limit for their currency, they will have more success at stabilizing the currency with a smaller amount of intervention if they publicly announce these limits ahead of time. By preannouncing the limits, policymakers can get speculators working for them rather than against them. This proposition cannot be tested with the dollar data from the late 1980s because the "reference range" that was reportedly established at the Louvre in February 1987 was not made public.[1] Indeed, the markets, operating for the

---

1. Tests on data from the European Monetary System show that the strict form of the target zone model, with perfect credibility, did not hold for European currencies in the 1980s (with the possible exception of the Dutch guilder vis-à-vis the deutsche mark). By 1990–91, a degree of EMS credibility had been established for most currencies (Rose and

most part under the belief that no such range had been established, soon breached the reported limits.

By August 1992, even the broader limits hypothesized by some had been breached, as the dollar fell through its all-time nominal low against the mark and the yen. The prospects for establishing a new rigid target zone for the dollar are dubious. All the foreign exchange reserves in the G-7 vaults are not enough to defend an exchange rate that investors, operating in modern capital markets, decide is inconsistent with fundamentals. If the United States has, for example, a persistently higher inflation rate or lower productivity growth rate than Japan or other major trading partners, it will eventually have to let the dollar depreciate.

Nevertheless, our finding that intervention is more potent than conventional economic wisdom—as reflected in the Jurgensen Report and elsewhere—has held it to be could be interpreted as one piece of evidence on the side of those favoring a flexible sort of target zone (or its weaker version of "reference ranges"). Economic logic suggests that a target zone is more likely to be sustainable when the central parities are allowed to change over time in line with fundamentals, such as rates of inflation and productivity growth, and less likely to be sustainable when it is fixed. This consideration supports the sort of target zone design proposed by Williamson (1985), as opposed to that of the troubled European Monetary System. But we do not in this study take a position, one way or the other, on formal target zone arrangements, let alone the more detailed and ambitious Williamson and Miller (1987) "blueprint" for policy coordination.

We do not think that major institutional changes in who makes intervention policy are in order. But we do endorse calls for better integration of the making of exchange rate policy and monetary policy. Regular meetings on the subject between the Treasury and the Federal Reserve System might help. There has been no shortage of contact and communication between the two agencies, from the secretary-chairman level on down. But there has been a temptation in the Treasury to focus exclusively on day-to-day "fire fighting," with insufficient pauses to formulate a longer-run view.

One possibility is quarterly meetings—including staff from the Federal Reserve Board, Federal Reserve Bank of New York, Treasury, Council of Economic Advisers, and other executive agencies—at which recent exchange rate developments could be evaluated in the light of trends regarding inflation, productivity, growth, the trade balance, monetary

---

Svensson 1991; Frankel and Phillips 1993)—until the crisis of September 1992. That crisis confirmed the precept that exchange rate rigidity is ultimately incompatible with integrated financial markets and macroeconomic policy autonomy, even though intervention and the declaration of fixed bands were able to maintain credibility and postpone adjustment until the month of the crisis.

policy, and fiscal policy. The discussion and consensus, if any, could then inform statements in the Federal Reserve Bank of New York's *Quarterly Review*, the Federal Reserve Board chairman's semiannual statements to Congress, the Treasury's regular reports to Congress under the Omnibus Trade and Competitiveness Act of 1988, and the Council of Economic Advisers' annual *Economic Report of the President*.

Our recommendations—that the authorities more often allow their interventions to be publicly known and that an interagency process regularly consider exchange rate developments in the light of fundamentals—do not mean that we recommend, as do other observers, that the entire process of exchange rate policymaking be "democratized," or opened up to include Congress and private-sector advisory committees. It is true that congressional and private-sector concern about the rising trade deficit and the danger of resulting protectionist legislation were in 1985 a major proximate cause of the administration's switch in exchange rate policy. This switch seems to us to have been a good thing. But it does not follow that such pressure would necessarily be a good thing in the future, or even that including these parties in exchange rate policy is more likely to produce good outcomes than bad.

On the other hand, our major trade partners should be brought into the policymaking process. The dollar, after all, belongs to the rest of the world as much as to the United States: it takes two to make an exchange rate. In addition to providing information and perspective on what policy changes we can make in our own interest, discussions with trading partners sometimes promote desired changes in foreign policies that can be negotiated as part of a beneficial coordinated package among all the trading partners. Furthermore, coordinated intervention in the foreign exchange market is often more effective than individual intervention (Dominguez 1990a). These judgments, of course, describe the ideas behind the concerted G-5 interventions begun in 1985, the G-7 effort to formalize a set of economic indicators to guide the adjustment process at the Tokyo Summit of May 1986, and the Louvre meeting to stabilize the dollar in February 1987.

Several observers have pointed out that the discussion of exchange rate policy and the discussion of macroeconomic policy are rather artificially separated in G-7 meetings. Responsible and knowledgeable observers recognize the danger of thinking of exchange rate policy as a tool that can be used independently of macroeconomic policy. When an uncomfortable exchange rate movement signals that something is wrong with monetary or fiscal policy, officials may be tempted to use exchange market intervention as a pill to suppress the symptom even when a fundamental cure is required. Integrating exchange rate and macroeconomic policy discussions in G-7 meetings as well as introducing a periodic long-term focus in Fed-Treasury consultations are ways of reducing the chance that a government will behave as if it can set an exchange rate that is independent of its monetary and fiscal policies.

Most official language of the last 10 years recognizes a single exception to the principle that intervention cannot be divorced from macroeconomic policy: the idea that intervention is called for in "disorderly markets." But disorderly markets, as reflected in such indicators as unusually wide bid-ask spreads, do not usually require a G-7 meeting.

We would like to add a more important exception to the principle: intervention may also be called for in the case of speculative bubbles. Sustained movements that are widely agreed to be speculative bubbles—that is, to be departures from fundamentals—are rare. Nevertheless, they do occasionally occur, as the events of 1984–85 show. In such occasions, intervention may be appropriate.

In the introduction to this study, we suggested an analogy for foreign exchange intervention: that it plays a role in the foreign exchange market analogous to the role played by herd dogs among cattle. When an individual steer begins to wander away from the herd in a disorderly manner, a dog can often be helpful in cajoling it to return. This is the "intervention to calm disorderly markets" that has all along been an accepted part of central bank wisdom. On the other hand, it is clear that a few dogs, who after all are smaller in size and fewer in number than the steers, probably could not sustain overall control of the herd for long without the sense of direction provided by the cowhands and would have little idea what to do with such control if they had it. This makes the point that intervention operations—which, after all, are small compared with the private market—probably could not sustain control of the foreign exchange market for long without the sense of direction provided by monetary policy and might be used to pursue inconsistent policy goals even if such control could be sustained.

But there is an important case that lies between the extremes of calming disorderly markets during a given day and divorcing the exchange rate from macroeconomic policy during a given presidential term. That case is the speculative bubble, which our cattle-herd analogy is ready-made to illustrate. On those rare occasions when a stampede gets under way because each panicked steer is following its neighbors, the herd can potentially wander quite far from the proper course. The dogs can be useful in heading off a stampede: if a few of them succeed in turning around a few key steers in a highly visible manner, the rest of the herd may turn to follow. Furthermore, the noisier the dogs are, the greater effect they are likely to have. Intervention does appear to have been instrumental in pricking the 1984–85 speculative bubble in the dollar.

Our results suggest that intervention can be effective, especially if it is publicly announced and concerted. It may be that sterilized intervention can only have effects in the short term. But if "short-term effects" include the bursting of a nine-month bubble earlier than it would otherwise have burst, then such an effect may be all that is needed. If policymakers cultivate the habit of explicitly considering how exchange rate developments relate to macroeconomic fundamentals, then they will be better equipped, not only to interpret what information the exchange rate has to offer on how the market perceives the current stance of macroeconomic policies, but also to recognize the next occasion when exchange rates deviate from fundamentals.

Our specific recommendations are quite modest: that the authorities make their interventions public, that an interagency process regularly consider exchange rate developments in light of the fundamentals, and that G-7 discussions on macroeconomic policy and exchange rates be integrated.

We do conclude, however, that foreign exchange intervention can "work" if properly conceived and executed. Intervention represents a more potent policy instrument than most officials and especially most outside analysts have in recent years imagined it to be. Hence, it can make a more significant contribution both to policy now and to the ongoing debate over how best to organize the international monetary system.

References

Abrams, Richard. 1980. "International Trade Flows Under Flexible Exchange Rates." *Economic Review*, Federal Reserve Bank of Kansas City, 3–10 March.

Adams, Donald, and Dale Henderson. 1983. "Definition and Measurement of Exchange Market Intervention." Board of Governors of the Federal Reserve System Staff Series, no. 126.

Akerlof, George A., and Janet Yellen. 1985. "Can Small Deviations from Rationality Make Significant Differences to Economic Equilibria?" *American Economic Review*, 708–35.

Akhtar, M. Akbar, and Spence Hilton. 1984. "Effects of Exchange Rate Uncertainty on German and U.S. Trade." *Federal Reserve Bank of New York Quarterly Review* 9, no. 1 (Spring): 7–16.

Baillie, Richard T., and Owen F. Humpage. 1992. "Post-Louvre Intervention: Did Target Zones Stabilize the Dollar?" Federal Reserve Bank of Cleveland Working Paper no. 9203.

Bank for International Settlements. 1988. "Exchange Market Intervention and Monetary Policy." Basel: Monetary and Economic Department, BIS (March).

Bank for International Settlements. 1990. "Survey of Foreign Exchange Activity." Basel: Monetary and Economic Department, BIS (February).

Bergsten, C. Fred. 1982. "What to Do About the U.S.-Japan Economic Conflict." *Foreign Affairs* (Summer).

Bergsten, C. Fred. 1984a. "The United States Trade Deficit and the Dollar." Statement before the Senate Committee on Banking, Housing and Urban Affairs, Subcommittee on International Finance and Monetary Policy, 6 June.

Bergsten, C. Fred. 1984b. "The Case for Leaning with the Wind." *Financial Times* (24 October).

Bergsten, C. Fred. 1991. "The Collapse of Bretton Woods: Implications for International Monetary Reform." NBER conference, Bretton Woods, N.H., October; also in Michael Bordo and Barry Eichengreen, eds., *Retrospective on the Bretton Woods System*, University of Chicago Press, Chicago, 1993.

Black, Stanley W. 1973. "International Money Markets and Flexible Exchange Rates." *Studies in International Finance* no. 25, Princeton University.

Black, Stanley W. 1993. "The Relationship of the Exchange Risk Premium to Net Foreign Assets and Central Bank Intervention." Department of Economics Working Paper No. 93-01, University of North Carolina at Chapel Hill, (February).

Boothe, P., Clinton, K., Cote, A., and Longworth, D. 1985. *International Asset Substitutability: Theory and Evidence for Canada*, Ottawa: Bank of Canada.

Bordo, Michael, and Anna Schwartz. 1990. "What Has Foreign Exchange Market Intervention Since the Plaza Agreement Accomplished?" NBER Working Paper No. 3562 (December).

Brada, J., and J. Mendez. 1988. "Exchange Rate Risk, Exchange Rate Regimes and the Level of International Trade." *Kyklos* 41, no. 2: 277.

Branson, William. 1979. "Exchange rate dynamics and monetary policy." In *Inflation and Employment in Open Economies*, ed. A. Lindbeck, Amsterdam: North Holland.

Branson, William, Hannu Halttunen, and Paul Masson. 1977. "Exchange Rates in the Short Run: The Dollar-Deutschemark Rate." *European Economic Review* 10, no. 3: 303–24.

Branson, William, and Dale Henderson. 1985. "The Specification and Influence of Asset Markets." In Ronald Jones and Peter Kenen, eds., *Handbook of International Economics*, vol. 2. Amsterdam: North Holland.

Caballero, Ricardo, and Vittorio Corbo. 1989. "The Effect of Real Exchange Rate Uncertainty on Exports: Empirical Evidence." *The World Bank Economic Review* 3, no.2 (May) 263–78.

Canzoneri, Mathew. 1985. "Monetary Policy Games and the Role of Private Information." *American Economic Review*, 1056–70.

Carlson, John A. 1977. "A Study of Price Forecasts." *Annals of Economic and Social Measurement*, 27–56.

Catte, P., G. Galli, and S. Rebecchini. 1992a. "Concerted Interventions and the Dollar: An Analysis of Daily Data." Ossola Memorial Conference, Banca d'Italia, Perugia, Italy, 9–10 July.

Catte, P., G. Galli, and S. Rebecchini. 1992b. "Exchange Markets Can be Managed!" *International Economic Insights* (September/October): 17–21.

Corden, W. Maxwell. 1983. "The Logic of the International Monetary Non-System." In F. Machlup et al., eds., *Reflections on a Troubled World Economy*. London: MacMillan.

Council of Economic Advisers. 1984. *Economic Report of the President* (February). Washington: CEA.

Cukierman, Alex, and Allan Meltzer. 1986. "A Theory of Ambiguity, Credibility and Inflation Under Discretion and Asymmetric Information." *Econometrica* 54, 1099–1128.

Danker, Deborah, Richard Haas, Dale Henderson, Steven Symansky, and Ralph Tryon. 1987. "Small Empirical Models of Exchange Market Intervention: Applications to Germany, Japan, and Canada." *Journal of Policy Modeling* (Spring): 143–73.

De Grauwe, Paul. 1988. "Exchange Rate Variability and the Slowdown in Growth of International Trade." *IMF Staff Papers* 35, 63–84.

Destler, I. Mac, and C. Randall Henning. 1989. *Dollar Politics: Exchange Rate Policymaking in the United States*. Washington: Institute for International Economics.

Dobson, Wendy. 1991. "Economic Policy Coordination: Requiem or Prologue?" POLICY ANALYSES IN INTERNATIONAL ECONOMICS 30. Washington: Institute for International Economics.

Dominguez, Kathryn. 1986. "Are Foreign Exchange Forecasts Rational? New Evidence from Survey Data." *Economic Letters* 21, 277–82.

Dominguez, Kathryn. 1990a. "Market Responses to Coordinated Central Bank Intervention." *Carnegie-Rochester Series on Public Policy*, vol. 32.

Dominguez, Kathryn. 1990b. "Have Recent Central Bank Foreign Exchange Intervention Operations Influenced the Yen?" Unpublished paper, Harvard University.

Dominguez, Kathryn. 1992a. "The Informational Role of Official Foreign Exchange Intervention Operations: The Signalling Hypothesis." In *Exchange Rate Efficiency and the Behavior of International Asset Markets*. New York: Garland Publishing Company.

Dominguez, Kathryn. 1992b. "Foreign Exchange Market Intervention," and "Coordinated Central Bank Intervention." In J. Eatwell, M. Milgate, and P. Newman, eds., *The New Palgrave Dictionary of Money and Finance*. London: Macmillan Press.

Dominguez, Kathryn. 1993. "Does Central Bank Intervention Influence the Volatility of Foreign Exchange Rates?" Unpublished paper, Harvard University.

Dominguez, Kathryn, and Jeffrey Frankel. 1993a. "Does Foreign Exchange Intervention Matter? The Portfolio Effect." *American Economic Review* (forthcoming).

Dominguez, Kathryn, and Jeffrey Frankel. 1993b. "Foreign Exchange Intervention: An Empirical Assessment." In J. Frankel, ed., *On Exchange Rates*. Cambridge, MA: The MIT Press (1993).

Dooley, Michael, and Peter Isard. 1982. "A Portfolio-Balance Rational-Expectations Model of the Dollar-Mark Rate." *Journal of International Economics* 12: 257–76.

Dooley, Michael, and Peter Isard. 1983. "The Portfolio Balance Model of Exchange Rates and Some Structural Estimates of the Risk Premium." *IMF Staff Papers*, 683–702.

Dornbusch, Rudiger. 1976. "Expectations and Exchange Rate Dynamics." *Journal of Political Economy* 84, 6 (December): 1161–76.

Dornbusch, Rudiger. 1982. Equilibrium and Disequilibrium Exchange Rates. *Zeitschrift für Wirtschafts und Sozialwissenshaften* 102, 6: 573–99. Reprinted in Dornbusch, R., *Dollars, Debts, and Deficits*. Cambridge, MA: MIT Press.

Dornbusch, Rudiger. 1983. "Exchange Risk and the Macroeconomics of Exchange Rate Determination." In R. Hawkins, R. Levich, and C. Wihlborg, eds., *The Internationalization of Financial Markets and National Economic Policy*. Greenwich, CT: JAI Press.

Dornbusch, Rudiger. 1986. "Flexible Exchange Rates and Excess Capital Mobility." *Brookings Papers on Economic Activity* 1: 209–26.

Dudler, Herrmann J. 1988. "Monetary Policy and Exchange Market Management in Germany." In Bank for International Settlements, ed., *Exchange Market Intervention and Monetary Policy*. Basel: BIS.

Edison, Hali. 1993. "The Effectiveness of Central Bank Intervention: A Survey of the Post-1982 Literature." *Special Papers on International Economics* 18, Princeton University (forthcoming).

Edison, Hali, and Michael Melvin. 1990. "The Determinants and Implications of the Choice of An Exchange Rate System." In W. Haraf and T. Willett, eds., *Monetary Policy For a Volatile Global Economy*. Washington: American Enterprise Institute.

Eijffinger, Sylvester C. W., and Noud P.D. Gruijters. 1991a. "On the Short Term Objectives of Daily Intervention by the Deutsche Bundesbank and the Federal Reserve System in the U.S. Dollar/Deutsche Mark Exchange Market." *Kredit and Kapital* 24: 50–72.

Eijffinger, Sylvester C. W., and Noud P.D. Gruijters. 1991b. "On the Effectiveness of Daily Interventions by the Deutsche Bundesbank and the Federal Reserve System in the U.S. Dollar/Deutsche Mark Exchange Market." Tilburg University (Holland), Research Memorandum FEW394. Forthcoming in E. Baltensperger and H. W. Sinn, eds., *Exchange Rate Regimes and Currency Union* (Basingstoke: Macmillan).

Engel, Charles M., and Rodrigues, Anthony P. 1989. "Tests of International CAPM with Time-Varying Covariances." *Journal of Applied Econometrics* (April-June): 119–38.

Feldstein, Martin. 1984. "The Dollar Exchange Rate." Remarks before the World Affairs Council of Philadelphia, 29 February.

Feldstein, Martin. 1986. "New Evidence on the Effects of Exchange Rate Intervention." NBER Working Paper No. 2052 (October).

Feldstein, Martin. 1988. "Thinking About International Economic Coordination." *Journal of Economic Perspectives* 2 (Spring): 3–13.

Feldstein, Martin, and Kathleen Feldstein. 1992. "Meddling with the Dollar." *The Boston Globe*, 18 August.

Frankel, Jeffrey. 1979. "The Diversifiability of Exchange Risk." *Journal of International Economics* 9 (August). Reprinted in J. Frankel, ed., *On Exchange Rates*. Cambridge, MA: MIT Press (1993).

Frankel, Jeffrey. 1982a. "A Test of Perfect Substitutability in the Foreign Exchange Market." *Southern Economic Journal* 46, no. 4, (April).

Frankel, Jeffrey. 1982b. "In Search of the Exchange Risk Premium: A Six-Currency Test Assuming Mean-Variance Optimization." *Journal of International Money and Finance* 1, (December). Reprinted in J. Frankel, ed., *On Exchange Rates*. Cambridge, MA: MIT Press (1993).

Frankel, Jeffrey. 1985. "The Dazzling Dollar." *Brookings Papers on Economic Activity* 1: 199–217.

Frankel, Jeffrey, and Charles Engel. 1984. "Do Asset Demand Functions Optimize Over the Mean and Variance of Real Returns? A Six-Currency Test." *Journal of International Economics* 17, 309–23.

Frankel, Jeffrey, and Kenneth Froot. 1987. "Using Survey Data to Test Standard Propositions Regarding Exchange Rate Expectations." *American Economic Review* 77, 1: 133–53. Reprinted in J. Frankel, ed., *On Exchange Rates*. Cambridge, MA: MIT Press (1993).

Frankel, Jeffrey, and Kenneth Froot. 1990a. "Chartists, Fundamentalists, and the Demand for Dollars." NBER Working Paper No. 1854. Final published version in A. Courakis and M. Taylor, eds., *Private Behavior and Government Policy in Interdependent Economies*, Oxford (UK): Clarendon Press.

Frankel, Jeffrey, and Kenneth Froot. 1990b. "Exchange Rate Forecasting Techniques, Survey Data, and Implications for the Foreign Exchange Market." IMF Working Paper No. 90/43 (May).

Frankel, Jeffrey, and Steven Phillips. 1993. "The European Monetary System: Credible at Last?" In J. Frankel, ed., *On Exchange Rates*. Cambridge, MA: MIT Press. Also published as NBER Working Paper No. 3819 (August 1991).

Frankel, Jeffrey, and Shang-Jin Wei. 1992. "Trade Blocs and Currency Blocs." Global Finance Lecture, University of Birmingham, UK, (November), and CEPR conference on *The Monetary Future of Europe*, La Coruna, Spain, 11 December 1992.

Friedman, Milton. 1953. "The Case for Flexible Exchange Rates." In *Essays in Positive Economics*. Chicago: University of Chicago Press.

Froot, Kenneth, and Jeffrey Frankel. 1989. "Forward Discount Bias: Is it an Exchange Risk Premium?" *Quarterly Journal of Economics* 104, no. 1 (February). Reprinted in R. Thaler, ed., *Advances in Behavioral Finance*. New York: Russell Sage Foundation, 1993.

Funabashi, Yoichi. 1988. *Managing the Dollar: From the Plaza to the Louvre*. Washington: Institute for International Economics.

Gaiotti, E., P. Giucca, and S. Micossi. 1989. "Cooperation in Managing the Dollar (1985-87): Interventions in Foreign Exchange Markets and Interest Rates." Temi di discussione del Servizio Studi, no. 119 (June).

Gartner, Manfred. 1987. "Intervention Policy Under Floating Exchange Rates: An Analysis of the Swiss Case." *Economica* 54: 439–53.

Ghosh, Atish R. 1992. "Is it Signalling? Exchange Intervention and the Dollar-Deutschemark Rate." *Journal of International Economics* 32: 201–20.

Giovannini, Alberto, and Philippe Jorion. 1989. "The Time-Variation of Risk and Return in the Foreign Exchange and Stock Markets." *Journal of Finance* 44, no. 2 (June): 307–24.

Girton, Lance, and Henderson, Dale. 1977. "Central bank operations in foreign and domestic assets under fixed and flexible exchange rates." In P. B. Clark, D. Logue, and R. Sweeney, eds., *The Effects of Exchange Rate Adjustments*. Washington: Government Printing Office.

Golub, Stephen. 1989. "Foreign-Currency Government Debt, Asset Markets, and the Balance of Payments." *Journal of International Money and Finance* 8, no. 2 (June): 285–94.

Goodhart, Charles. 1988. "The foreign exchange market: A random walk with a dragging anchor." *Economica* 55: 437–60.

Greene, Margaret. 1983a. "U.S. Experience with Exchange Market Intervention: January 1974–March 1975." Board of Governors of the Federal Reserve System Staff Series No. 127 (September). Washington: Federal Reserve Board.

Greene, Margaret. 1983b. "US Experience with Exchange Market Intervention: September 1977–December 1979." Staff Studies No. 128. Washington: Federal Reserve Board.

Haltiwanger, John, and Michael Waldman. 1985. "Rational Expectations and the Limits of Rationality: An Analysis of Heterogeneity." *American Economic Review*, 326–40.

Hamada, K. 1976. "A strategic analysis on monetary interdependence." *Journal of Political Economy* 84: 677–700.

Hardouvelis, Gikas. 1988. "Economic News, Exchange Rates and Interest Rates." *Journal of International Money and Finance* 7.

Henderson, Dale. 1984. "Exchange Market Intervention Operations: Their Role in Financial Policy and Their Effects." In J. Bilson and R. Marston, eds., *Exchange Rate Theory and Practice*. Chicago: University of Chicago Press.

Henderson, Dale, and Stephanie Sampson. 1983. "Intervention in Foreign Exchange Markets: A Summary of Ten Staff Studies." *Federal Reserve Bulletin* 69 (November): 830–36.

Hogan, Ked, Michael Melvin, and Dan Roberts. 1991. "Trade Balance News and Exchange Rates: Is There a Policy Signal?" *Journal of International Money and Finance* 10 (March): S90–S99.

Hooper, Peter, and Steven Kohlhagen. 1978. "The Effect of Exchange Rate Uncertainty on Prices and Volume of International Trade." *Journal of International Economics* 8, (November): 483–511.

Humpage, Owen. 1989. "On the Effectiveness of Exchange-Market Intervention." Unpublished paper, Federal Reserve Bank of Cleveland.

Humpage, Owen. 1990. "Post-Louvre Intervention: Some Initial Estimates." Unpublished paper, Federal Reserve Bank of Cleveland.

Hung, Juann. 1991. "The Effectiveness of Sterilized U.S. Foreign Exchange Intervention: An Empirical Study Based on the Noise Trading Approach." Federal Reserve Bank of New York Research Paper No. 9118 (May).

Ito, Takatoshi. 1990. "Foreign Exchange Rate Expectations: Micro Survey Data." *American Economic Review* 80, no. 3 (June): 434–49.

Jacobson, Laurence. 1983. "Calculations of Profitability for US Dollar–Deutsche Mark Intervention." Board of Governors of the Federal Reserve System Staff Series No. 131. Washington: Federal Reserve Board.

Jurgensen, P. 1983. "Report of the working group on exchange market intervention [Jurgensen Report]." Washington: Treasury Department (March).

Kaminsky, Graciela, and Karen Lewis. 1993. "Does Foreign Exchange Intervention Signal Future Monetary Policy?" Finance and Economic Discussion Series No. 93-1. Washington: Federal Reserve Board (February).

Kenen, Peter. 1988. *Managing Exchange Rates.* New York: The Royal Institute of International Affairs, Council on Foreign Relations Press.

Kenen, Peter, and Dani Rodrik. 1986. "Measuring and Analyzing the Effects of Short-term Volatility in Real Exchange Rates." *Review of Economics and Statistics*, 311–15.

Klein, Michael. 1992. "The Accuracy of Reports of Foreign Exchange Intervention." National Bureau of Economic Research Working Paper No. 4165. Cambridge, MA: NBER (September).

Klein, Michael, Bruce Mizrach, and Robert Murphy. 1991. "Managing the Dollar: Has the Plaza Agreement Mattered?" *Journal of Money, Credit and Banking* 23, no. 4, (November): 742–51.

Klein, Michael, and Karen Lewis. 1991. "Learning About Intervention Target Zones." National Bureau of Economic Research Working Paper No. 3674. Cambridge, MA: NBER.

Klein, Michael, and Eric Rosengren. 1991. "Foreign Exchange Intervention as a Signal of Monetary Policy." *New England Economic Review* (May/June): 39–50.

Kouri, P., and Porter, M. 1974. "International capital flows and portfolio equilibrium." *Journal of Political Economy* 82: 443–67.

Krugman, Paul. 1985. "Is the Strong Dollar Sustainable?" In *The U.S. Dollar—Recent Developments, Outlook, and Policy Options*. Kansas City: Federal Reserve Bank of Kansas City.

Krugman, Paul. 1991. "Target Zones and Exchange Rate Dynamics." *Quarterly Journal of Economics* 3 (August): 669–82.

Leahy, Michael. 1989. "The Profitability of US Intervention." Board of Governors of the Federal Reserve System International Finance Discussion Paper No. 343. Washington: Federal Reserve Board.

Lewis, Karen. 1988. "Testing the Portfolio Balance Model: A Multi-Lateral Approach." *Journal of International Economics* 24, 109–27.

Loopesko, Bonnie. 1984. "Relationships Among Exchange Rates, Intervention, and Interest Rates: An Empirical Investigation." *Journal of International Money and Finance* 3, 257–77.

Marris, Stephen. 1985. "Deficits and the Dollar: The World Economy at Risk." POLICY ANALYSES IN INTERNATIONAL ECONOMICS 14. Washington: Institute for International Economics.

Marston, Richard. 1988. "Exchange Rate Policy Reconsidered." In Martin Feldstein, ed., *International Economic Cooperation*. Chicago: University of Chicago Press.

McKinnon, Ronald. 1984. "An International Standard for Monetary Stabilization." POLICY ANALYSES IN INTERNATIONAL ECONOMICS 8. Washington: Institute for International Economics.

Merrill Lynch. 1992. "Central-Bank Intervention and the Determination of Exchange Rates." Special Study Series on Currency Forecasting: Theory and Practice, no.7. New York: Merrill Lynch (October).

Mishkin, Frederic S. 1981. "Are Market Forecasts Rational?" *American Economic Review* (June): 295–306.

Mulford, David. 1991. "The G7 Strikes Back!" Interview in *The International Economy* (July/August): 15–23.

Mundaca, B. Gabriela. 1989. "A GARCH-Switching Simultaneous Equations Model: The Effect of Official Interventions on the Exchange Rate Volatility." Oslo: Research Department, Norges Bank (December).

Mussa, Michael. 1981. *The Role of Official Intervention*. Group of Thirty Occasional Papers No. 6. New York: Group of Thirty.

Mussa, Michael. 1990. "Exchange Rates in Theory and in Reality." *Essays in International Finance* No. 179 (December). Princeton, N.J.: Princeton University.

Neumann, Manfred. 1984. "Intervention in the Mark/Dollar Market: the Authorities' Reaction Function." *Journal of International Money and Finance* 3: 223–39.

Neumann, Manfred, and Jurgen von Hagen. N.d. "Monetary Policy in Germany." In Michele Fratianni and Dominik Salvatore, eds., *Handbook of Monetary Policy*. Westport, CT: Greenwood Press (forthcoming).

Obstfeld, Maurice. 1982. "The capitalization of income streams and the effects of open-market policy under fixed exchange rates." *Journal of Monetary Economics* 9: 87–98.

Obstfeld, Maurice. 1983. "Exchange Rates, Inflation and the Sterilization Problem: Germany 1975–1981." *European Economic Review* 21: 161–89.

Obstfeld, Maurice. 1990. "The Effectiveness of Foreign-Exchange Intervention: Recent Experience, 1985–1988." In Branson, Frenkel, and Goldstein, eds., *International Policy Coordination and Exchange Rate Fluctuations*. National Bureau of Economic Research conference volume. Chicago: University of Chicago Press.

Putnam, Robert, and Nicholas Bayne. 1987. *Hanging Together: The Seven-Power Summits*. Cambridge, MA: Harvard University Press (2nd edition).

Redburn, Tom. 1990. "The Fed Has the Edge on the Economic Policy Front." *The International Economy* (June/July): 61–63.

Rogoff, Kenneth. 1983. "Time Series Studies of the Relationship between Exchange Rates and Intervention: A Reivew of the Techniques and Literature." Board of Governors of the Federal Reserve System Staff Studies No. 132 (September).

Rogoff, Kenneth. 1984. "On the Effects of Sterilized Intervention: An Analysis of Weekly Data." *Journal of Monetary Economics* 14, 133–50.

Rogoff, Kenneth. 1985. "Can international monetary policy coordination be counterproductive?" *Journal of International Economics* 18: 199–217.

Rose, Andrew, and Svensson, Lars. 1991. "Expected and Predicted Realignments: The FF/DM Exchange Rate During the EMS." International Finance Discussion Paper No. 395. Washington: Board of Governors of the Federal Reserve System.

Schulmeister, Stephen. 1987. "An essay on exchange rate dynamics." Research Unit Labor Market and Employment Discussion Paper 87-8. Berlin: Wissenschaftzentrum Berlin für Sozialforschung.

Schulmeister, Stephen, and Michael B. Goldberg. 1989. "Noise Trading and the Efficiency of Financial Markets." In G. Luciani, ed., *Structural Change in the American Financial System*. Rome: Centro di Studi Americani.

Smith, Ralph W., and Brian F. Madigan. 1988. "Exchange Market Management and Monetary Policy in the United States." In Bank for International Settlements, ed., *Exchange Market Intervention and Monetary Policy*. Basel: BIS.

Stein, Jeremy C. 1989. "Cheap Talk and the Fed: A Theory of Imprecise Policy Announcements." *American Economic Review* (March): 32–42.

Stockman, Alan. 1979. "Monetary control and sterilization under pegged exchange rates." University of Rochester. Mimeo.

Takagi, Shinji. 1990. "Foreign Exchange Market Intervention and Domestic Monetary Control in Japan, 1973–89." Unpublished manuscript, University of Osaka, Japan.

Taylor, Dean. 1982. "Official Intervention in the Foreign Exchange Market, Or, Bet Against the Central Bank." *Journal of Political Economy* 90-2 (April): 356–68.

Taylor, Mark, and Helen Allen. 1992. "The use of technical analysis in the foreign exchange market." *Journal of International Money and Finance* 11, 3 (June): 304–14.

Tobin, James. 1978. "A proposal for international monetary reform." *Eastern Economic Journal* 3: 3-4 (July/October), reprinted in his *Essays in Economics: Theory and Policy*. Cambridge, MA: MIT Press.

Truman, Edwin. 1992. "Comments on 'Concerted Interventions and the Dollar: An Analysis of Daily Data.' " Ossola Memorial Conference, Banca d'Italia, Perugia, Italy, 9–10 July.

Tryon, Ralph. 1983. "Small Empirical Models of Exchange Market Intervention: A Review of the Literature." Board of Governors of the Federal Reserve System Staff Studies No. 134 (September).

von Hagen, Jurgen. 1989. "Monetary Targeting with Exchange Rate Constraints: The Bundesbank in the 1980s." *Federal Reserve Bank of St. Louis Review* 71, 5 (October): 53–69.

Wallich, H. 1984. "Institutional cooperation in the world economy." In J. Frenkel and M. Mussa, eds., *The World Economic System: Performance and Prospects*. Dover: Auburn House.

Watanabe, Tsutomu. 1991. "Essays on Sterilized Intervention Signalling and Currency Composition of Government Debt." Unpublished dissertation, Harvard University.

Williamson, John. 1985. "The Exchange Rate System." POLICY ANALYSES IN INTERNATIONAL ECONOMICS 5. Washington: Institute for International Economics.

Williamson, John, and Marcus Miller. 1987. "Targets and Indicators: A Blueprint for the International Coordination of Economic Policy." POLICY ANALYSES IN INTERNATIONAL ECONOMICS 22. Washington: Institute for International Economics.

Wonnacott, Paul. 1982. "U.S. Intervention in the Exchange Market for DM, 77–80." Princeton Studies in International Finance, no. 51. Princeton, N.J.: Princeton University, International Finance Section.

Appendix: Exchange rate policy news reports, by date and source,* 1983–90

19-Apr-83 WSJ — Volcker expresses a preference for modest intervention in foreign exchange markets to help calm extreme fluctuations

21-Apr-83 WSJ — Bundesbank sold between $300 million and $400 million on 19 April to support the deutsche mark

22-Apr-83 WSJ — Haruo Maekawa, head of Bank of Japan, urges "international concerted action" when forex rates exceed an acceptable level

29-Apr-83 WSJ — Volcker recommends that the major industrialized countries consider intervention in forex markets to dampen volatility

19-May-83 WSJ — Volcker remarks that lower US interest rates wouldn't necessarily depress the dollar

29-Jul-83 WSJ — three central banks intervene to stabilize exchange markets

02-Aug-83 WSJ — US, Germany, and Japan intervene to stabilize forex markets

03-Aug-83 WSJ — more intervention efforts by four governments

---

* News accounts of exchange rate policy may have been reported in more than one newspaper, but only one source is listed above. The news search was performed sequentially through various newspapers, the source listed is the first report of its kind found in the search. Newspapers included *Wall Street Journal* (WSJ), *London Financial Times* (LFT), *The New York Times* (NYT)

04-Aug-83 WSJ	— Fed, in an effort to offset the expansionary effect of US intervention in forex markets, is using its domestic operations to maintain tight monetary control; LFT—forex intervention by several central banks
08-Aug-83 NYT	— intervention by various European central banks
09-Aug-83 WSJ	— continued intervention
12-Aug-83 WSJ	— intervention
14-Sep-83 WSJ	— Regan says the US intervention in forex markets in the 29 July–5 August period was for extenuating circumstances and didn't represent a change in policy
08-Nov-83 WSJ	— Bundesbank intervention
15-Dec-83 WSJ	— Bundesbank intervenes to support DM
19-Dec-83 WSJ	— intervention by European central banks
06-Jan-84 WSJ	— Fed intervenes in forex market
10-Jan-84 WSJ	— US and Bundesbank intervene in forex market to defend mark
09-May-84 WSJ	— Bundesbank intervenes in forex markets in support of DM
10-May-84 WSJ	— Bundesbank intervention
11-May-84 WSJ	— third successive day of Bundesbank intervention
24-May-84 WSJ	— US and Japan agree on measures to expand international use of the yen
20-Jun-84 WSJ	— sizable Bundesbank intervention
22-Aug-84 WSJ	— Bundesbank intervenes on behalf of DM
18-Sep-84 WSJ	— European central bank intervention yesterday
24-Sep-84 WSJ	— Bundesbank intervention cited for 21 October
25-Sep-84 WSJ	— substantial Bundesbank intervention
27-Sep-84 WSJ	— West German intervention
02-Oct-84 WSJ	— intervention
17-Oct-84 WSJ	— Bundesbank intervention
29-Oct-84 WSJ	— Bundesbank intervention
15-Nov-84 WSJ	— intervention by Bundesbank
16-Nov-84 WSJ	— modest Bundesbank intervention
03-Dec-84 WSJ	— Volcker states that the Fed plans to assure "adequate growth in money and liquidity" to promote economic growth
07-Dec-84 WSJ	— Bundesbank purchases marks, and other central banks intervene
10-Dec-84 WSJ	— Bundesbank intervention
11-Dec-84 WSJ	— Bundesbank sells dollars
17-Jan-85 WSJ	— G-5 in Washington, DC; leaders commit to coordinated intervention
18-Jan-85 NYT	— Reagan seems to ease restrictions on currency market intervention

19-Jan-85	LFT	— five major industrial powers unite to curb excessive surges by the dollar
21-Jan-85	WSJ	— US join Britain, France, West Germany, and Japan in trying to stabilize forex markets
22-Jan-85	WSJ	— concerted intervention
23-Jan-85	WSJ	— concerted European central bank intervention
24-Jan-85	WSJ	— intervention
30-Jan-85	WSJ	— intervention
01-Feb-85	WSJ	— BOJ, West German, and Fed foreign exchange intervention
04-Feb-85	WSJ	— BOJ and Bundesbank intervention
05-Feb-85	WSJ	— intervention by West Germany, United Kingdom, and Japan
06-Feb-85	LFT	— leading Japanese officials state that domestic interest rates will not be raised in order to try to halt the slide in the value of the yen against the dollar on foreign exchange markets; central bank intervention
08-Feb-85	LFT	— senior West German monetary officials not optimistic that the US will take part in concerted intervention to depress the dollar on forex markets
14-Feb-85	LFT	— Reagan hints at concern over dollar
19-Feb-85	LFT	— intervention
20-Feb-85	WSJ	— West German intervention
26-Feb-85	WSJ	— BOJ intervention
27-Feb-85	WSJ	— Volcker suggests that the intervention efforts by central banks should have been more forceful; intervention by European central banks
28-Feb-85	WSJ	— massive intervention
01-Mar-85	WSJ	— intervention by Bundesbank and BOJ
02-Mar-85	LFT	— European central banks launch another major attack on the dollar; Bundesbank intervention
04-Mar-85	WSJ	— intervention
05-Mar-85	WSJ	— light intervention
07-Mar-85	WSJ	— Volcker speculates that the dollar could fall sharply once the downward trend began
09-Mar-85	LFT	— Fed doubtful about effectiveness of central bank intervention designed to stem rise of the dollar in face of "fundamental" economic trends
01-Apr-85	LFT	— Volcker concerned at volatile dollar
04-Apr-85	WSJ	— Bank of England buys dollars
26-Apr-85	WSJ	— Congress expresses unwillingness to support a new round of world trade liberalization negotiations until Reagan administration reduces the value of dollar and stabilizes exchange rates

30-Apr-85 WSJ	— Baker says that US will adhere to policy of intervening in periods of disorderly conditions
02-May-85	— Bonn Summit
03-May-85 WSJ	— Reagan and Kohl agree on new round of trade talks
24-Jun-85 WSJ	— Finance ministers and central bankers from Group of 10 express support for floating exchange rates; LFT—Fed aim still is lower dollar
02-Jul-85 LFT	— danger of "crash landing" of the dollar is growing as a result of the continuing rise in US current account deficit and rapid buildup of US debt, Bundesbank president says
15-Jul-85 WSJ	— Baker says that Reagan administration isn't unhappy about drop in dollar
18-Jul-85 WSJ	— rumors of intervention; LFT—Volcker warns of inflation threat if dollar collapses
08-Aug-85 WSJ	— Bank of England intervened
23-Sep-85 WSJ	— Plaza Agreement announced by G-5; LFT—US says dollar must come down
24-Sep-85 WSJ	— massive BOJ and Fed (and three other central banks) intervention
25-Sep-85 WSJ	— BOJ intervention
26-Sep-85 WSJ	— coordinated intervention
27-Sep-85 WSJ	— intervention
30-Sep-85 WSJ	— coordinated intervention
01-Oct-85 LFT	— Bundesbank intervention; BOJ sells dollars
03-Oct-85 WSJ	— intervention
04-Oct-85 WSJ	— central bank intervention
07-Oct-85 WSJ	— intervention
08-Oct-85 WSJ	— Bundesbank and BOJ intervention
09-Oct-85 WSJ	— Bundesbank and BOJ intervention
10-Oct-85 WSJ	— BOJ intervention
11-Oct-85 WSJ	— intervention
14-Oct-85 WSJ	— intervention
15-Oct-85 WSJ	— Japan announces stimulus package to support dollar
16-Oct-85 WSJ	— Bundesbank and BOJ intervention
17-Oct-85 WSJ	— intervention by three central banks
18-Oct-85 WSJ	— concerted intervention
21-Oct-85 WSJ	— intervention
22-Oct-85 WSJ	— Fed intervention
23-Oct-85 WSJ	— Fed and BOJ intervention
24-Oct-85 WSJ	— BOJ intervention
25-Oct-85 WSJ	— US, Japanese, and West German intervention
29-Oct-85 WSJ	— BOJ intervention
30-Oct-85 WSJ	— intervention by central banks
31-Oct-85 WSJ	— intervention

04-Nov-85 WSJ	—	BOJ sells dollars
07-Nov-85 WSJ	—	Fed and BOJ intervention; LFT—Fed anxious about effects of sharp dollar fall
09-Nov-85 LFT	—	central banks act quickly to stem sudden surge by the dollar on forex markets
13-Nov-85 WSJ	—	intervention
18-Nov-85 WSJ	—	Sprinkel and Baker disagree on appropriate Fed policy toward dollar
26-Nov-85 WSJ	—	Bundesbank disputes charges that it is not living up to Plaza Agreement
06-Dec-85 LFT	—	further 10 percent decline in value of the dollar would help to stabilize US trade deficit, US Trade Representative Clayton Yeutter says
12-Dec-85 WSJ	—	West Germany, UK, and France intervene
19-Dec-85 WSJ	—	Japanese signal they may stop bolstering yen
20-Jan-86 WSJ	—	G-5 agrees to keep pressure on the dollar
27-Jan-86 WSJ	—	BOJ says they would be comfortable with a stronger yen
06-Feb-86 WSJ	—	White House budget proposal warns that currency realignment might be necessary to ease US trade deficit
20-Feb-86 WSJ	—	Volcker tells House panel that he is worried that slide in dollar could worsen inflation; LFT—cross-talk act on the dollar
18-Mar-86 WSJ	—	BOJ intervention
21-Mar-86 WSJ	—	BOJ intervention
02-Apr-86 WSJ	—	BOJ intervention
29-Apr-86 WSJ	—	intervention by Bundesbank and BOJ
01-May-86 WSJ	—	Pöhl indicates that Germany will continue to intervene in the forex market to support dollar
06-May-86 WSJ	—	G-7 nations agree on a plan seeking less currency volatility; joint intervention is major part of the proposal
09-May-86 WSJ	—	Volcker restates his concern that the dollar, once it begins a decline, could then tumble rapidly
14-May-86 LFT	—	US indicates unease at dollar fall
19-May-86 LFT	—	leading US central bank official warns on slide of the dollar
20-May-86 WSJ	—	intervention by Japan
29-May-86 WSJ	—	intervention
30-May-86 LFT	—	Reagan says dollar fall has begun to correct trade deficit
04-Jun-86 LFT	—	Baker warns on further changes in exchange rates
07-Jul-86 WSJ	—	intervention by Japan

24-Jul-86 WSJ	— Volcker indicates that he has become less worried about a collapse in the dollar
05-Sep-86 LFT	— Fed denies intervening to support dollar
22-Sep-86 LFT	— EEC ministers seek to persuade US to stabilize dollar
24-Sep-86 WSJ	— unconfirmed report that the EC agreed to bolster the dollar
30-Sep-86 WSJ	— intervention by Bundesbank
01-Oct-86 WSJ	— intervention by Bundesbank
06-Oct-86 WSJ	— British central bank is expected to intervene to support pound against the DM
08-Oct-86 WSJ	— intervention by European central banks
10-Oct-86 WSJ	— European intervention
14-Oct-86 WSJ	— Bundesbank intervention
15-Oct-86 WSJ	— intervention
16-Oct-86 WSJ	— intervention
31-Oct-86 WSJ	— Baker-Miyazawa accord
01-Nov-86 LFT	— Japan and US forge bilateral link on the yen
02-Jan-87 LFT	— Pöhl warns that a further marked fall in the dollar would jeopardize growth in West Germany
06-Jan-87 WSJ	— Bundesbank intervention
13-Jan-87 WSJ	— massive BOJ intervention
14-Jan-87 WSJ	— BOJ intervention
16-Jan-87 LFT	— West German Finance Minister Gerhard Stoltenberg is skeptical about chances of agreement with the US on stabilizing the sliding dollar
19-Jan-87 WSJ	— frantic BOJ intervention
20-Jan-87 LFT	— Japan finance chief plans US visit to seek action on dollar
22-Jan-87 WSJ	— Baker and Miyazawa recognize "temporary instability" in forex markets but stop short of pledge to act
23-Jan-87 LFT	— Delors accuses the US of seeking to blackmail its trading partners by letting the dollar fall
26-Jan-87 WSJ	— Pöhl indicates that Bundesbank is now prepared to support dollar
27-Jan-87 WSJ	— Bundesbank intervenes
28-Jan-87 WSJ	— first dollar purchase by Fed since the Plaza Agreement; LFT—West Germany intervenes
29-Jan-87 WSJ	— BOJ intervenes
03-Feb-87 WSJ	— Volcker says drop in the dollar has reached the danger point and that further declines will trigger inflation
06-Feb-87 WSJ	— Reagan administration says it has no differences with Volcker over the dollar
07-Feb-87 LFT	— US is not concerned about pushing the dollar down further

09-Feb-87 WSJ	— coordinated central bank action
10-Feb-87 WSJ	— under proposal by Baker, US offers to cooperate with Germany and Japan in stabilizing exchange rates if those countries stimulate their economies
11-Feb-87 NYT	— Baker announces that dollar has declined enough against the yen
17-Feb-87 LFT	— Baker remarks that currency's decline so far has been orderly
19-Feb-87 WSJ	— G-5 has reached a modest agreement aimed at reducing dollar turmoil in return for vows by Germany and Japan to try and stimulate their economies
23-Feb-87 WSJ	— Louvre Accord announced
26-Feb-87 WSJ	— expectations of intervention
04-Mar-87 WSJ	— Bank of England intervention
11-Mar-87 WSJ	— Fed sold dollars
13-Mar-87 WSJ	— rumors of central bank intervention
24-Mar-87 WSJ	— BOJ intervenes; unconfirmed Fed intervention
25-Mar-87 WSJ	— central bank intervention
26-Mar-87 WSJ	— heavy intervention by central banks
27-Mar-87 WSJ	— intervention by G-6
30-Mar-87 WSJ	— BOJ intervention
31-Mar-87 WSJ	— Fed and BOJ intervention
01-Apr-87 WSJ	— intervention by BOJ
02-Apr-87 WSJ	— intervention
03-Apr-87 WSJ	— Fed intervention
06-Apr-87 WSJ	— Fed intervention
16-Apr-87 WSJ	— Japanese officials indicate plans to bolster forex activity to support dollar
17-Apr-87 WSJ	— comments by Baker signal market that Reagan administration is prepared to bolster the dollar
21-Apr-87 WSJ	— Baker, seeking to boost support for the dollar, voiced confidence in Fed's anti-inflationary policies
22-Apr-87 WSJ	— BOJ intervenes to support dollar
24-Apr-87 WSJ	— seven major central banks intervene, buying dollars and selling yen
01-May-87 WSJ	— US and Japan are moving jointly to stem dollar's decline
02-May-87 LFT	— Fed statement on support for dollar
29-May-87 LFT	— US plays down talk of Venice initiative on dollar
12-Jun-87 WSJ	— Reagan, in commenting on the Venice summit, misstated US policy on the dollar
24-Jun-87 WSJ	— rumors of intervention by one or more central banks
29-Jun-87 WSJ	— rumors of a pact by central banks to maintain exchange rate zones
01-Jul-87 WSJ	— rumors of market intervention

03-Jul-87 WSJ	— Japan's central bank chief makes remark that Fed has acted to avert a further drop in the dollar
09-Jul-87 WSJ	— intervention rumors involving the Fed and Bundesbank
10-Jul-87 WSJ	— intervention rumors involving Fed and Bundesbank
31-Jul-87 WSJ	— rumors of Fed intervention
05-Aug-87 WSJ	— Fed intervention
06-Aug-87 WSJ	— intervention by Bundesbank
07-Aug-87 WSJ	— intervention by Bundesbank and Fed
10-Aug-87 WSJ	— intervention by central banks
11-Aug-87 WSJ	— intervention by central banks
20-Aug-87 WSJ	— US and Japan intervene
21-Aug-87 WSJ	— Japan intervenes
25-Aug-87 WSJ	— BOJ intervention
02-Sep-87 WSJ	— Fed and three other central banks intervene
03-Sep-87 WSJ	— concerted intervention
09-Sep-87 WSJ	— six central banks intervene
20-Oct-87 WSJ	— Baker and German officials agree in surprise meeting to support unspecified changes in Louvre Accord on exchange rate and economic-policy cooperation
26-Oct-87 LFT	— central bank intervention to back dollar but Fed involvement is uncertain
29-Oct-87 LFT	— central bank intervention; Delors says that the US was ready to let dollar fall to DM1.60
30-Oct-87 LFT	— central bank intervention
02-Nov-87 WSJ	— Wayne Angell states that dollar should not be allowed to free fall
03-Nov-87 LFT	— BOJ and other central banks intervene
05-Nov-87 LFT	— Bundesbank acts to prop up dollar
06-Nov-87 NYT	— Baker states that the US will not support the dollar if it means recession; LFT—Baker says US remains committed to Louvre Accord; LFT—European and Japanese central banks launch coordinated attempt at dollar stabilization
09-Nov-87 NYT	— central banks meet to discuss Fed and US dollar; central bank intervention
11-Nov-87 LFT	— Reagan says dollar has fallen far enough; BOJ and central banks attempt to control dollar's slide
26-Nov-87 LFT	— modest Bundesbank intervention
01-Dec-87 WSJ	— intervention
02-Dec-87 WSJ	— coordinated central bank intervention; LFT—Fed absent from concerted intervention
04-Dec-87 LFT	— central banks drive European interest rates down to help dollar
07-Dec-87 WSJ	— Fed intervention

11-Dec-87 WSJ	—	central bank intervention
15-Dec-87 LFT	—	White House tries to halt slide of dollar with its remarks
16-Dec-87 WSJ	—	White House remarks that US isn't seeking a weaker dollar
23-Dec-87 WSJ	—	G-7 reaffirmed coordinated intervention policies
24-Dec-87 WSJ	—	intervention by six central banks
28-Dec-87 WSJ	—	eight central banks intervene
29-Dec-87 LFT	—	central bank intervention
30-Dec-87 WSJ	—	intervention by six central banks
31-Dec-87 WSJ	—	intervention by as many as eight central banks; LFT - central banks intervene for third day running to support dollar
01-Jan-88 LFT	—	BOJ and Bundesbank intervention
04-Jan-88 WSJ	—	intervention by central banks
05-Jan-88 WSJ	—	central banks actively buy dollars
06-Jan-88 LFT	—	West German minister says recent events prove G-7 doing everything it can to stabilize rates
08-Jan-88 LFT	—	officials admit that G-7 agreement exists on intervention; BOJ intervention
11-Jan-88 WSJ	—	official dollar buying by central banks
13-Jan-88 LFT	—	US-Japan agreement on intervention to support dollar
21-Jan-88 LFT	—	Bundesbank defends intervention policy in support of dollar
27-Jan-88 WSJ	—	Manuel Johnson makes statement in support of dollar; LFT—German Finance Minister defends Bundesbank intervention policy
04-Feb-88 WSJ	—	Stoltenberg and Baker make joint statement in support of dollar
01-Mar-88 LFT	—	Brady makes statement strongly supporting exchange rate stabilization
25-Mar-88 WSJ	—	Fed intervention
28-Mar-88 WSJ	—	Fed intervention
29-Mar-88 LFT	—	BOJ and Fed intervention
30-Mar-88 WSJ	—	continuing intervention by BOJ and Fed
08-Apr-88 WSJ	—	West German intervention
14-Apr-88 WSJ	—	Fed and seven other major central banks intervene in support of dollar
15-Apr-88 LFT	—	coordinated intervention
25-Apr-88 WSJ	—	BOJ affirms G-7 intervention policy
10-May-88 WSJ	—	central bank action
27-May-88 WSJ	—	Fed intervention
31-May-88 WSJ	—	Bundesbank intervention
03-Jun-88 WSJ	—	UK intervenes

09-Jun-88 WSJ	— Bundesbank intervenes; LFT—Bundesbank chief backs strong DM
10-Jun-88 WSJ	— Bundesbank intervention
13-Jun-88 LFT	— change in BOJ attitude toward dollar support; WSJ-central banks send mixed signals
14-Jun-88 WSJ	— Bundesbank intervention
15-Jun-88 LFT	— intervention; WSJ—Bundesbank intervention
16-Jun-88 LFT	— intervention
24-Jun-88 WSJ	— US officials confirm that G-7 is coordinating intervention efforts
27-Jun-88 WSJ	— Fed and Bundesbank intervention
28-Jun-88 WSJ	— Fed and Bundesbank (and European central bank) intervention
29-Jun-88 WSJ	— third day of Fed and Bundesbank intervention; LFT—BOJ intervention
08-Jul-88 LFT	— intervention
11-Jul-88 WSJ	— coordinated intervention by Bundesbank, Fed and five other European central banks
12-Jul-88 LFT	— widespread intervention
18-Jul-88 WSJ	— BOJ and Bundesbank intervention
19-Jul-88 WSJ	— coordinated BOJ intervention
20-Jul-88 WSJ	— Fed and Bundesbank intervention
21-Jul-88 WSJ	— central bank intervention
22-Jul-88 WSJ	— intervention
27-Jul-88 WSJ	— central bank intervention
28-Jul-88 WSJ	— Fed intervention; LFT—central bank intervention
29-Jul-88 WSJ	— central bank intervention
04-Aug-88 WSJ	— intervention
05-Aug-88 WSJ	— intervention
08-Aug-88 WSJ	— intervention by Fed and Bundesbank
09-Aug-88 WSJ	— Fed intervention
11-Aug-88 WSJ	— warnings by West German official that dollar must fall
17-Aug-88 LFT	— Fed and Bundesbank intervene
18-Aug-88 WSJ	— Fed intervention in thin market
19-Aug-88 WSJ	— Fed intervention
22-Aug-88 WSJ	— intervention
23-Aug-88 WSJ	— intervention
26-Aug-88 WSJ	— Bundesbank defends mark
29-Aug-88 LFT	— intervention
31-Aug-88 WSJ	— BOJ comments weaken yen
07-Sep-88 WSJ	— Mulford reassures G-7 that Baker's departure will not alter US exchange rate policy
14-Sep-88 WSJ	— Fed intervention
22-Sep-88 WSJ	— Fed forex action

23-Sep-88 LFT	— G-7 reaffirms commitment to intervention against dollar
26-Sep-88 WSJ	— central bank intervention
27-Sep-88 WSJ	— Brady reaffirms US commitment to G-7 intervention coordination
14-Oct-88 WSJ	— rumors of intervention
18-Oct-88 WSJ	— official remarks by central bankers in support of dollar
19-Oct-88 WSJ	— BOJ's new exchange rate stance suggests authorities see inflation waning
24-Oct-88 WSJ	— jawboning by BOJ in support of dollar
27-Oct-88 WSJ	— BOJ intervention
31-Oct-88 WSJ	— intervention; LFT—Fed intervention
01-Nov-88 WSJ	— intervention by Fed and BOJ
02-Nov-88 WSJ	— BOJ and Fed intervene for third straight day
10-Nov-88 WSJ	— BOJ urges coordinated intervention
11-Nov-88 WSJ	— German officials talk up mark, and Brady denies rumors that US seeks lower dollar
14-Nov-88 WSJ	— Fed and BOJ intervene in support of dollar; LFT - government statements and intervention in support of dollar
16-Nov-88 WSJ	— Fed intervention
17-Nov-88 WSJ	— Fed and Bundesbank (and eight other nations) intervene in support of dollar
18-Nov-88 LFT	— intervention; WSJ—Brady says he is not worried about dollar's level
22-Nov-88 WSJ	— intervention
29-Nov-88 WSJ	— BOJ and Fed support dollar
05-Jan-89 WSJ	— Bundesbank intervention
06-Jan-89 NYT	— Bundesbank: dollar won't weaken, selling not aimed at slowing dollar rise
08-Jan-89 LFT	— Pöhl: strong dollar may cause tension with EMS
09-Jan-89 WSJ	— official jawboning and intervention
10-Jan-89 WSJ	— Fed selling, Bundesbank remarks confusing
11-Jan-89 WSJ	— intervention by central banks
12-Jan-89 LFT	— central bank intervention
13-Jan-89 NYT	— coordinated central bank intervention
14-Jan-89 LFT	— coordinated central bank intervention
19-Jan-89 WSJ	— central banks force dollar lower
20-Jan-89 NYT	— concerted intervention
21-Jan-89 LFT	— intervention
23-Jan-89 WSJ	— intervention
24-Jan-89 LFT	— continued central bank intervention
25-Jan-89 WSJ	— Fed and BOF sell US unit
26-Jan-89 WSJ	— intervention by Fed

28-Jan-89	LFT	— central bank intervention
29-Jan-89	WSJ	— G-7 shows little inclination to shift policies
31-Jan-89	LFT	— Fed chairman stresses need for exchange rate stability through G-7 cooperation
03-Feb-89	NYT	— concerted dollar sale, G-7 agrees to keep dollar at current level
06-Feb-89	WSJ	— central banks intervene
07-Feb-87	LFT	— central bank dollar selling continues
09-Feb-89	WSJ	— intervention
14-Feb-89	WSJ	— Bush makes bearish remarks
27-Feb-89	WSJ	— sales of sterling by Bank of England
08-Mar-89	WSJ	— Fed intervention
15-Mar-89	WSJ	— European central banks intervene
17-Mar-89	LFT	— central banks support DM
18-Mar-89	LFT	— central banks intervene
20-Mar-89	WSJ	— Fed intervention
28-Mar-89	WSJ	— intervention
29-Mar-89	WSJ	— intervention by major central banks
30-Mar-89	WSJ	— intervention
02-Apr-89	WSJ	— G-7 warns markets not to push dollar higher, prepared to stop them
03-Apr-89	WSJ	— intervention by BOJ to drive dollar lower
10-Apr-89	WSJ	— intervention
11-Apr-89	WSJ	— Fed intervention
28-Apr-89	NYT	— central banks sell dollars
01-May-89	WSJ	— intervention by BOJ and Fed
02-May-89	WSJ	— intervention
03-May-89	WSJ	— central bank intervention
04-May-89	WSJ	— bullish comments by Fed; LFT—Bundesbank leads central bank intervention
05-May-89	WSJ	— central bank intervention
08-May-89	WSJ	— central bank intervention
09-May-89	NYT	— US officials dampen speculation of change in G-7 policy
10-May-89	WSJ	— bearish remarks by Japanese and West German officials
11-May-89	WSJ	— Treasury wants weaker dollar, Fed less committed
12-May-89	WSJ	— coordinated assault on dollar by central banks
16-May-89	LFT	— central bank intervention
17-May-89	WSJ	— central banks prepare big new intervention
18-May-89	WSJ	— massive intervention; NYT—Murayama warns forex speculators
19-May-89	WSJ	— central banks give mixed signals on their resolve to stem dollar rally

20-May-89 LFT	—	absence of Bundesbank from currency market operations sparks speculation that there is rift within G-7 over dollar policy
22-May-89 WSJ	—	intervention; NYT—Fed officials and White House remarks suggest concern with rising dollar
23-May-89 LFT	—	US administration reaffirms commitment to international cooperation; WSJ—intervention
24-May-89 WSJ	—	Bush states concerns with rising dollar; LFT—central bank intervention
25-May-89 WSJ	—	intervention
25-May-89 LFT	—	Fed leads efforts to push dollar down
27-May-89 LFT	—	concerted intervention that includes the Bundesbank
30-May-89 NYT	—	central bank dollar-selling
31-May-89 LFT	—	strong selling by central banks
01-Jun-89 WSJ	—	Brady warns of stronger dollar
06-Jun-89 WSJ	—	Fed intervenes
13-Jun-89 WSJ	—	Fed and others intervene; NYT—Bush unhappy, but dollar increase only temporary, no strong effort to halt it
14-Jun-89 WSJ	—	intervention
21-Jun-89 WSJ	—	central bank intervention
22-Jun-89 WSJ	—	intervention
28-Jun-89 WSJ	—	intervention
29-Jun-89 WSJ	—	intervention
07-Jul-89 LFT	—	senior officials comment on welcome fall of dollar but need for stability
16-Jul-89 LFT	—	G-7 endorses existing exchange rate policies
11-Aug-89 WSJ	—	central bank intervention
12-Aug-89 LFT	—	widespread central bank intervention
24-Aug-89 LFT	—	G-7 agrees to halt dollar
27-Aug-89 LFT	—	G-7 central banks sell $4 billion to drive dollar down
29-Aug-89 WSJ	—	Japanese central bank intervenes
01-Sep-89 WSJ	—	intervention
05-Sep-89 WSJ	—	central bank intervention
06-Sep-89 LFT	—	central bank action
07-Sep-89 WSJ	—	intervention
08-Sep-89 WSJ	—	central bank intervention
14-Sep-89 WSJ	—	intervention
19-Sep-89 WSJ	—	US intervenes; LFT—Lawson on dollar: level tolerable, but no rise
20-Sep-89 WSJ	—	intervention
21-Sep-89 WSJ	—	central bank intervention
22-Sep-89 LFT	—	heavy intervention
24-Sep-89 WSJ	—	G-7 officials, concerned about dollar rise, vow to cooperate; NYT—intervention by several central banks

25-Sep-89 WSJ	—	intervention efforts by central banks
26-Sep-89 WSJ	—	intervention by central banks; Brady: G-7 works
27-Sep-89 WSJ	—	third intervention day
28-Sep-89 WSJ	—	intervention
29-Sep-89 NYT	—	US and allies intervene
30-Sep-89 LFT	—	G-7 countries continue to intervene
02-Oct-89 WSJ	—	intervention by central banks
03-Oct-89 LFT	—	new round of concerted central bank intervention in line with G-7 agreement
04-Oct-89 WSJ	—	intervention by central banks in Asia and Europe; pound stirs Bank of England to intervention
05-Oct-89 WSJ	—	Bundesbank and others boost interest rates to weaken dollar
06-Oct-89 NYT	—	US and allies sell dollars
07-Oct-89 LFT	—	seven other central banks join Fed intervention
09-Oct-89 LFT	—	some Fed governors criticize G-7 on dollar strength
11-Oct-89 WSJ	—	central bank intervention
12-Oct-89 LFT	—	suspicion that G-7 policy is in disarray with Fed refusing to ease monetary policy; BOJ governor concedes discount rate increase aimed at weakening dollar
13-Oct-89 LFT	—	Treasury secretary concedes differences over dollar policy between administration and Fed
25-Oct-89 LFT	—	Greenspan comments on limited effectiveness of intervention to force dollar down
28-Dec-89 WSJ	—	dollar selling by some European central banks
02-Jan-90 WSJ	—	Federal Reserve Board intervenes to slow the rise of dollar
04-Jan-90 WSJ	—	surprise selling by Bundesbank
12-Jan-90 LFT	—	Japanese finance minister expresses confidence in ability of G-7 to maintain currency stability
18-Jan-90 WSJ	—	two Fed officials indicate they no longer support easier credit
19-Jan-90 NYT	—	article on aggressive strategy of Bundesbank to strengthen mark
20-Feb-90 WSJ	—	Greenspan comments that interest rates are not likely to decline soon
23-Feb-90 NYT	—	BOJ buys heavily to halt dollar's rise against yen
27-Feb-90 WSJ	—	US and Japanese central bank intervention
02-Mar-90 WSJ	—	Fed Vice Chairman Manuel Johnson says he views the dollar as basically stable and is comfortable with its current levels; LFT—central banks intervene to cut dollar's rise
05-Mar-90 WSJ	—	world's leading central banks intervene
07-Mar-90 WSJ	—	large, repeated dollar sales by central banks

08-Mar-90 WSJ	—	intervention by Federal Reserve Board
09-Mar-90 WSJ	—	dollar-weakening intervention
12-Mar-90 LFT	—	tension between Fed and administration over intervention
13-Mar-90 WSJ	—	CB intervention; LFT—Federal government stresses unease with large-scale dollar intervention
19-Mar-90 WSJ	—	BOJ boosted its discount rate to shore up yen; Japanese finance minister concerned over falling yen
20-Mar-90 WSJ	—	BOJ discount-rate increase aimed at yen exchange rate
21-Mar-90 NYT	—	Japanese government efforts to bolster the plummeting yen; Bush administration says that talks between US and Japan are intended to weigh moves to check recent fall of yen
23-Mar-90 NYT	—	Japan asks US for help in checking fall of yen
27-Mar-90 NYT	—	rift between Fed and Treasury over the dollar
28-Mar-90 WSJ	—	Japan's Finance Ministry denies rumors that it has urged investors to curb their purchases of dollar-denominated securities
29-Mar-90 WSJ	—	BOJ intervention; US Treasury and FRB officials began to put aside their differences to prepare a uniform US position on boosting the Japanese yen when the subject comes up at an April 1990 G-7 meeting
30-Mar-90 WSJ	—	efforts by Japan and six other industrialized nations to support yen
04-Apr-90 WSJ	—	G-7 meets to shore up the yen
06-Apr-90 WSJ	—	G-7 says the yen's recent decline has undesirable consequences for world economic adjustment but brushes aside Japanese calls for coordinated interest-rate actions to support the shaky currency; NYT—Treasury Secretary Nicholas Brady says yen's value is not outside bounds of stability
09-Apr-90 WSJ	—	modest intervention by central banks
11-Apr-90 WSJ	—	round of token intervention by central banks
07-May-90 WSJ	—	G-7 meeting has little effect on trading because of a lack of new initiatives announced; LFT—G-7 delegates express concern over yen
11-Jun-90 LFT	—	Bank for International Settlements report calls for enhanced coordination in international exchange rate policy
06-Jul-90 WSJ	—	US attempts to prop up the yen
12-Jul-90 WSJ	—	Greenspan says the Fed is ready to ease monetary policy for sake of the dollar
27-Jul-90 WSJ	—	easing of dollar by the Fed expected
17-Aug-90 WSJ	—	traders say central banks may move to bolster dollar

06-Sep-90 WSJ	— Fed expected to ease dollar
07-Sep-90 NYT	— Treasury Secretary Nicholas Brady calls for Fed to sanction a cut in interest rates and says dollar's fall is not precipitous
13-Sep-90 WSJ	— Greenspan remarks hint at a move to cut interest rates to help dollar
17-Sep-90 WSJ	— G-7 to meet 22 September to discuss the decline of US dollar
03-Oct-90 WSJ	— Greenspan announces that the budget package is credible and would "most certainly" cause a decline in interest rates and the dollar
19-Oct-90 WSJ	— US officials likely to stand by and watch the dollar fall another 5 to 10 percent without taking action
23-Oct-90 WSJ	— central bankers' comments fall on deaf ears
30-Oct-90 NYT	— Bush administration concerned about recent sharp decline in dollar
06-Nov-90 WSJ	— rumors and remarks by central banks buffet market
08-Nov-90 LFT	— French minister calls for G-7 meeting to discuss decline of dollar
09-Nov-90 LFT	— Bundesbank unconcerned by dollar's fall
16-Nov-90 WSJ	— Fed in an easing mode, unconcerned with dollar fall
28-Nov-90 WSJ	— Fed comments bolster dollar
30-Nov-90 LFT	— French finance minister calls for meeting of G-7 to discuss the decline of the dollar
11-Dec-90 WSJ	— indications that G-7 may meet in January 1991 to discuss the dollar's frailty
14-Dec-90 WSJ	— French economics minister calls for a meeting of G-7 to address the dollar's depreciation

Index

Abrams, Richard 35
Adams, Donald 65, 72
Adaptive expectations 125, 126, 134
Akerlof, George A. 110
Akhtar, M. Akbar 34
Allen, Helen 43
Assets
  diversified holdings of foreign and domestic
    36, 58–59, 103–06
  offsetting net changes in 57, 66, 87

Baillie, Richard T. 108
Baker, James A. 12–15, 17, 18, 20, 48–51, 112
Bandwagon expectations 42, 43, 61, 125, 134
Bank for International Settlements 52, 66, 72
Bank of England 88
Bank of Japan. *See also* Japan; Yen-dollar rates
  daily intervention in 1989 21
  daily intervention in 1990 22
  daily intervention in 1991 24
  discount rate set by 14
  dollar purchases of 15, 21, 22, 86, 87
  dollar sales of 13, 20
  Foreign Exchange Fund Special Account of
    the Central Government 65
  Foreign Exchange Fund Special Account of
    the National Budget 65
  market survey by 88
  resistance to appreciation of yen 83
  yen support in 1987 86
Bayne, Nicholas 10
Bear squeeze 19, 23, 86, 89, 91, 101

Bergsten, C. Fred 10, 11, 25, 46, 64, 134
Black, Stanley W. 58, 106
Blumenthal, Michael 6, 14
Boothe, P. 104
Bordo, Michael 88
Brada, J. 35
Bradley, Senator Bill 50, 51
Brady, Nicholas 20, 50
Branson, William 58, 104
Bretton Woods 1, 5, 29, 78
Budget deficit, US 8, 10, 46, 48, 106
Bundesbank. *See also* Germany; Mark-dollar
    rates
  attempts to strengthen European currencies
    46
  daily intervention in 1985 90
  daily intervention in 1987 91
  daily intervention in 1988–89 92
  daily intervention in 1989 21
  daily intervention in 1990 22
  daily intervention in 1991 24
  dollar purchases of 21, 22, 24, 76, 83, 91, 92
  dollar sales of 12, 13, 21, 22, 24, 74, 76, 83,
    92
  effect on exchange rate volatility 108
  frequency of intervention operations of 73,
    75
  obtaining intervention data from 72, 74, 82
  reaction function of 83–85, 88
  responsibilities of 65, 66
  size of intervention operations of 21, 22, 24,
    76, 90–92
  sterilization procedure of 57
Bush, President George 19, 20

Caballero, Ricardo 34
Camdessus, Michel 9
Canzoneri, Mathew 71
Carlson, John A. 110
"Carter" bonds 6
Carter, President Jimmy 6
Catte, Pietro 16, 21, 22, 24, 85, 86, 101, 106
Central banks. *See also* Bank of Japan;
  Bundesbank; Federal Reserve; Swiss
  National Bank
  credibility of 71
  customer transactions and 64
  daily intervention in 1989 21
  daily intervention in 1990 22
  daily intervention in 1991 24
  disorderly markets and 64
  dollar purchases of 15, 16, 21, 22, 24, 76, 83,
    86, 87, 91, 92
  dollar sales of 12, 13, 20, 21, 22, 24, 74, 76,
    82, 83, 92
  foreign exchange portfolio of 67
  preference for secrecy 71
  reputation for truthful signals 63
  signaling of market operations 72, 135
"Chartists" 43
China 51
Clinton, K. 104
Congress, US 11, 46, 50, 51, 138
Coordinated intervention
  accuracy of reported operations 73
  definition of 56
  fixed-rate systems and 63
  floating rate systems and 63
  to halt dollar slide in 1992 26
  investor confidence and 63
  nonsterilized operations and 62
  number reported, 1982–90 75
  spillover effects on exchange rates 62
  sterilized operations and 62
  success of 101, 118, 120
  versus unilateral intervention 116, 138
Corbo, Vittorio 34
Corden, W. Maxwell 47
Cote, A. 104
Council of Economic Advisers 10, 12, 46, 52,
  137, 138
"Crowding out" 8
Cukierman, Alex 71
Customer transactions 56, 64, 65, 72

Danker, Deborah 104
Darman, Richard 12
De Grauwe, Paul 35
Destabilizing speculation 42
Destler, I. Mac 9, 12, 19, 50–53
Discreet intervention *See* Secret intervention
Disorderly markets 9, 61, 64, 78, 107, 139
Dobson, Wendy 12, 14, 15, 19, 20, 23, 52

Dollar. *See also* Dollar appreciation; Dollar
  depreciation; Mark-dollar rates; Yen-dollar
  rates
  and mark as substitute international
    currencies 26
  Plaza Agreement and 12, 14, 64, 136
  price-adjusted exchange value of 40
  as a "safety valve" 46
Dollar appreciation
  "safe haven" view of 10
  during Reagan administration 7, 8
  in the late 1980s 19
  protectionism and 46
Dollar depreciation
  demand for US bonds and 18
  after Plaza meeting 14
  before Plaza meeting 12
Dominguez, Kathryn M. 34, 106–09, 124, 135
Dooley, Michael 104, 105
Dornbusch, Rudiger 37, 39
Dudler, Herrmann J. 57

Edison, Hali 34, 88, 103
Eijffinger, Sylvester C. W. 70, 77
Engel, Charles M. 105
European Monetary Cooperation Fund
  (EMCF) 66
European Monetary System (EMS) 25, 57, 136
European Monetary Union (EMU) 25
Ex post excess returns 105
Exchange rate determination
  asset-pricing models of 59
  monetary model 36, 44, 57, 106
Exchange rate expectations
  adaptive 125, 126, 134
  bandwagon 42, 43, 61, 125, 134
  extrapolative 125, 134
  intervention's influence on 36, 109, 135–36
  investors' one-month ahead 128
  investors' pooled 129
  investors' three-month ahead 126
  lagged expectation and 125
  lagged spot rate and 125
  long-run equilibrium and 125
  measuring investors' 34
  problems of measuring 104
  rational expectations methodology and
    33–34, 39, 41, 44, 104, 105
  rationality of market and 109
  stabilizing versus destabilizing 126, 127
  static 126
  use of survey data to measure 109, 124
Exchange Rate Mechanism 47
Exchange rate policy
  democratization of 49, 52, 138
  East Asia and US 51
  legislation and 50
  macroeconomic fundamentals and 138, 140

proposals to integrate with monetary policy 52, 137, 138

trade partners and 138

Exchange rate volatility. *See also* Free-floating exchange rates; Magnification effect; Overshooting effect; Speculative bubble

bilateral studies of 34–35

long-term effects of 35

real versus nominal effects of 30–31

time-conditional 107–08

Exchange rates. *See also* Exchange rate determination; Exchange rate expectations; Exchange rate policy; Exchange rate volatility; Mark-dollar rates; Yen-dollar rates

daily versus weekly movements in 108

direction of changes in 96

movement in concert with intervention 89, 96–100

nominal vs. real 36

as signal of inappropriate policy 47

supply-siders view of 10

Exchange Stabilization Fund 50, 65

Expectations. *See* Exchange rate expectations

Extrapolative expectations 125, 134

Federal Reserve Act 49

Federal Reserve Bank of New York 49, 60, 87, 137, 138

Federal Reserve

accuracy of reported intervention of 73

daily intervention in 1985 90

daily intervention in 1987 91

daily intervention in 1988–89 92

daily intervention in 1989 21

daily intervention in 1990 22, 92, 93

daily intervention in 1991 24, 93

dollar purchases of 15, 24, 74, 76, 77, 91–93

dollar sales of 13, 21, 22, 24, 74, 76, 77, 90–93

effect on exchange rate volatility of 108

increased intervention after Plaza Agreement 74

market survey by 88

predictability of intervention in the 1980s 77

press reports of intervention of 75

reaction function of 77–80

reasons for intervention 74, 77, 78

signaling of market operations 72

size of intervention operations of 21, 22, 24, 90–93

size of operations vis-á-vis Bundesbank's 74

target rates and 82

Treasury and 52, 60, 137, 138

yen support in 1987 86

Feldstein, Martin 10, 12, 14, 18, 46, 48

Feldstein, Kathleen 48

Financial Times (London) 73, 112

Fixed exchange rates 5, 29, 32, 40

Forecasts, basis of. *See also* Exchange rate expectations

momentum models as 43

technical analysts as 42

Foreign exchange rates. *See* Exchange rates

Forward exchange market 32–35, 38, 67

Forward exchange rate, as forecast of future spot rate 39

Forward exchange rate, as measure of investor expectations 124

Frankel, Jeffrey A. 7, 34, 106, 109, 124, 134

Free-floating exchange rates

arguments for 29, 30

cost on international transactions of 31

efficiency of 39

as equilibrating the trade balance 31

monetary policy and 36

national policy independence and 47

system of 6

volatility of 29, 35

Friedman, Milton 9, 36, 42, 106, 107

Froot, Kenneth 11, 34, 43, 109, 124, 125, 134

Funabashi, Yoichi 11–14, 17, 78, 79, 82–84, 86

Gaiotti, E. 83, 86, 88

Galli, Giampaolo 16, 21, 22, 24, 85, 86, 101, 106

Gartner, Manfred 87

Germany 17, 27, 65, 74, 83, 88. *See also* Bundesbank

Ghosh, Atish R. 106, 109, 135

Giovannini, Alberto 105

Girton, Lance 58

Giucca, P. 83, 86, 88

Goldberg, Michael B. 43

Goodhart, Charles 43

Greene, Margaret 6, 7

Greenspan, Alan 18, 48, 50

Group of Five (G-5) 11, 51, 64, 74, 86, 138

Group of Seven (G-7) 9, 52, 103, 138

Gruijters, Noud P. D. 70, 77

Haas, Richard 104

Hagen, Jurgen von 57, 88

Haltiwanger, John 110

Halttunen, Hannu 104

Hamada, K. 62

"Hard landing" 18

Hardouvelis, Gikas 112

Henderson, Dale 58, 65, 70, 72, 103, 104

Henning, C. Randall 9, 12, 19, 50–53

Hidden reserves 69

Hilton, Spence 34

Hogan, Ked 112

Hooper, Peter 34

Humpage, Owen 108, 116

Hung, Juann 89, 127

Initial intervention 116, 120

Interest rates. *See also* Interest rates, Eurodollar; Interest rates, Euromark; Interest rates, German; Interest rates, US
change in asset demand and 133
decline after Plaza Agreement 14
differential in US and trading partners' 39–40
effect on risk premium 129

Interest rates, Eurodollar 130

Interest rates, Euromark 130

Interest rates, German 25–27

Interest rates, US
budget deficit and 10
difference in real and nominal 7
dollar depreciation against mark and 26
long-term real 8
nominal vs. real 31
Reagan administration view of 10
recession of 1981–82 and 7
stock market crash and 48

Intervention. *See also* Central banks; Coordinated intervention; Initial intervention; Intervention data; Intervention policy; Public intervention; Sterilized intervention; Unilateral intervention
as an independent policy tool 2, 5, 45, 52, 62, 139
as both stock and flow 130
central bank motives for 64, 77, 78
central banks' definition of 55, 56
coincidence with exchange rate changes 89, 95–101
commercial banks and 72
consistency with macroeconomic policy 61
effect on domestic money base 66, 87
effect of frequency on spot rate changes 117
effect of past changes in spot rate on 78
funds designated for 65
how central banks conduct 55, 72
how operations are financed 65
news reports of 73, 75, appendix A. *See also* News reports, effect of
nonsterilized 56, 57
operations to support fellow central banks 66, 78
profitability criterion for 106, 107
role in bursting 1984–85 speculative bubble 139
size of 74, 76, 88–89, 93, 115, 121–123
Treasury's role in financing 65

Intervention data
availability of 69–71
reserves to serve as a proxy for 103
secrecy of 70

Intervention policy. *See also* Exchange rate policy

as predictor of monetary policy 108, 109, 135
democratization of 49, 52, 138
dollar-mark target and 108
dollar-yen target and 108
effects on exchange rate volatility 107
proposals to integrate with monetary policy 137–38
trading partner coordination of 138

Isard, Peter 104, 105

Italy 27

Ito, Takatoshi 42, 124

Jacobson, Laurence 107

Japan 65, 74, 83, 88. *See also* Bank of Japan

Johnson, Manuel 50

Jorion, Philippe 105

Jurgensen, P. (report) 9, 12, 70, 103, 137

Kaminsky, Graciela 109, 135

Kenen, Peter 34, 89

Klein, Michael 73, 77, 109, 112

Kohlhagen, Steven 34

Korea 51

Kouri, P. 58

Krugman, Paul 11, 136

Laissez-faire policy 11, 30, 38, 39

Leahy, Michael 107

Leaning against the wind 56, 63, 64, 78, 82, 84, 85, 114, 118, 120

Leaning with the wind 56, 64, 84

Lewis, Karen 77, 105, 109, 135

Livingston, Joseph 110

Longworth, D. 104

Loopesko, Bonnie 70, 106

Louvre Accord 15, 78, 82, 84, 108, 113, 136, 138

Lundine, Rep. Stan 51

Madigan, Brian F. 60

Magnification effect 36

Managed float 6

Mark-dollar rates 20, 23, 74, 78, 88, 89, 94–101, 107, 108, 137

Marris, Stephen 18

Marston, Richard 7

Masson, Paul 104

McKinnon, Ronald 88

Meltzer, Allan 71

Melvin, Michael 34, 112

Mendez, J. 35

Micossi, S. 83, 86, 88

Miller, Marcus 137

Misalignment 35

Mishkin, Frederic S. 109

Miyazawa, Kiichi 15, 17
Mizrach, Bruce 112
Monetary policy. *See also* Intervention policy;
 Exchange rate policy
 central bank support for 59
 conflict between internal and external
  balance and 57
 decentralization of authority and 49
 dollar support from 17
 exchange rate policy and 47, 51, 52, 138
 expectations of 59, 71, 108, 109, 124, 135
 German 88
 as a given constraint 46
 independence of 27
 inflation in US and 50
 interest rate gap and 26
 Japanese 14, 23
 national sovereignty and 62
 news reports and 109
 reserves as predictor of 109
 Swiss 88
 target zones and 47, 48
Money Market Services, International (MMS)
 43, 110, 124–25, 127
Money "surprises" 108
Mulford, David 13, 20, 50, 89
Mundaca, B. Gabriela 108
Murphy, Robert 112
Mussa, Michael 40, 59

Neumann, Manfred 57, 70
New York Times, The 73, 112
News reports, effect of
 on daily changes in the spot rate 113–15
 on dollar appreciation 120
 on dollar-mark expectations 127
 intervention and 111
 on investor expectations 124, 126, 128, 129
 reducing the simultaneity bias and 112
 size of intervention and 76
 on weekly changes in the spot rate 118, 119,
  121, 123
Nominal anchor 29, 30, 48

Obstfeld, Maurice 12, 15, 18, 48, 58, 88
Omnibus Trade and Competitiveness Act of
 1988 51, 138
Overshooting effect 36, 37, 39, 42, 43

Passive intervention 5, 64, 65, 72. *See also*
 Customer transactions
Phillips, Steven 137
Plaza Agreement
 absence of monetary policy discussion at 52
 change in US policy after 11–13
 dollar depreciation and 136

incidence of coordinated intervention and 2,
 73
 increased Fed operations after 74, 77
 statement on Japanese monetary policy 14
 support of dollar trend 64
 US exchange rate policy and 50, 136
Porter, M. 58
Portfolio-balance channel 37, 38, 56, 58, 62,
 103–06, 109, 120, 136
Public intervention 3, 56, 59–61, 72–74, 108,
 112, 120, 133, 136, 139
Purchasing-power parity 79, 81, 85, 125
Putnam, Robert 10

Random walk 101
Rational expectations methodology 33–34, 39,
 41, 44, 104, 105
Reaction functions of central banks 77–88
Reagan, President Ronald 2, 7, 8, 10–12, 48,
 50, 112
Rebecchini, S. 16, 21, 22, 24, 85, 86, 101, 106
Redburn, Tom 50
Reference range 17, 25, 136. *See also* Target
 zones
Regan, Donald 49
Repurchase agreements 67
Reserve holdings 78
Reserves, as proxy for intervention policy 109
Reserves, data on 69
Risk premium 33, 34, 38, 39, 105, 124, 127–33
Roberts, Dan 112
Rodrigues, Anthony P. 105
Rodrik, Dani 34
Rogoff, Kenneth 62, 70, 104, 105
Rose, Andrew 136
Rosengren, Eric 109

Sampson, Stephanie 70, 103
Schulmeister, Stephen 43
Schwartz, Anna 88
Secret intervention
 central banks' preference for 60–61, 70–71,
  74
 definition of 56
 disorderly markets and 61
 effect on exchange rate volatility 108, 114
 effect on investor expectations 126, 128, 129,
  136
 impact of 120, 132
 institutional conflict and 60
 portfolio adjustment transactions and 62
 versus public intervention after the Plaza 13
 relative frequency of 73
 weekly changes in the spot rate and 119
Select Oversight Committees, proposals for 52
Shadow Open Market Committee 9
Signaling channel 56, 58–60, 63, 71, 108, 109,
 124, 135

Other Publications from the
Institute for International Economics

POLICY ANALYSES IN INTERNATIONAL ECONOMICS Series

28 **The Progress of Policy Reform in Latin America**
John Williamson/*January 1990*
ISBN paper 0-88132-100-1   106 pp.

29 **The Global Trade Negotiations: What Can Be Achieved?**
Jeffrey J. Schott/*September 1990*
ISBN paper 0-88132-137-0   72 pp.

30 **Economic Policy Coordination: Requiem or Prologue?**
Wendy Dobson/*April 1991*
ISBN paper 0-88132-102-8   162 pp.

31 **The Economic Opening of Eastern Europe**
John Williamson/*May 1991*
ISBN paper 0-88132-186-9   92 pp.

32 **Eastern Europe and the Soviet Union in the World Economy**
Susan M. Collins and Dani Rodrik/*May 1991*
ISBN paper 0-88132-157-5   152 pp.

33 **African Economic Reform: The External Dimension**
arol Lancaster/*June 1991*
ISBN paper 0-88132-096-X   82 pp.

34 **Has the Adjustment Process Worked?**
Paul R. Krugman/*October 1991*
ISBN paper 0-88132-116-8   80 pp.

35 **From Soviet disUnion to Eastern Economic Community?**
Oleh Havrylyshyn and John Williamson/*October 1991*
ISBN paper 0-88132-192-3   84 pp.

36 **Global Warming: The Economic Stakes**
William R. Cline/*May 1992*
ISBN paper 0-88132-172-9   128 pp.

37 **Trade and Payments After Soviet Disintegration**
John Williamson/*June 1992*
ISBN paper 0-88132-173-7   96 pp.

BOOKS

IMF Conditionality
John Williamson, editor/*1983*
ISBN cloth 0-88132-006-4   695 pp.

Trade Policy in the 1980s
William R. Cline, editor/*1983*
ISBN cloth 0-88132-008-1   810 pp.
ISBN paper 0-88132-031-5   810 pp.

Subsidies in International Trade
Gary Clyde Hufbauer and Joanna Shelton Erb/*1984*
ISBN cloth 0-88132-004-8   299 pp.

International Debt: Systemic Risk and Policy Response
William R. Cline/*1984*
ISBN cloth 0-88132-015-3   336 pp.

Trade Protection in the United States: 31 Case Studies
Gary Clyde Hufbauer, Diane E. Berliner, and Kimberly Ann Elliott/*1986*
ISBN paper 0-88132-040-4   371 pp.

Toward Renewed Economic Growth in Latin America
Bela Balassa, Gerardo M. Bueno, Pedro-Pablo Kuczynski, and Mario Henrique
Simonsen/*1986*
(out of stock)   ISBN paper 0-88132-045-5   205 pp.

Capital Flight and Third World Debt
Donald R. Lessard and John Williamson, editors/*1987*
(out of print)   ISBN paper 0-88132-053-6   270 pp.

The Canada-United States Free Trade Agreement:
The Global Impact
Jeffrey J. Schott and Murray G. Smith, editors/*1988*
ISBN paper 0-88132-073-0   211 pp.

World Agricultural Trade: Building a Consensus
William M. Miner and Dale E. Hathaway, editors/*1988*
ISBN paper 0-88132-071-3   226 pp.

Japan in the World Economy
Bela Balassa and Marcus Noland/*1988*
ISBN paper 0-88132-041-2   306 pp.

America in the World Economy: A Strategy for the 1990s
C. Fred Bergsten/*1988*
ISBN cloth 0-88132-089-7   235 pp.
ISBN paper 0-88132-082-X   235 pp.

Managing the Dollar: From the Plaza to the Louvre
Yoichi Funabashi/*1988, 2d ed. 1989*
ISBN paper 0-88132-097-8   307 pp.

United States External Adjustment and the World Economy
William R. Cline/*May 1989*
ISBN paper 0-88132-048-X   392 pp.

Free Trade Areas and U.S. Trade Policy
Jeffrey J. Schott, editor/*May 1989*
ISBN paper 0-88132-094-3   400 pp.

Dollar Politics: Exchange Rate Policymaking in the United States
I. M. Destler and C. Randall Henning/*September 1989*
ISBN paper 0-88132-079-X   192 pp.

Latin American Adjustment: How Much Has Happened?
John Williamson, editor/*April 1990*
ISBN paper 0-88132-125-7   480 pp.

The Future of World Trade in Textiles and Apparel
William R. Cline/*1987, 2d ed. June 1990*
ISBN paper 0-88132-110-9   344 pp.

Completing the Uruguay Round: A Results-Oriented Approach to the GATT Trade
Negotiations
Jeffrey J. Schott, editor/*September 1990*
ISBN paper 0-88132-130-3   256 pp.

Economic Sanctions Reconsidered (in two volumes)
Economic Sanctions Reconsidered: History and Current Policy
(also sold separately, see below)
Economic Sanctions Reconsidered: Supplemental Case Histories
Gary Clyde Hufbauer, Jeffrey J. Schott, and Kimberly Ann Elliott/*1985, 2d ed.*
December 1990

ISBN cloth 0-88132-115-X	928 pp.
ISBN paper 0-88132-105-2	928 pp.

Economic Sanctions Reconsidered: History and Current Policy
Gary Clyde Hufbauer, Jeffrey J. Schott, and Kimberly Ann Elliott/*December 1990*

ISBN cloth 0-88132-136-2	288 pp.
ISBN paper 0-88132-140-0	288 pp.

Pacific Basin Developing Countries: Prospects for the Future
Marcus Noland/*January 1991*

ISBN cloth 0-88132-141-9	250 pp.
ISBN paper 0-88132-081-1	250 pp.

Currency Convertibility in Eastern Europe
John Williamson, editor/*October 1991*

ISBN cloth 0-88132-144-3	396 pp.
ISBN paper 0-88132-128-1	396 pp.

Foreign Direct Investment in the United States
Edward M. Graham and Paul R. Krugman/*1989, 2d ed. October 1991*

ISBN paper 0-88132-139-7	200 pp.

International Adjustment and Financing: The Lessons of 1985-1991
C. Fred Bergsten, editor/*January 1992*

ISBN paper 0-88132-112-5	336 pp.

North American Free Trade: Issues and Recommendations
Gary Clyde Hufbauer and Jeffrey J. Schott/*April 1992*

ISBN cloth 0-88132-145-1	392 pp.
ISBN paper 0-88132-120-6	392 pp.

American Trade Politics
I. M. Destler/*1986, rev. June 1992*

ISBN cloth 0-88132-164-8	400 pp.
ISBN paper 0-88132-188-5	400 pp.

Narrowing the U.S. Current Account Deficit
Allen J. Lenz/*June 1992*

ISBN cloth 0-88132-148-6	640 pp.
ISBN paper 0-88132-103-6	640 pp.

The Economics of Global Warming
William R. Cline/*June 1992*

ISBN cloth 0-88132-150-8	416 pp.
ISBN paper 0-88132-132-X	416 pp.

U.S. Taxation of International Income: Blueprint for Reform
Gary Clyde Hufbauer, assisted by Joanna M. van Rooij/*October 1992*

ISBN cloth 0-88132-178-8	304 pp.
ISBN paper 0-88132-134-6	304 pp.

Who's Bashing Whom? Trade Conflict in High-Technology Industries
Laura D'Andrea Tyson/*November 1992*

ISBN cloth 0-88132-151-6	352 pp.
ISBN paper 0-88132-106-0	352 pp.

Korea in the World Economy
Il Sakong/*January 1993*

ISBN cloth 0-88132-184-2	328 pp.
ISBN paper 0-88132-106-0	328 pp.

NAFTA: An Assessment
Gary Clyde Hufbauer and Jeffrey J. Schott/*February 1993*

ISBN paper 0-88132-198-2	92 pp.

Pacific Dynamism and the International Economic System
C. Fred Bergsten and Marcus Noland, editors/*May 1993*

ISBN paper 0-88132-196-6	424 pp.

Economic Consequences of Soviet Disintegration
John Williamson, editor/*May 1993*

ISBN paper 0-88132-190-7	664 pp.

Reconcilable Differences? United States–Japan Economic Conflict
C. Fred Bergsten and Marcus Noland/*June 1993*

ISBN paper 0-88132-129-X	296 pp.

Does Foreign Exchange Intervention Work?
Kathryn M. Dominguez and Jeffrey A. Frankel/*September 1993*

ISBN 0-88132-104-4	192 pp.

SPECIAL REPORTS

1 Promoting World Recovery: A Statement on Global Economic Strategy by Twenty-six Economists from Fourteen Countries/ *December 1982*

(out of print) ISBN paper 0-88132-013-7	45 pp.

2 Prospects for Adjustment in Argentina, Brazil, and Mexico: Responding to the Debt Crisis
John Williamson, editor/*June 1983*

(out of print) ISBN paper 0-88132-016-1	71 pp.

3 Inflation and Indexation: Argentina, Brazil, and Israel
John Williamson, editor/*March 1985*

ISBN paper 0-88132-037-4	191 pp.

4 Global Economic Imbalances
C. Fred Bergsten, editor/*March 1986*

ISBN cloth 0-88132-038-2	126 pp.
ISBN paper 0-88132-042-0	126 pp.

5 African Debt and Financing
Carol Lancaster and John Williamson, editors/*May 1986*

(out of print) ISBN paper 0-88132-044-7	229 pp.

6 Resolving the Global Economic Crisis: After Wall Street
Thirty-three Economists from Thirteen Countries/*December 1987*

ISBN paper 0-88132-070-6	30 pp.

7 World Economic Problems
Kimberly Ann Elliott and John Williamson, editors/*April 1988*

ISBN paper 0-88132-055-2	298 pp.

Reforming World Agricultural Trade
Twenty-nine Professionals from Seventeen Countries/*1988*
ISBN paper 0-88132-088-9   42 pp.

8   **Economic Relations Between the United States and Korea: Conflict or Cooperation?**
Thomas O. Bayard and Soo-Gil Young, editors/*January 1989*
ISBN paper 0-88132-068-4   192 pp.

FORTHCOMING

Reciprocity and Retaliation: An Evaluation of Tough Trade Policies
Thomas O. Bayard and Kimberly Ann Elliott

The Globalization of Industry and National Economic Policies
C. Fred Bergsten and Edward M. Graham

The New Tripolar World Economy: Toward Collective Leadership
C. Fred Bergsten and C. Randall Henning

The United States as a Debtor Country
C. Fred Bergsten and Shafiqul Islam

The Dynamics of Korean Economic Development
Soon Cho

Third World Debt: A Reappraisal
William R. Cline

Equilibrium Exchange Rates for Global Economic Growth
Rudiger Dornbusch

Global Competition Policy
Edward M. Graham and J. David Richardson

International Monetary Policymaking in the United States, Germany, and Japan
C. Randall Henning

The New Europe in the World Economy
Gary Clyde Hufbauer

The Costs of U.S. Trade Barriers
Gary Clyde Hufbauer and Kimberly Ann Elliott

Comparing the Costs of Protection
Gary Clyde Hufbauer and Kimberly Ann Elliott, editors

Toward Freer Trade in the Western Hemisphere
Gary Clyde Hufbauer and Jeffrey J. Schott

A World Savings Shortage?
Paul R. Krugman

Migration and Trade: The Case of NAFTA
Philip Martin

Sizing Up U.S. Export Disincentives
J. David Richardson

Adjusting to Volatile Energy Prices
Philip K. Verleger, Jr.

The Future of the World Trading System
John Whalley

Trading and the Environment: Setting the Rules
John Whalley and Peter Uimonen

Equilibrium Exchange Rates: An Update
John Williamson

The Politics of Economic Reform
John Williamson

For orders outside the US and Canada please contact:

Longman Group UK Ltd.
PO Box 88
Harlow, Essex CM 19 5SR
UK

Telephone Orders: 0279 623925
Fax: 0279 453450
Telex: 817484